PENGUIN

Best of Friends

Suzy Baldwin has been a researcher, book editor, editor of the *Australian Harper's Bazaar* and *24 Hours* magazine, and the presenter of Sunday Afternoon on ABC TV. As a features writer and book reviewer, she has written for the *Australian*, the *Bulletin*, *Vogue Australia* and the *Sydney Morning Herald*. She was general editor of the bestselling Bicentennial book *Unsung Heroes and Heroines of Australia* and wrote many of its two hundred stories. Suzy spent her early life in Melbourne in the fifties and sixties and now lives in Sydney, where she is Deputy Arts Editor of the *Sydney Morning Herald*. She has two sons.

best of friends *Suzy* BALDWIN

AUSTRALIAN WOMEN TALK ABOUT FRIENDSHIP

PENGUIN BOOKS

Penguin Books Australia Ltd
487 Maroondah Highway, PO Box 257
Ringwood, Victoria 3134, Australia
Penguin Books Ltd
Harmondsworth, Middlesex, England
Penguin Putnam Inc.
375 Hudson Street, New York, New York 10014, USA
Penguin Books Canada Limited
10 Alcorn Avenue, Toronto, Ontario, Canada M4V 3B2
Penguin Books (NZ) Ltd
Cnr Rosedale and Airborne Roads, Albany, Auckland, New Zealand
Penguin Books (South Africa) (Pty) Ltd
5 Watkins Street, Denver Ext 4, 2094, South Africa
Penguin Books India (P) Ltd
11, Community Centre, Panchsheel Park, New Delhi 110 017, India

First published by Penguin Books Australia Ltd 2001

10 9 8 7 6 5 4 3 2 1

Cover designed by Sandy Cull, Penguin Design Studio; actors for
photograph referred by La Mama Theatre, Melbourne
Text designed by Jenny Grigg, Penguin Design Studio
Typeset in Goudy by Post Prepress, Brisbane, Queensland
Made and printed in Australia by Australian Print Group, Maryborough,
Victoria

National Library of Australia
Cataloguing-in-Publication data:

Baldwin, Suzy.
Best of friends: Australian women talk about friendship.

Bibliography.
ISBN 0 14 100055 4.

1. Friendship – Australia. 2. Women – Australia – Attitudes. I. Title.

302.340994

www.penguin.com.au

For Ben and Josh

It is for aid and comfort through all the relations and passages of life and death. It is fit for serene days and graceful gifts and country rambles, but also for rough roads and hard fare, shipwreck, poverty and persecution . . . We are to dignify to each other the daily needs and offices of man's life, and embellish it by courage, wisdom and unity. It should never fall into something usual and settled, but should be alert and inventive and add rhyme and reason to what was drudgery.

RALPH WALDO EMERSON

Friendship is love made bearable.

RITA MAE BROWN

Contents ¶

FIRST THINGS FIRST

WE ARE ON A bus coming home from the shops. My mother, Jennifer and me. Jennifer and I are both four. She is my first best friend.

Jennifer is the blonde that little girls are supposed to be in 1950, like all the princesses in my books. Even the beautiful non-princesses have golden hair. I don't have golden hair. My hair is black, the colour of a raven's wing as it says in the fairytales. But children know that ravens are not a good sign. Whenever they're mentioned something terrible happens; someone dies and it's usually those raven-haired girls – the wicked stepmother, the malign fairy, the evil queen. The bad brunettes. Sure, they get to wreak havoc first, but that's not much comfort. Especially as the beautiful, virtuous, long-suffering blondes marry the princes and live happily ever after. It is clear to me, even at the age of four, that the angels are on the side of the blondes, and we raven-haired girls will just have to fend for ourselves as best we can.

Apart from its colour, Jennifer's hair is just like mine – ear-lobe length, glassy, straight and shiny, with a part on one side and on the other a bobby pin and a bow of satin ribbon, care-fully ironed but slightly limp from repeated tying. Like me, she wears a pale lemon woollen sweater and a pleated tartan skirt, white cotton socks turned over at the ankles, and pol-ished brown lace-up shoes that we also wear for best. On the bus we sit side by side, and we talk. I tell Jennifer everything. Unlike my mother, she never looks worried or calls me over-imaginative. To her, my regular visitations from fairies and goblins are as commonplace as these visits to the grocer.

The bus stops. Four women bump on with lumpy string bags. Everyone shuffles up a bit to make room. Women in suburban Melbourne in 1950 have big bottoms, and children are supposed to get out of their way, but as one of these bottoms lowers itself towards Jennifer, it is clear that she is about to be squashed. I burst into tears and tug at my mother's arm: 'Mummy, she's going to sit on Jennifer.' The bus turns to watch. The bottom finishes seating itself and its owner looks sternly at my mother to remind her that children should be seen and not heard. My mother blushes and apologises. I hear the word 'imaginary'. Like most children of my generation, I am well behaved in public but this calumny is too much to bear. I feel the blood rise to my face and I sob, 'She isn't made up! She's real! She's my *friend*.' Jennifer survives the squashing but my mother never really forgives me.

I discovered Jennifer when we were both three. For years she was my playmate, my confidante, co-conspirator and constant companion. She co-starred in my complicated stories, shared my fears and my fabulous dreams, and laughed at my jokes. If a child's life seems small to adults, it's because they forget that a child's imagination does not see the boundaries that limit and diminish a grown-up's universe. To a child, all things are possible, if not in the visible world then in some other – more inspired, more beautiful, more vivid and more real. For me, and for Jennifer, the world in my head had an existence as real as my own. She comforted me, had faith in me, and that gave me courage. She was trusting and absolutely trustworthy, the most reliable presence I knew. She was my soulmate, my other self. My best friend.

Are we born with certain habits of mind, or do they just form so early that they seem bred in the bone? A bit of both, it would seem. But whether driven by peculiarities of nature or nurture, isolated and unhappy children find love and solace where they can. And the invisible friend seems to me the necessary creation of the imaginative solitary child. For as long as I can remember, my most constant friends of the heart and mind have lived in books and in my imagination, mutually sustaining worlds that are more alive to me than what is commonly called real life. I was no longer a child when I first read Keats's 'On First Looking Into Chapman's Homer' but I immediately recognised where I was. I too had much travelled in the realms of gold and many goodly states and kingdoms did I see. And there my friends dwelt. The wild and wonderful inhabitants of a parallel but more intense world, they were – are still – passionate, brilliant, beautiful and heroic. Like the ancient gods (indeed, some of them *are* the ancient gods), they are certainly flawed, but they are never boring and are often wickedly funny. How was 'real life' – too often flat, dull and dun-coloured – ever going to match that? Many years before I could articulate it, and long before I had ever heard of William Blake (although, thanks to my father and his rugby club friends, I could sing all the words to 'Jerusalem' by the time I was three), I believed that the real life is the life of the imagination 'that liveth forever'. It is not an entirely unalloyed blessing.

However we acquire them, these early habits of mind, and the forces that shape them, colour all our days. Old loves and lovelessness, old losses, old griefs do not disappear. We do not, in that harsh phrase, 'get over them'. They lie, buried perhaps, concreted over, but waiting to emerge and remind us that 'The past is not over. It is not even the past.' Our earliest patterns of affection, or lack of it, our confidence or anxiety about it, inform all our relationships – our passionate loves, our friendships great and small.

I don't know where she went, or why, but in the forty-odd years since Jennifer vanished, I have had several best friends who have shared, illuminated and helped me survive various stages of my life – what I now think of as my several lives. Although to the rest of the world those friends had a more obvious corporeal reality than Jennifer, in some ways they were not so different.

Intimate, uninhibited conversation remained at the core of those relationships, although I no longer had to do all the voices and there was no longer any guarantee that my best friend would agree with me quite so often, or understand so absolutely what I was saying. We shared experiences and deep affection, offered each other solace and support, and made each other laugh. I would like to tell you that with the best of them I felt that same sense of complete belonging, of being fully known, totally accepted and unconditionally loved that I had with Jennifer, but it's not the truth.

I am told by those more pragmatic, or more bitter, than I that no frail mortal can live up to those creatures of the imagin-ation, or recreate the intense, passionate, mutually sustaining bond of those ideal soulmates. However, the very essence of the imagination is its refusal to be cut down to workable size. Ralph Waldo Emerson, American scholar, poet and transcendentalist, recognises the paradox in his 1840s essay 'Friendship':

> The higher the style we demand of friendship, of
> course, the less easy to establish it with flesh and
> blood. We walk alone in the world. Friends such
> as we desire are dreams and fables. But a sublime
> hope cheers ever the faithful heart . . .

If we were capable of ideal friendship we would be self-sufficient enough to live without it. As we're not, lumbered as we are with our mortal flaws and desires, most of us find that, for at least some stages of our lives, close friendships are essential to our growth, our sense of who we are, our enjoyment of life, and even to our very survival. If you conduct a quick straw poll, you'll find virtually everyone will agree with Bette Midler: 'You've got to have friends.' But do we have to have friends? And what kind of friends?

For the young, the evidence is pretty conclusive. Children and adolescents *do* have to have friends. Alliances, visible or invisible and however temporary, are essential to help us navigate the jungle of childhood and adolescence without losing life, limb or sanity. And girls, it would appear, have to have *best* friends, those intense, exclusive relationships that teach us not only what intimacy is, but also how bitter its loss.

Adults are a different matter. Probe deeper, ask how someone defines a friend – especially an intimate friend – look at how a life is actually lived, and it becomes clear that for some adults the feeling is not always so strong. There are of course various degrees of friendship. Some adults, and this seems especially true for women, have more than one best friend. Some have two or three, perhaps a handful of 'best' friends – a description that I realise is grammatically nonsensical but which denotes the emotional significance and the intimate, one-to-one quality of the friendships I am exploring here.

However, not everyone seems to need the kind of friends that most women count on. Many men, and some women too, live without intimate friends. They might have acquaintances, workmates or colleagues, be part of a community, spend much of their lives in a permanent crowd of social friends, but have no intimate friend, no trusted confidante. True intimate friendship, *best* friendship, is not a group affair. Although we might have more than one best friend, each of those friendships is an exclusive entity – it exists outside the group, is inimical to it and subversive of it. You can be a best friend and also be part of a group, but they are journeys in different directions, involving different parts of your self.

Many women go through stages in their lives when the demands of family and work make intimate friendships hard to maintain, but they continue to value their friendships even when they feel they are undernourishing them. For most women the feeling is overwhelming – we *do* have to have friends. And we have to have intimate friends. For women this need can be so intense that it is primal, as essential to survival as air.

A close and trusted friend can often help us find our way through a dark wood. Women often say, and mean it, that there have been times when a close friend has saved not only their sanity but their lives. Medical research seems to confirm this. Dr David Spiegel, for example, professor of psychiatry at Stanford University, found that cancer patients with close friends live longer than those without, in some cases twice as long – but this is only true of intimate, conversational, emotionally supportive friendships, which he identifies as the female model.

The women in Spiegel's test groups behaved like most women friends – they gave each other time, energy, attention and support; they talked honestly about their feelings and fears, and they made each other laugh. The uninhibited laughter that characterises so many female friendships, and female institutions, is not only metaphorically heart-warming, it also prompts physiological changes which benefit the immune system and reduce the effects of stress – it is physically good for you.

Even faced with the prospect of imminent death, however, most of us are unlikely to give living longer as the prime reason we need our intimate friends. There is little point in living longer unless we feel that life is worth hanging onto. And for most of us, it is our affectionate relationships – the people we love and those who love and care about us – that are most likely to make us feel it's worth the effort. In a world where families disappoint and disintegrate, romantic and sexual relationships routinely break down, and work is increasingly stressful, many of us find that our warmest, most supportive and sustaining, most stimulating and most purely enjoyable affection comes from our close friends. The affections, as Emerson wrote, 'from the highest degree of passionate love to the lowest degree of good-will . . . make the sweetness of life'. It is our affections that make us most fully human, the quality of our connections with other people that makes us who we are and informs all that we do. As Yeats, who enjoyed great friendships and suffered from great loves, knew, 'all the ladders start/In the foul rag-and-bone shop of the heart'.

Conservative politicians would have us believe that the ladders start, and finish, in the family. In the last few years they have given us an earbashing about the importance of 'family values', implying that families are the sole repositories of all that makes life meaningful and humane. As the sad but indisputable evidence is that the family is too often the perpetrator and breeding ground of violence – physical, emotional and psychological, all doing us lasting damage – I have always been mystified by this. What *are* these values that operate only within families and why should we want to encourage them? Dorothy Rowe, a London-based Australian clinical psychologist, was also mystified and set out to define what 'family values' might be. In an article in the *Guardian* entitled 'The Formula for Happy Families', a wise and refreshingly acerbic reflection on friends and family prompted by spending a relaxed and happy Christmas with friends where no-one cried in the kitchen or escaped to the pub, she identifies four values exclusive to families: 'You are my possession and I can do with you what I want' (parent to child); 'You owe me' or 'You have to make up to me what your existence has deprived me of' (sibling to sibling); 'You have been given a role in the family which is yours for life. You cannot escape it' (everyone to everyone else); and 'Anyone who isn't family isn't important' (parents and grandparents to anyone younger).

As Rowe observes:

> Of the families I knew that adhered to some or all of these four values, none could be described as happy. Many of these families would say that they loved one another, but love alone does not promote happiness, especially when 'I love you' has the corollary 'therefore you must do what I want'. The only love which promotes happiness is that which says: 'I love you and wish you well, even if that "well" does not include me.' [Happy families] are not closed in upon themselves, with few friends and fearful of the world outside. They are hospitable, kind, and interested in people and all that the world has to offer.

These are the families that encourage friendship in their children. However, Rowe concludes:

> loving, wishing the other person well, treating people as people, not objects, treating people with generosity, respect and dignity, valuing friendship, accepting the other person's point of view, being flexible, patient, tolerant, truthful, loyal, co-operative, hospitable, kind, interested

in people and events are all wonderful values but
they are not values specific only to happy families. These are the values of friendship.

For some women, family is the place where they learn friendship. A rare few find their best friends inside the family. But for
many women, families are not such friendly places; for them, the
affectionate bonds of friendship can be thicker than blood. Our
most intimate friends can be kinder, more understanding and
more likely to give honest and affectionate counsel than partners
or family. They comfort us when those other relationships fail us,
supply what those relationships cannot and are more generous
with allowing us to be, and become, ourselves. Our best friends
see us. While families tend to see us as fixed in one role – the
smart one, the stupid one, the baby – and find it hard to see us
any other way, no matter how old we become, friends allow us to
try out different selves. As we grow older, the friends with whom
we share a history are often our only witnesses to the people we
once were, but, at the same time, the friends who genuinely love
us and wish us well don't fix us in aspic. They allow us to change
and encourage us to grow – indeed, sometimes their most valuable act of friendship is to kick-start us when they can see we're
stuck and can't help ourselves. In short, our closest friends are
agents for change in all aspects of our lives. They are part of who
we are. We trust them to know us and to reflect us honestly, but
with affection and goodwill, back to ourselves.

Frances Partridge, born in 1900 and the oldest surviving
Bloomsberry, commented when she was eighty and looking
back on a lifetime of richly rewarding friendships:

> Why, I wonder, have writers paid so little honour
> to friendship? Sustaining, warming, refreshing and

endlessly stimulating, it should surely have had almost as many poems written to it as have been dedicated to love [. . .]

Blood is thicker . . . well, in a sense it is true, but love of family is genetic and static in comparison: one is born possessing it, and although it may persist staunchly [. . .] its capacity for development is limited. The exciting truth about friendship is that it is founded on choice; its possibilities of growth and change are manifold. It fertilises the soil of one's life, sends up fresh shoots, encourages cross-pollination and the creation of new species.

The ideal of intimate friendship, of a pair of best friends, has a long and noble history – at least in theory. Aristotle described friendship as 'one soul inhabiting two bodies'. Cicero, writing in 44 BC, argued for a more elevated kind of friendship than the usual pragmatic Roman exchanges of political allegiance and material benefit. He defined true friendship as 'a complete identity of feeling about all things in heaven and earth [. . .] With the single exception of wisdom, I am inclined to regard it as the greatest of all gifts the gods have bestowed on mankind.'

But his ideal of friendship is not for everybody. Cicero makes it clear that he is not speaking about 'ordinary, commonplace friendships, delightful and valuable as they can be', but about 'the authentic, truly admirable sort of relationship [. . .] embodied in those rare pairs of famous friends'. Rare indeed. There were only four pairs of those famous friends, the most familiar to us probably Achilles and Patroclus. They were all heroes, warriors, and all men. Cicero doesn't mention women but they must have been presumed to be busy elsewhere when the gods bestowed this greatest of gifts.

The Renaissance revived the classical world's interest in friendship, as in much else. It was taken up by the two illustrious fathers of the modern essay, Michel de Montaigne, whose essays were first published in 1580 but were a life's work in progress until his death in 1592, and Francis Bacon, whose final edition of essays appeared in 1625.

Bacon, that pragmatic Elizabethan politician, philosopher and scientist, regarded one function of friendship as having someone to act on your behalf and in your interests, praising you and interceding to gain your advancement while you were alive, and carrying out your wishes after you were dead – not an unusual view of friendship at the time, nor, indeed, in some circles now. However, this was the last of Bacon's three 'fruits of friendship'. The first two, more passionately espoused, were the unburdening of the heart and an illumination of the understanding. 'A true friend,' wrote Bacon, is one 'to whom you may impart griefs, joys, fears, hopes, suspicions, counsels, and whatsoever lieth upon the heart to oppress it, in a kind of civil shrift or confession [. . .] Those that want [ie. lack] friends to open themselves unto are cannibals of their own hearts', but the 'communicating of a man's self to his friend [. . .] redoubleth joys and cutteth griefs in half.' Without true friends 'the world is a wilderness', which for Bacon would have had professional and political as well as personal implications.

However it was Montaigne, French gentleman, who put real passion into friendship. His essay traditionally called 'On Friendship', but more accurately translated as 'On Affectionate Relationships', is primarily an elegy for his loving friendship with Etienne de La Boëtie, who died in 1563, leaving

Montaigne utterly bereft. Theirs was a friendship of only four years but it was 'the peak of perfection', and, wrote Montaigne, compared to those years of friendship with La Boëtie, the rest of his life was 'but smoke and ashes, a dark night and dreary'.

Montaigne's rhapsodic account of his first meeting with La Boëtie describes love at first sight: 'so seized by each other, so known to each other and so bound together that from then on none was so close [. . .] Our souls were yoked together.' However, Montaigne, like Cicero, is at pains to stress the rarity of such a relationship. It is 'so perfect and so entire that [. . .] no trace at all of it can be found among men today [. . .] it is already something if Fortune can achieve it once in three centuries [. . .] Let nobody place those other common friendships in the same rank as this.'

Given this ecstatic description, it is not surprising that for Montaigne this friendship takes precedence over all other affectionate relationships. Echoing Aristotle, Montaigne says that he and La Boëtie were 'one soul in bodies twain' and closes by quoting Catullus: 'all my soul is buried with you [. . .] I shall love you always.'

Montaigne, who also had a wife and children and writes elsewhere of conjugal love, is at pains to point out that this was not a homosexual relationship. Nor is it to be compared with sexual love, which is 'but a mad craving for something which escapes us'. Friendship 'is a matter of the mind, with our souls being purified by practising it [. . .] scornfully watching the other racing along way down below'. In the Renaissance cosmology implied in this, friendship belongs to the soul, our closest link to the angels, while sexual passion belongs to the flesh, the part we share with the beasts.

Women, according to Montaigne, 'are in truth not normally capable of responding to such familiarity and mutual confidence as sustain the holy bond of friendship, nor do their souls seem firm enough to withstand the clasp of a knot so lasting and tightly drawn'. However, he does consider the possibility of *parfait amitié* – the most perfect loving relationship of all, between man and woman, in which both souls and bodies would be one: 'if it were possible to fashion such a relationship, willing and free, in which not only the souls had this full enjoyment but in which the bodies too shared in the union – *where the whole human being was involved* [my italics] – it is certain that the loving friendship would be more full and more abundant'. But, he adds, 'there is no example yet of woman attaining to it and by the common agreement of the Ancient schools of philosophy she is excluded from it'.

Emerson doesn't mention women at all but paints a heartbreakingly beautiful picture of intimate friendship. He concedes that ideal friendship is such a glorious notion it is more likely to exist in the imagination than on earth. However, even though 'friendship, like the immortality of the soul, is too good to be believed', we all spend our lives in search of it because the affections, 'these fine inward irradiations', have the power to transform our lives and our selves:

> The moment we indulge our affections, the earth is metamorphosed; there is no winter and no night; all tragedies, all ennuis vanish, – all duties even; nothing fills the proceeding eternity but the forms all radiant of beloved persons. Let the soul be assured that somewhere in the universe it should rejoin its friend, and it would be content and cheerful alone for a thousand years.

To Emerson friendship and solitude are not antithetical. Indeed, he is anxious not to exhaust great friendship, and by the end of the essay he has created an image of the true friend as one who allows him to be creatively alone. For Emerson there are two equal elements in friendship, truth – a friend is someone with whom he can be sincere – and love. It must be a mutual relationship and a robust one: 'I do not wish to treat friendship daintily but with roughest courage.' The only hitch that Emerson can see is the very slim chance of finding the soulmate we hope for, 'those rare pilgrims whereof only one or two wander in nature at once'.

To a modern female eye, there are three very striking things about these sublime and passionate descriptions of ideal best friendship. The first is how hard it is to recognise in them a picture of contemporary Western male friendship. Modern men's friendships with each other, particularly those of heterosexual men, are more likely to be based on doing things together than on frank and intimate conversation. Men share time and activities – building a fence or a business, running, riding a bike, fishing, watching football, drinking – rather than their selves. If they bare their souls to anyone, it is most likely to be to a woman.

The second is that if you add sex to these descriptions you would have the modern ideal of the loving, companionate, sexual relationship. Montaigne was right about that: he was only wrong in assuming that it is impossible because women are incapable of it. A relationship that involves the whole human being is what most modern women dream of sharing with their sexual partners. However, as things are, most women find that marriage or long-term heterosexual partnership is not enough. While many men say that their wives or female lovers are their best friends – and often their only close friend – very few women say the same about their husbands or male lovers. Even women who describe themselves as happily married are likely to become depressed if they are for too long without a close friend.

Third, it's not so surprising that all these writers emphasise the rarity of loving friendships, writing as they are about relationships between men. If you shift the focus to women, you find that loving friendship is what many women – not in an ideal world, but in this one – share with their best friends. Not all women's best friendships are as exalted as these ideal descriptions, it's true – extraordinary relationships of any kind are, by definition, always rarer than their more commonplace cousins – but many women experience something very like it, often more than once in their lives. And while very few men would describe their friendships in anything remotely approaching the emotionally intense terms used by Cicero, Montaigne, Bacon and Emerson, many women do. And always have.

The nature of women's friendship and its difference from that of men can hardly be called one of history's secrets. Men have always recognised its power, although they have not all regarded it as an unequivocally good thing. Chaucer has his Wife of Bath (a lively and still extraordinarily fresh embodiment of 'the woman question', circa 1387) say of her best friend and confidante, her 'gossip' Alisoun, 'she knew my heart and my secrets [. . .] To her I revealed everything.' William Congreve, in his great Restoration comedy of 1700, *The Way of the World*, has the lovers Mirabell and Millamant set out the conditions under which they might agree to marry. Mirabell's first condition to his love Millamant is that 'you admit no sworn confidante, or intimate of your own sex; no she-friend to screen her affairs under your countenance, and tempt you to make trial of mutual secrecy'. Women might not have held political or economic power, but their friendships, as Mirabell well understood, could be highly subversive.

Shakespeare understood the qualities of women's best friendships so well that many of his women are not only play-ful and comforting confidantes, but brave, outspoken and loyal friends who take extraordinary risks for each other. A handful of years after Montaigne's death, Shakespeare's Beatrice was such a friend to Hero, putting her own life, happiness and future husband on hold to clear her friend of vicious slander. So too was Paulina to Hermione, risking her life to defy and castigate her king and defend her queen; and Celia to Rosalind, a loyal, witty and sharp-eyed companion who defied her father and chose exile and possible death rather than abandon her friend. These are fictional characters, perhaps, but their relationships are a mirror of loving friendships more often realised and more vividly alive, faults and all, than Montaigne's idealised recollections.

Women's novels, letters and diaries from the eighteenth, nineteenth and first half of the twentieth centuries abound with intimate female friendships, often expressed in language so intensely passionate and romantic that some readers feel prompted to see a lesbian or two in every shared bed or house. While that might sometimes have been the case, it more often was not. Even when it might have been partly the case – in the shared 1920s London household of the writers Vera Brittain and her 'second self' Winifred Holtby, for example, which con-tinued after Brittain married, it is possible that Holtby was lesbian while Brittain was not – sex was neither the basis nor a component of the friendship. An intensely loving, intimate friendship, including delight in the other's physical presence, is exactly what Cicero, Montaigne, Bacon and Emerson have ennobled as true friendship. It is certainly a matter of the heart, often with all the sweet tenderness of a romance, but Eros in his carnal aspect is not its presiding deity.

Hannah Arendt and Mary McCarthy were just such a pair of intimate, loving, passionate best friends. Theirs was one of Cicero's 'authentic, truly admirable [. . .] rare pairs of famous friends'. Indeed, so luminously loving and enduring a friendship was it that many people who observed it over the years were impressed and moved by it, regardless of whether or not they liked the participants.

Even those who have never heard of Hannah Arendt would recognise the phrase coined by the subtitle of her 1963 book *Eichmann in Jerusalem: A Report on the Banality of Evil*. A German-Jewish philosopher, teacher, writer and critic, Arendt arrived in America in 1941 with her second husband, Heinrich Blücher. She was thirty-five, already a formidable intellectual, with a sceptical wit and a deliciously dry sense of humour. She had had a youthful love affair with her university teacher, the philosopher Martin Heidegger (she was his star pupil and he was *the* love of her life, according to her best friend), and had been both a refugee in Paris and an inmate of a French internment camp. In 1944, in Manhattan's Murray Hill Bar, she met Mary McCarthy, six years her junior and one of America's most prominent, prolific and sharp-tongued writers, then married to her second husband, the critic Edmund Wilson.

It was not loving friendship at first sight. In 1945, at a New York party of the city's literary intelligentsia, McCarthy made a cavalier remark about Hitler. Arendt, whose experience of Hitler was rather more personal than McCarthy's, took umbrage. Three years later, they made it up: 'We think so much alike,' said Hannah, which was generous if not entirely true.

There began one of the twentieth century's most successful, sustaining (and well-documented) best friendships, twenty-five years of intense and intimate loving relationship that ended only with Hannah's death in 1975.

In the view of writer Elizabeth Hardwick, a close friend of Mary's, Hannah was one of only two people outside Mary's family circle for whom 'she felt a kind of reverence' (the other was the Italian cultural and social critic Nicola Chiaramonte). In her foreword to Mary's posthumously published *Intellectual Memoirs*, Hardwick wrote:

> Mary was, quite literally, enchanted by Hannah's mind, her scholarship, her industry, and the complexities of her views. As for Hannah, I think perhaps she saw Mary as a golden American friend, perhaps the best the country could produce, [. . .] a sort of New World, blue-stocking *salonière* [. . .] The friendship of these two women was very moving to observe in its purity of respect and affection.

Fortunately for us, although not necessarily for them, for much of their friendship Mary and Hannah lived in different cities, often different countries, and they were letter writers. Hannah, particularly later in her life, would pick up the telephone, but Mary was an incurable correspondent.

Their letters are a vivid portrait of a long, intimate female friendship. They exude vitality, immediacy, and have that free-ranging, all-inclusive quality that characterises feminine conversation, encompassing and exploring in detail everything of importance in the two women's lives – matters philosophical, intellectual, literary, political and personal, affairs of the world and of the heart and mind, along with wickedly acute gossip and observations on frocks and food. The women discuss their profession of writing, offering detailed, thoughtful comments on each other's work. There is personal confession from Mary, who hurled herself into love affairs and marriages convinced that each was the great true love, to which Hannah responds with sage and humane advice. Intelligent and highly informed opinion on current events and public figures sits alongside (and is often one and the same as) lively commentary on the doings of their circle, a leftist literary and intellectual web of friends, past lovers, husbands, allies, enemies, and those it was hard to categorise, in particular 'the boys' from the journal *Partisan Review*.

On 10 August 1954 Mary wrote to Hannah from Wellfleet on Cape Cod where she and her third husband were spending the summer. If you had to pick one letter that encapsulates the range and spirit of the friendship, this could be it. An ironic account of social life on the Cape ('we've been responding like invertebrates to the mysterious call of social duty [. . .] huge parties [. . .] one can smell the fumes of alcohol half a mile off'), leads into problems with her current novel, questions about the 'shattered science of epistemology', a gallop past Nietzsche, Kant and Hume, discussions of Hannah's latest article on ideology and terror, of Philip Rahv (*Partisan Review* editor and a former lover of Mary's), Marxism, the Oppenheimer case, Alfred Kazin 'cutting me dead', and the irritation of 'shivering at social slights, even from people you don't care for'.

There was a clear recognition that their lives were intellectual *and* social. Although both were intellectuals and Hannah taught at the New School in New York and the University of Chicago, neither was an academic theorist immured in a tenured ivory tower. Mary had a hunger for the society of her peers, while Hannah, although sociable and excellent company, was more able to live and work in a kind of 'exalted solitude' that struck Mary as essentially and enviably European. However it was Hannah who would remind Mary that a life of the mind divorced from a love of the world – the *amor mundi* which was at the heart of Hannah's philosophy – was not worth living.

According to Mary McCarthy's biographer and editor of their letters to each other, Carol Brightman, Hannah had 'a genius for the kind of friendship in which much is given, little demanded'. Her twenty-five years of unwavering loyalty and affection for Mary, whose parents had died when she was six, seemed to give Mary a solid emotional ground that she appears never to have found with the many men in her life, although her last marriage, to Jim West, seems to have come close. Hannah treated each of Mary's relationships with men with the great kindness and generosity that characterises her friendship. She was sympathetic, wise, patient, honest, and firm when she felt it was required – a classic example of the combination of kind heart and shrewd counsel that the best women friends provide for each other.

Indeed, Mary called Hannah 'my wise counsellor', and confessed that she wrote with Hannah's reaction in mind:

> I have you horribly on my conscience every time sex appears. You are tugging at my elbow saying 'stop' during a seduction scene I've just been writing. And your imagined remonstrances are so effective that I've rewritten it . . . But you still won't like it, I'm afraid [. . .] I have misgivings about the taste of this novel [*A Charmed Life*], which localize around your anticipated or feared reaction.

Hannah was Mary's moral yardstick and intellectual mentor as well as her closest friend. Mary's son Reuel describes her as his mother's 'intellectual conscience'. And the American historian Arthur Schlesinger observed that Hannah 'made Mary put her marvellous brain to work'. In her turn, Mary read Hannah's manuscripts with an editor's care, gave her excellent literary advice, and defended Hannah fiercely and publicly when she was attacked, most importantly after the publication of *Eichmann in Jerusalem*, her book on the trial of Adolf Eichmann for his role in the Holocaust.

Both women needed defending in 1963. *Eichmann* was published in May, having earlier appeared as a series of essays in the *New Yorker*, and Mary's novel *The Group* hit the bookstores in August. The New York intellectuals went to town on both of them, their swipes at Mary paling only beside their furious attacks on Hannah for what they saw as her slandering of the Jewish victims of the Holocaust and what she insisted was simply the reporting of the facts of the trial. The boys of the *Partisan Review*, to which both women contributed, turned against Hannah, Lionel Abel most viciously in his review of *Eichmann*. Hannah was so shocked by the response to her book that she remained silent, a stance that Mary understood but always felt to be a mistake. Mary was so angry that she wrote a twelve-page rebuttal of Abel for *Partisan Review*.

The Group, Mary's novel about eight Vassar girls from the class of 1933 making their way in the world, was published to mixed critical response, the attack led by Norman Mailer who called it 'a lady-book'. It also quickly moved onto the bestseller lists, which must have irritated the hell out of the boys. Hannah wrote to Mary that it was 'beautifully written [. . .] and often hilariously funny'. The critics, Hannah observed, 'have forgotten how it is to *laugh*'.

Both were deeply hurt by the vehemence of the attacks on them: Mary wrote to Hannah, 'I have no cheek left to turn'. *The Group* made McCarthy's name and was eventually to sell five million copies, which cheered Mary somewhat. The reception of *Eichmann* would always trouble Hannah.

Their unfailing support for one another in rough times – and these were professionally the roughest – was also deeply personal. In 1955 Hannah flew from New York to be with Mary in Venice, 'to hold me up' as Mary says, when she was at a very low ebb. She had just had a miscarriage, her third marriage was in crisis, and she was working on something she was unsure of. When Hannah's husband died in 1970, Mary flew immediately from Paris where she was living to be with Hannah in New York.

As with all friends, there were occasional temporary mis-understandings, usually on Mary's part. 'Envy *is* a monster,' Hannah wrote to Mary after Alfred Kazin attacked both Mary's character and her writing in 1965. It was a monster that at times sunk its claws into Mary, who could be ferociously jealous of Hannah's other friends, particularly intellectual women such as Susan Sontag, whom she suspected of wanting to 'seduce' Hannah away from her. Her greatest rage was vented on Lillian Hellman, who, Mary was convinced, was determined to replace her as Hannah's best friend. To Mary, her friendship with Hannah was unique and irreplaceable, her most important relationship apart from the current man in her life and her son. It was just as important to Hannah, but even these two remark-able women were human, and Mary's human frailties were especially close to the surface.

Tact as well as honesty was necessary in this, as in all inti-mate friendships. While some of Mary's close friends would comment on her extravagance and her taste for luxury, Hannah would say nothing. She regarded it as none of her business, and her loyalty to Mary meant that she would never criticise her to anyone else. 'Their relationship had a moral quality,' wrote Elizabeth Hardwick, who was herself not averse to a swipe at Mary. It also had the what-shall-I-wear aspects of female friendship. Mary suggested a hairdo to cover Hannah's scar from an accident in Paris, and when, in the year before her death, Hannah was awarded Denmark's Sonning Prize – the first woman and the first US citizen to be so honoured – it was Mary who made sure that she bought a new dress for the award ceremony.

As well as letters, they sent each other presents, flowers, and went to stay with one another as often as they could. Despite their talents as correspondents, letters could not take the place of each other's company, and at times their longing to see one another is palpable. Hannah to Mary: 'I count the days until you come.' 'Dearest, I miss you in countless ways.' Mary to Hannah: 'I am homesick for you.' And in 1968 Hannah wrote, 'Times are lousy and we should be closer to each other.'

They were both attractive women. Mary's sharp American good looks are still clear in later photographs, while Hannah's generous, lived-in face is beginning to look a bit like W.H. Auden's. However she was a beautiful younger woman – many men seem to have been reduced to rubble by her – and remained flirtatious and intensely feminine until the end. She was sexy, with huge brown eyes and terrific legs, and she was charming: Brightman describes her saying, 'Szee here . . .' in her gruff warm voice, a cigarette in one hand. But, like the very best of friends, Mary saw more. In the eulogy at Hannah's funeral, Mary spoke of the Hannah she loved as an 'alluring, seductive, feminine' beauty, 'who had heard a voice such as spoke to the prophets'.

When Hannah died, Mary laid aside her own work to edit Hannah's Gifford Lectures, which were posthumously published as *The Life of the Mind*. It was three years of solid work which, combined with her task as executor of Hannah's estate, Hardwick says, 'could only be called sacrificial'. Mary acknowledges it was 'a heavy job' but one that 'kept going an imaginary dialogue with her', the dialogue that their friendship had so profoundly and rewardingly been. 'She was full of vitality, an extraordinary electric vitality,' Mary said of her best friend ten years after her death. 'She filled me with delight and wonder.'

The relationship between Hannah and Mary was clearly an intimate friendship of the highest order. If I asked Australian women about their best friends, I wondered, was this the kind of friendship they would describe? Would they speak of friendships as entire as this? What would they say their most intimate friendships were based on – affection, loyalty, common values, shared interests and experience, thinking alike? Would the extent to which a friend would put herself out for you prove to be important? Or was affection alone enough? And would they say they confided everything, and counted on each other always to be there, or were there boundaries?

Would women's best friends always turn out to be women, or did they also have men as best friends? If so, were those men heterosexual or homosexual, and how was that different from having a woman as a best friend? If the woman and the male friend were both heterosexual, did the man have to be a former lover or husband so that the question of sex, however implicitly or explicitly it hovered, had already been dealt with? And was it because sex was (usually) a non-issue that women's friendships with gay men could be the most liberated and liberating of all? Indeed, was it this freedom, combined with a sense of affinity, that made gay men the only men with whom some women could be absolutely themselves?

Would women say they expected best friends to be lifelong relationships, or would they also speak of the betrayals, the painful disappointments, the losses of intimate friendship? Would some say that there had been times when a best friend was an absolute necessity and others when the need was not so great, or that they sometimes needed a different kind of friendship? Might some women with fulfilling and satisfying lives say that they did not have a best friend, did not have intimate friends at all? And would there be some women for whom Emerson's blissful vision of perfect, soul-united friendship – that is, an ideal, imagined relationship rather than a real-life one – was more familiar than something approaching Hannah Arendt and Mary McCarthy's twenty-five years of unfailing mutual devotion and admiration?

I wanted to know what women thought best friendship was, whether it was important to them, and if so, how they did it. So I asked them. The conversations in this book are what they told me.

At the heart of women's friendship, and one of its greatest joys, I discovered, is feminine conversation – the dialogue that was such a loss to Mary McCarthy when Hannah was gone and which shaped their friendship, and both of them, for all those years. The intimacy of one-to-one talk is essential for best friends. We might have more than one best friend, but our deepest, most intimate and most satisfying relationship with each of them is the communication we have when it is just the two of us. Intellectual conversation, the exchange and sparking and testing of ideas, is a crucial part of intimate friendship for many women, but so is the freedom to appear ridiculous or angry or defeated or confused. Women exchange intimate details of their lives – how they feel, what they think, what they should do – and in these conversations find not only stimulation and growth, but also relief and affirmation, sustenance and good counsel.

These are the kinds of conversations that I had with all the women to whom I talked for this book. The place of best friends in our lives is as mutable with time and experience as everything else, so I talked to women with a range of experience and a decent chunk of life under their belts. The published conversations begin with a playwright of thirty-something and end with a couple of wise, fiercely alive women in their seventies, but I talked to many others whose words do not appear here directly. All spoke with the great generosity, frankness and good humour that is the hallmark of the best of women's conversations.

In these conversations we talked about whether relationships actually matter, and, if so, which ones. If close friends are important, what is expected of them and how are they sustained? Where do friends stand in relation to lovers, husbands or partners, children, family, other friends? How to juggle friends and work? As well as friendship, we talked about love, children, work, the things we value and believe in, because best friendship, or the idea of best friendship, its luxury or its necessity, its possibility or impossibility, cannot be separated from any of these.

This is not an 'isn't it gorgeous having a girlfriend' kind of book, a feel-good but superficial celebration that glosses over the pain and the pitfalls. It is, however, full of five-star friendships: pairs of best friends, including one pair of sisters; individual halves of best friendships; women with several best friends. One woman whose several brilliant and creative best friends are a kind of family, one whose husband is her best friend, another whose female partner is, one who says she doesn't believe in best friends even though she has lived for eighteen years with what many would see as the ideal best friend. And two women who have had famous friendships, one of whom keeps on making intimate friends, the other of whom, despite being utterly enchanting, says that she has no best friend and does not believe in friendship, that her work is her friend.

This is not an objective sampling of all women and their best friends, but that is not what I set out to do. I set out to talk to particular women who seemed to me to have or have had especially passionate, intense, sustained and sustaining intimate friendships – what, for ease of reference, I have called best friends, although they might not – and whose experiences and insights into those relationships could help us understand our lives, and each other, more fully.

Our best friends are among the most important relationships in our lives. They are also perhaps the least recognised. The loss of a lover is understood by others as a grievous blow; sympathy is offered, allowances are made. But the loss of a friend is scarcely acknowledged, although the grief it causes can still bring tears to women's eyes many years later.

It also struck the rawest nerve in the conversations I had for this book. Women talked as freely about their lost best friends as about all other aspects of their lives, but those with the most painful stories did not want to be identified publicly with them. As you would expect, they told the common tale of sexual betrayal – best friend sleeps with lover – but that troubled them least of all. Much more grief-stricken was the woman who spoke of feeling utterly abandoned and bereft when her best friend of many years married and took on another life that utterly excluded her, and those women who had been caught in the complicated webs of envy, possessiveness and resentment that turn intimate friendship into a war zone. One woman spoke of an intimate friend who simply shut the door in her face one day – now, many years later, she believes that she made such excessive demands that the friend broke off all contact for her own survival, but she wept over the loss for years. Another spoke of a friendship in her twenties that was so intense it had to be abandoned if the two women were to have any other relationships, another of a friendship of her thirties that gave both friends the courage to take on the world but which, perhaps inevitably, broke apart once it had allowed them to grow into their mature, very different and separate selves. Another told of returning, heartbroken and vulnerable, from a year away in a brief and disastrous late marriage to have her three closest friends, the women she thought of as her sisters, rise up in judgement against her like avenging angels and write a letter formally ending the friendship. All feel the loss of these friends as a huge hole in their lives that they are unlikely ever to fill again.

These losses appear to be more private experiences than the loss of a lover. Intertwined with the pain of loss are feelings of profound humiliation and shame, a sense of having failed at being human and certainly of having failed at being female. After all, women are supposed to be good at having friends. How could we have so misjudged this person, or, worse, so misjudged ourselves? Variations on these emotions are often present at the breakup of a love affair or a marriage, but in those circumstances at least we know we share that experience with much of the rest of the Western world. We are accustomed to sex and romantic love throwing a serious spanner into most people's works, driving us to behave irrationally if not utterly insanely, in spite of all our best instincts and intentions. Living together is difficult: passion and domesticity are not always an easy fit, and the strains on a marriage can often sink it. We see it all the time so are not surprised when sexual and romantic relationships end in tears. Sadly, we recognise that this is a universal experience, the way of the world. But when a best friend abandons us, we cannot escape the fact that the person whom we love and trust most directly, uncomplicated by sexual or familial bonds, can let us down – deliberately betray us, turn cold and implacable just like a lover who loses interest – can become malicious and wilfully cruel. Without sex or family to blame, we can seldom avoid the suspicion that, through some terrible personal flaw, we have brought this on ourselves.

People, even those who are friends, can deeply disappoint one another: that's one of the harshest and most bitter of life's lessons, and one most of us would prefer not to learn. And because this somewhat pessimistic view of humanity seems to be a shameful secret, so little admitted to in public, we are often left with the nagging suspicion that we might be one of the few unfortunates who have to learn it.

Women begin learning about friendship, its importance and its power, its consolations and its treachery, as girls. While boys are learning to do things in groups, girls are gravitating to the intimacy of the pair. It's not at all sugar and spice and all things nice; on the contrary, girls' friendships are red in tooth and claw. And they're complicated by girls' relationships with their mothers, the first intimate relationship that sets the course, one way or another, for all others. Of course, this is most children's primary relationship, regardless of gender, but the merging of mother and daughter makes it far messier for girls and more fraught with peril. Whereas boys are expected eventually to split off from their mothers and identify with the men, girls have to juggle their desire for independence with their feelings of identification with the one person they have to leave in order to become independent. Even women who get on well with their mothers are terrified of turning into them. I suspect that it's the common girlhood experience of mothers and best friends – from whom we need and expect so much and who can wound us so deeply – that makes it much easier for some women to forgive a man than to forgive another woman.

Nine- and ten-year-old girls have usually not read Kafka. They don't need to. They know what it is to be punished brutally for a crime they have not committed, to be cast out, not to be the best friend any more of the girl with whom you have eaten lunch all term, who has walked through the playground with her arm around your shoulder while you whispered secrets in each other's ear, who has slept in your bed with you, scratching your back and talking and giggling until your mother appears in her nightie and tells you to shush. And not to know why.

Moreover, not only is your best friend not your best friend any more, but she has taken your second and third best friends with her, and now they giggle together, torment and shame you with your most intimate secrets now made public, and make your life an utter misery. Sometimes you feel so abject that you will do anything to be allowed back into favour. It is a cycle of cruelty and betrayal that makes most opera plots look anaemic and sends chills of bitter memory down the spine of any woman watching.

I don't remember my best friends at primary school, not as individuals. They were not affectionate choices but brief, temporary, desperate – and essential – alliances against the intolerable. I do remember, however, the triumphal tone of the words 'You're not my best friend any more', and the sense of betrayal that always followed. It wasn't the being alone that I minded, it was being an outcast.

I didn't care for other children much, or not the other children I came across. They were a poor substitute for the fantastic cast of characters who lived in my head, and weren't nearly as much fun as the adults – my parents' friends, especially the rugby-playing British 'boys' my father had taken under his wing, with whom I felt much more at home than I did with the children I knew. Children seemed to me slow, stupid and mean, and the boys coarse, aggressive and incomprehensibly violent as well. The dislike was mutual. I was odd, what was called then 'highly strung'. I talked to myself. I was a misfit in just about every way possible – a plain, fat, clever girl at a rough state primary school in suburban Melbourne in the early fifties, a deadly decade and a stultifying place, where boys ruled and the landscape was littered with things that girls 'couldn't do'. Clever girls were considered abnormal, untrustworthy and probably dangerous (sadly, the last often proved to be true, although the gravest danger was always to themselves). I have since discovered that there were enlightened families and schools in Australia then, but our paths didn't cross.

I'm sure that other children thought I was a pain in the neck – I always had my nose in a book, I *hated* sport and I could spell Czechoslovakia. I could draw pictures and tell stories. I knew the words not only to 'Jerusalem' but to 'The German Band', 'Foggy Foggy Dew' and every other song likely to be sung on a Saturday night by Rugby Union players. But these were solitary pleasures, illicit in that time and place, not the qualities that made friends in the classroom or the playground, although they are the things that enable you to do without them.

Margaret Atwood remembers with chilling clarity the bloodbath that is the friendship of nine- and ten-year-old girls. In *Cat's Eye*, the most autobiographical of her novels, a successful middle-aged painter, returning to the city in which she grew up, recalls her childhood tormentors, the girls who, among other barbarities, buried her alive in a hole in the back-yard and left her to drown in an icy river. These girls who persecuted and nearly killed her were also her 'best friends':

> This is how it goes. It's the kind of thing girls of this age do to one another, or did then, but I'd had no practice in it. As my daughters approached this age, the age of nine, I watched them anxiously [. . .] I asked them leading ques-tions: "Is everything all right? Are your friends all right?" And they looked at me as if they had no idea what I was talking about, why I was so anxious [. . .] Or maybe it was worse. Maybe my daughters were doing this sort of thing them-selves, to someone else [. . .] Most mothers worry when their daughters reach adolescence, but I was the opposite. I relaxed, I sighed with relief. Little girls are cute and small only to adults. To one another they are not cute. They are life-sized.

Adolescent girls are also life-sized to one another – and larger than life-sized to everyone else. As Mary Pipher says in *Reviving Ophelia*, her wise book on teenage girls, 'Think of them as constantly on LSD . . . Compared to stable adults, they all look crazy.' And when it's all girls, *only* girls, they look even crazier.

I am eleven. It is the first day of school, so I am allowed to walk through the main door usually reserved for parents and Canon

Cooper, our religious leader, head of the school council and the only man we see at school apart from the gardener. It is an all-girls school, Anglican, private, hats and gloves and no eating in the street. On my first day it is hushed, hostile, and terrifying. I will soon find that underneath that prim exterior it is, like all girls' institutions, an hysterical hothouse.

I have won a scholarship to come here but, unfortunately, there is nothing intellectually distinguished about this school. It is not at all the kind of educational establishment for girls that Virginia Woolf had in mind and that I had dreamed of – there is no Greek, no Latin, no great library. This school's primary concern is to turn out well-behaved, middle-class suburban housewives – 'ladies' – not scholars, intellectuals, artists, or women equipped for careers. Its principal values are obedience and disciplined godliness – prayers every morning and church at least once a week.

Like many of Melbourne's fine Victorian buildings, including its most famous gaol, the school church is built of bluestone, which is not blue at all but a dark charcoal, grim and cold and forbidding, especially in a Melbourne winter. There Canon Cooper thunders at us, threatening fire and brimstone for the most minor transgressions, while above his head two impossibly cheerful cherubs hold a sugary-pink scroll inscribed in gold: 'God is Love'. I can't see, then or now, how Canon Cooper and the cherubs can both be right.

We spend a lot of time on our knees with our heads bowed, faces buried in our arms, hidden by the pew in front – a perfect position for whispering secrets, passing notes and spying, as both the Vatican and the Tudor Church of our founders could have told our keepers. As in those two venerable institutions, any natural tendencies towards secrecy and duplicity are honed to a perverse kind of perfection by the repressive rule

and wilful cruelties of the tyrant who is our head. She is probably in her early forties, unmarried, and shapeless as an ice
chest in her severe suit, her hair cut brutally short by the local
men's barber. A sadist in a skirt.

First form is presided over by a lesser monster, the aptly
named Miss Hard. Ancient, shrunken and stooped, her nose
and chin almost meeting, her few wisps of hair incongruously
dyed black and in a bun, she is my first real crone, like the
witch in 'Hansel and Gretel'. I talk and laugh too much and am
prey to explosive attacks of the giggles. She sends me outside.
I still talk and laugh too much, so the hours I spent standing in
corridors over the next six years did me no good at all.

Two desks away from me is a quiet girl with olive skin and
thick, blue-black hair that hangs in a heavy plait down her
back. Irene. Along with six or seven other girls, she is perma-
nently excused from church. I am impressed. How does she
manage that? 'She's Jewish,' another girl whispers, as though it
is something exotic and secret, which, to me, it is. I have no
idea what being Jewish means. I know there are Catholics and
Protestants, although I don't know what that's about either,
except that we used to shout insulting rhymes at each other in
the street coming home from primary school. And occasionally
my mother whispers, 'They're Catholics,' as if it were one of the
most shameful of fates and explained everything. I know there
are Jews in the Bible but I can't connect this placid, round-
limbed girl with them. Anyway, if they're in the Bible, why
don't they go to church?

'Are you Jewish?' I ask Irene. 'Yes.' 'What does that mean?
Don't you believe in God?' I'm not sure that I do myself, but I
know that everyone is supposed to. 'We believe in God,' she says
matter-of-factly, 'but we don't believe in Jesus.' I am a bit mystified as I am under the impression that if you take one, you get

them both, with the holy ghost thrown in. But at eleven, my theology is a bit hazy. So we eat lunch together and sometimes I go home with her to her apartment, which is not far from school, and on two or three Saturday nights I go to stay with her.

I have never met a family who live in an apartment. The only flats I have ever been in belong to the rugby-playing friends of my parents – 'boys living in digs', as my mother calls them – and they are like campsites ravaged by bears. Irene's place is not at all like that. To me, an Anglo-Celtic child living in a lower middle-class Melbourne suburb in 1957, everything about it is exotic.

Irene is Polish. Her parents and the aunt who seems to live with them call her Irka. They have thick accents, and numbers tattooed on their arms. I am shocked when I see those crudely formed blue-black figures running up Irene's mother's tiny bird-like forearm. There is something so incongruous about their roughness above her perfect crimson fingernails that it is clear to me, even at eleven, that she cannot have chosen to put them there. Irene's mother is the first camp survivor I have seen, although by no means the last. Arms with numbers on them are to become very familiar in the Caulfield and Balaclava of my schooldays and the St Kilda and South Yarra of my twenties.

At Irene's we eat. For afternoon tea, the most delicious cakes I've ever tasted, rich and sweet and juicy, a world away from my mother's teacakes or the aptly named rock cakes we make in domestic science. For breakfast Irene's mother scrambles the eggs right in the frying pan. They are rich and eggy and silky, unlike my mother's scrambled eggs which she first beats with milk in a bowl then cooks in a saucepan. They always leak a disgusting thin liquid all over the toast, which immediately goes soggy and makes my stomach turn. (A few years later a Jewish boyfriend makes me scrambled eggs exactly as Irene's mother has done. In retrospect I see Jewish scrambled eggs as the first culinary revelation of my life.)

The sheets on the bed are so crisp that they crackle when I wriggle between them. I am mystified as to how they come to be so stiffly starched and ironed into perfect squares. No matter how carefully my mother and I fold the sheets at home, they are never really smooth, even though we fold them straight from the line.

And on a record player that is itself a luxury beyond my imagining – I am sixteen before I have one of my own, my father's last gift – Irene's father plays music that I have never heard before. It is, I now know, Bach and Mozart, and it briefly and tantalisingly opens a door onto another world that it will take me many years to find again.

Irene is an only child. She is never allowed to come to my house. We don't remain best friends, although we never have one of those terrible, bitter girls' breakups. Perhaps we are both trying out alliances to find one that we can live with. And I find Diana.

At twelve Diana is carelessly pretty, with the lean, straight body of a boy. With adolescence she develops the generous bosom of all the women in her family, while the rest of her remains boyish – slim hips, narrow thighs, good legs. She looks fabulous in pants. She has fine pale brown hair that she ties up with an old shoelace and a daisy, and which curls in wisps around her face, like a Botticelli angel, as another friend recalls. Only her feet and hands reveal her other self. They are the rough extremities of a workman, broad, flat and serviceable, with paint under the fingernails, gashes in the fingers, and a layer of hard skin about an inch thick on the soles of the feet. Diana can walk barefoot on asphalt on the hottest summer day without flinching, an achievement I thereafter aspire to but never quite match. I marvel at how intrepid she is, and how impervious to discomfort. She loves camping. When she is

married, she camps for years with two small children in a succession of houses that are in a constant state of renovation, and
builds a weekend shack in the bush with no bathroom and no
running water. For years I feel ashamed of my extreme fastidiousness and my need for a proper lavatory and a shower with an
inexhaustible supply of hot water.

I notice Diana because of her laugh, her looks, her drawing,
which even an eleven-year-old can see is the work of an exceptional talent, and her vague, good-natured, careless ease –
irresistibly attractive, even to a child. Like me, she is often in
trouble but it never seems to bother her. Nothing much seems
to bother her. She has the confidence of a child who doesn't
question that she is safe and sane and secure, doesn't doubt for
a second that people love her just as she is and will support her
whatever she does. She belongs to a big, close family where the
women are strong, fearless and dauntingly capable, and the
men quietly blend into one. Her maternal great-grandmother
owned a horse that won the Melbourne Cup.

One year I go to New Year's Day lunch with the clan at one
of their beach houses. The Cup-winning great-granny is dead
by now, but Diana's mother, her aunts and her grandmother are
unmistakably each other's kin, uncannily alike in shape, habit
and voice as they organise a vast table of food for twenty or
thirty people. These are the women that Diana and her sister
will become. I remember nothing about the men except that
they were there.

Diana's family life was as much a revelation to me as Irene's
had been. A middle child, she lived with an older brother, a sister two years younger and their parents in an old rambling
weatherboard house with wide verandahs and high ceilings and
large comfortable rooms – my first down-filled sofas, my first
William Morris linen – surrounded by the first bush garden I

had ever seen, opposite the beach at Beaumaris. When, many years later, I came across the work of Clarice Beckett, my heart leapt at the sight of that familiar landscape – the rock pools, the flat, luminous planes of sand and sea, the long shadows, the scrub that hides the water from the road, and the beach, wide and grey and empty in the rain.

Each summer holiday I would go with Diana and her family to Point Lonsdale where, on the back beach, we suffered the delights (hers) and torments (mine) of being adolescents. I was thin enough by then, although I didn't think so. The sand dunes that guarded the beach were high and wide and much too hot to walk on after ten in the morning, so we'd take lunch in a basket and live on the beach until late afternoon with a moving population of adolescent male surfers in board shorts and zinc cream, most of whom hung around Diana like adoring Labrador puppies. We'd eat the ham and cheese rolls first, before the cheese turned to oil and the ham went grey, and survive for the rest of the day on hot lemonade and slowly stewing peaches. Basted with baby oil, Diana would instantly turn an edible chocolate brown. I would burn, so badly in the year of our first bikinis that I had to stay on my bed for a couple of days covered in calamine lotion, until my skin peeled off in sheets.

At school we were a gang of five for most of the six years. Like many groups of adolescents, we were bizarrely mismatched and became more so as we grew older, but Diana came with the others attached – she had acquired them in her vague, friendly way in primary school and they stuck. We remained a group of sorts until we left school, even when two or three of us came to loathe each other and fought with the fury of old couples who heartily wish for the other to vanish but remain together out of habit.

Diana and I were the black sheep, the only girls in our matriculation class of twenty-five who were not made prefects or probationers. However, between the ages of about thirteen and sixteen, we were all – even the more conventional, well-behaved members of the gang of five – perpetually over-excited. Everything we did was immoderate. We looked crazy and, for at least part of the time, we were. We were susceptible to mass hysteria, most memorably one morning in third form when, for no particular reason, the five of us dissolved into racking sobs that we managed to keep up for three hours. More often we shrieked and giggled and laughed uncontrollably – oh, the *noise* of teenage girls – gave each other nicknames, often nonsensical, invented worlds and had all kinds of adventures, both real and fantastic, the membrane between them fairly permeable.

One of the tasks of adolescence is to try on selves for size, and that group of friends was one of the audiences on whom I tested out versions of myself. My mother, clinging to cliché in the face of what she saw as certain catastrophe, kept imploring me to 'Just be yourself.' But who was that? Which of the dozens of selves that elbowed each other to get in first every time I opened my mouth? What my mother meant was not *my* self at all, but the self that she, against all the evidence, wanted me to be. That, of course, was the one option I had already discarded.

Was I in love with any of my friends? No, although I burned with the grandest of passions, and had I found a true soulmate that is the friendship we might have had. I loved Diana and we were a powerful alliance but we were intellectually and emotionally disparate, our dreams very different and our needs far apart. We wore each other's clothes, used each other's toothbrushes and slept in each other's beds, but we were never passionately devoted, never mutually absorbed, were never absolutely everything to each other. We were never an exclusive pair, prepared to do anything rather than be separated. Then, suddenly, when I was sixteen, my father died. I was on the other side of the glass from my friends, visible but shut off from everyone, beyond friendship's reach. I still craved a soulmate, but I now needed one that I wasn't going to find among schoolgirls.

A couple of years ahead of us at school were two girls who clearly were an inseparable pair, although I have no idea what the private nature of their friendship was. In sixth form they still called each other Biggles and Algie, and amused themselves by treating much of school life as though it were a W.E. Johns adventure, which in retrospect is an even more inspired idea than it seemed at the time. They were good-humoured, funny, popular, athletic – one of them was the sports captain, the other the school captain – and always together. Probably because we adored them (crushes on one or other of them were commonplace), none of us girls regardèd the intense intimacy of this friendship as unusual. It was a girls' school, after all – all of our relationships were intense.

Only a handful of years before I first noticed Biggles and Algie, one of the most infamous of intimate girls' friendships had come to its grisly climax just across the Tasman. In June 1954, in Christchurch, Pauline Rieper and Juliet Hulme had brutally murdered Pauline's mother, apparently because she had tried to separate them and had refused to allow her daughter to go to England with her friend. This intense, passionate, 'us against the world' relationship is so accurately portrayed in the 1995 film *Heavenly Creatures* that women in cinemas wherever it was screened felt their pulses race with recognition. They remembered the emotional intensity, the ecstasy, and they recognised the idealism and the pair's belief in their intellectual and emotional superiority. Rieper and Hulme believed that they had found the key to the fourth dimension and that they possessed 'an extra part of the brain' that 'only about 10 people' have. 'The outstanding genius of this pair is understood by few, they are so rare', Rieper is reported to have written of herself and Hulme.

At the time of the crime, much was made of Rieper and Hulme's 'unnatural' sexuality, presumably by men with not the faintest idea about teenage girls, and by women who drew back from connecting their girlhood feelings for a best friend with either sex or murder. But whether the relationship was actively sexual or not is largely irrelevant. What's most interesting about any pair of inseparable girls is that their relationship can be of such passionate intensity and completeness, such exalted aims and noble desires, such exhilarating and intoxicating *happiness*, that they attain the Platonic ideal – the dream of two souls as yolk and white of one egg. Few, if any, relationships with a man will ever match it.

Probably because Diana and I were not heavenly creatures we endured. We were bridesmaids at each other's first weddings, at which we married another pair of best friends. Some years later, when I had left my husband and was living with someone else, we were pregnant together with our first babies, who were due on the same day and were born within two weeks of one another.

When I returned to Australia after many years of living abroad, Diana and I were once again part of each other's lives. She helped me survive the divorce from hell, the breakup of a serious affair and three house moves. At the first of these, when the removalists, all big burly blokes, shook their heads and went home, she persuaded me that the two of us could manoeuvre my desk – a ten-foot-long solid timber table with stretchers around the base, so that to move it was like handling a giant coffin – through the front window of a small Paddington terrace house.

And we did. At my next house, we planned and planted the garden together.

Over forty years the friendship has waxed and waned. We have grown apart. In the past several years neither of us seems to have been the friend the other needed. The friendship has faded, and despite attempts to repair it, contact has become less and less frequent. After a couple of years of spasmodically returned calls, no time for cups of coffee and, eventually, silence, I assumed that we had both retreated, hurt and sad. And I mourned the loss of my oldest best friend.

Sudden, cataclysmic breakups of friendship, however painful, are at least clearly identifiable. Betrayal, unforgivable behaviour, an unbridgeable disagreement – although usually much regretted – bring a distinct end with a definite cause. But when longtime best friends drift apart, the causes are harder to identify and the pain is more prolonged. There is no real sense of an ending, no body to bury and grieve over, just the guilt-ridden, drawn-out anguish of 'What have I done?'

What causes longtime best friends to withdraw, to stop feeling deeply connected to each other? It can be all the other things life throws at one, or both, of them: the end of a marriage, a new love, family crises, serious illness, demanding and exhausting work. You might think this is when we most need our best friends, but others feel that all they can do is batten down the hatches and try to survive. Sometimes one friend feels left behind by the other, feels that the gulf between what she sees as her life's chaos and the friend's apparent success is too painful to be around. This mix of envy, guilt and resentment appears to be too shameful for even the closest of friends to talk about, so it remains unspoken, unresolved and always painfully baffling to the rejected friend, who, unlikely to see her life as enviable, remains forever in the dark.

There are also times when best friends come to the realisation that they now have little in common, that they share a past rather than a present. Even the most passionate of intimate friendships – like the most passionate love affairs – can turn out to have a finite life. We change, grow apart, and what once connected us so closely vanishes into air. And there are times, especially as we grow older, when we turn inward and find that there are things that friendship, or the friendships that we have, cannot provide.

Out of the blue, Diana calls. 'Good heavens no,' she says, cheery as ever, when I ask if I have done something to offend her. 'I still think of you as my best friend. I've just been busy. Has it really been two years?'

Yes, it has. Nonetheless the friendship's roots run deep, and while its leaves fall and its branches drop off, those still hold firm. We share a history, know things about one another that no-one else knows. We have been important in each other's lives, and, apart from kin, who know us very differently, we are each other's sole witnesses to those earlier selves. The relationship has changed, contracted, but something indestructible remains. What, exactly?

Frances Partridge, that last surviving Bloomsberry, born in 1900, offers the wisdom of long experience on this. She was eight when she met Julia Strachey, a niece of Lytton's who became her best friend and remained in the forefront of her life until Julia's death. Reading *Memories*, Frances's memoir, and her six volumes of diaries that cover more than thirty years, it is apparent that Julia, who was a true original, creative, acutely intelligent and often highly entertaining, was also one of the most difficult and infuriating of friends. She was wilful, selfish, utterly eccentric when not downright mad, and extremely fastidious about her own comfort, so nothing was ever quite right – a serious difficulty for the friends of one who spent much of her life staying in other people's houses. She could be very *grande dame* and appears to have had not a skerrick of tact.

When she and Frances were in their sixties Julia suddenly, coldly, cut Frances off over some imagined slight and wouldn't speak to her for years, a situation that wounded Frances deeply even as she realised that it was partly the result of Julia's depression and increasing instability. However, Frances continued to love her, worry about her, help her financially, and when Julia got over whatever it was and they became friends again, Frances once more delighted, as she had always done, in the 'ever surprising entertainment her company provided', even though, until the end of her life, being around Julia was like walking through a minefield. When Frances was eighty she wrote:

> I have realised, now that she is dead, that a very early friend is more than a mere influence; she is in some sense a part of one; she has provided some of the ingredients in the cake that has become one's self, for good or ill – in other words a self is not a discrete entity but has a permeable shell like that of an egg, and its very yolk and white are infiltrated by the personalities of early friends.

And so it is with Diana and me.

Joanna Murray-Smith ¶

As schoolgirls, trying on different lives for size, we often make friends of people who are everything we are not and, although we might not know it at the time, are never likely to become. When she is fourteen, Georgia, the narrator of Joanna Murray-Smith's autobiographical novel *Truce*, has for her best friend an American girl, Hilary De Salle. The De Salles are a wealthy, ridiculously good-looking, perpetually sun-tanned family with a mother who looks like Lauren Bacall and 'does everything the modern way', which, in seventies Melbourne, meant 'instant pavlova mix in the shape of a giant plastic egg', and cream in an aerosol can. Georgia's family, like Joanna's own, is literary and left-wing, with a Polish-Jewish refugee mother and a Melbourne Establishment father. Their world is one of intellectuals, political radicals, artists, of summers on an island in Bass Strait, of wine, and a fridge crammed with pungent homemade food for drop-ins. A world in which friends, passionately engaged in argument, singing and laughter, are vital. ¶ AT THE DE SALLES', 'the gentle swinging of squash-toned limbs to the best of Perry Como is as violent as life gets. There is no poignancy. There is no constant presence of injustices and violations. Life is blessed, it's unimprovable, it's the latest model.' No wonder the girls often 'look at each other and say: Swap?' ¶ *TRUCE* CAME OUT of a crisis in Joanna's life, the death in 1988 of her father, Stephen

45

Murray-Smith – academic, historian, founder and editor of *Overland*, former communist and one of Australia's best known men of letters – and her breakdown that followed it. The book, like its author intense, passionate and lyrical, is dedicated to her parents and to 'Raymond Gill, who waited for me'. Ray is now Joanna's husband. He is also her best friend. ¶ IN 1995 JOANNA, Ray and their baby son Sam moved to New York for a year when Joanna took up a Rotary Ambassadorial Scholarship to Columbia University. The following year her play *Honour* was given a public reading in New York with Meryl Streep and Sam Waterston in the leads, and in 1998 it opened on Broadway. Now in her late thirties, Joanna lives with Ray and Sam in a big light loftlike space in one of Melbourne's most urban inner suburbs. She is writing, among other things, a Hollywood screenplay, an opera libretto and a second novel. And she is spending more time in New York, where she sees the friends that she was surprised, but delighted, to make.

───────

I DON'T HAVE lots of close friends. And I worry about that. I've never had that sort of girly-girly friendship, that one where you tell each other everything. Perhaps because I met Ray quite young, at twenty or so, at university, and we were each other's best friends before we were lovers, I've always felt a stronger loyalty to him than to anybody else. Which means that I don't have those discussions with women about my relationship with my husband because I've always felt on some level that it was a betrayal of him.

I have a number of good friends but I have one really great friend whom I've known from childhood. When we went to university, I was at Melbourne and she was at ANU in Canberra, so there were various times where we saw very little of each other. But I suppose I'd say that, after Ray, she was definitely my closest friend. That's Isobel Williams. There's a picture of her up there [on a bookcase] as a little girl by her father, Fred Williams. She's lovely.

Isobel is the same age as me and she's very, very unlike me in most easily identifiable ways. She's very smart but she's not particularly interested in intellectual issues. I can take life too seriously and she is full of joy. She's not working – she's got two young children and she hasn't been working for quite some time. And the things we spend money on are completely different. Just in those sorts of ways we're very, very different. But there is a pure, deep love that runs between us and I'm very affected by that. Perhaps because we don't work in the same area or because we have those differences there's no envy, there's no competition. And we share the privileges and the burdens of having fathers who lived both intense inner lives and very public ones.

I didn't expect to make another really close friend, but I must say I'm surprised that at my age I'm beginning to have crushes. I've had this amazing crush on a woman who was going out with a friend of mine and has ended up directing one of my plays. There are a lot of things about her I don't know. But there's been this tremendous exhilaration of natural intimacy recently, which is not to do with the work. Of course the work is part of it and that's lovely, but it's on another level entirely. And she makes me laugh. We're at the beginning of our journey together as friends, but I feel as if it's going to last forever. There's an integrity to her. There are other people that I'm very close to who, if it came to the crunch, I'm not quite sure how loyal they'd be, and I think that forces a shallowness. I'm aware of the possible limitations of friendships.

Do you feel you could call any of them at three in the morning in a crisis?

There are only a handful of people I could call – I would say there are only five people in the world.

That's pretty good. You're very lucky.

[Laughs] I was feeling so embarrassed about that. Yes, I think there are five people in the world who would do anything, who would go to the ends of the earth if I asked it of them.

When Ray and I broke up and I had a breakdown, I was going through terrible trauma and I had an enormous, enormous fight with a friend. I can't remember ever having fought with friends until then. It was a friend of mine from school days, whom I loved and I love again now, but at that difficult time I asked her to do something – it was something quite trivial but it was to do with my being in a state of collapse – and I felt that she was not willing to go the distance. I had a clear sense then that she was very much into friendship in the good times, but that in the bad times it wasn't there. Now that may or may not be true – it's a bit unfair, she's not here to defend herself, and we got over it when we had children because that brought us back together – but that was the first time I consciously considered issues of duty and morality in the context of friendship.

In my twenties I had never asked anything of my friends and they had never asked anything of me. We had led such comfortable and protected lives that there had never been an opportunity to demonstrate the limits of fidelity or love, or all of those things that are aspects of friendship. This was my one time and she was the only person that I called upon, and it wasn't there. It was then I began to feel that perhaps friendship is somehow or other not properly investigated by those who are protected economically. That somehow – I wondered about this and I don't know the answer to it – perhaps the middle class has less intense, less dependable, less complex notions of what friendship means because friends are so rarely asked to put themselves out for you.

There was a time in my life, before I was married, when I had an ongoing relationship with Ray and I also had another relationship with someone else. And they both knew. They represented different things and amongst my friends there was that sense of, Well, when she wants something that's real and meaningful, she can go home. And when she wants to do something glamorous, she can go off and do that. It is a genuinely obnoxious idea, but I was living it for a little while and there was definitely a sense that my friends were judging that. But I can honestly say that, if I'd been them, I would have been judging it too.

I think they were a bit at a loss about what to do. They were prepared to help me keep all systems running, but they could see that I was collapsing and that I had lost my powers of perception, which I had, and that I was deluded about everything being all right when it clearly wasn't. I mean, I was sick, really.

They'd say things like, 'You can't go on this way.' But no-one ever really sat me down and talked straight to me. And when I think about one of my closest friends now, there are aspects of her life that I'm very worried by. She is very unhappy, and I'm not sure which is more important: for one person in her life to sit down and gently, gently, try to make her see what the problem is, or for her to have one friend who, through thick and thin, lets her be deluded when she needs to be deluded. And who, when she is awakened to her problems, is there to listen, and who, when she makes decisions to change her life, is supportive of that but does not contribute to her stress or her lack of confidence by saying, 'You're doing things all wrong.' I don't know the answer to that. No-one did that with me and I regret that. I actually think it would have made my sense of friendship more substantial if someone had. I don't know how I would have responded, but I wish someone had. They supported me in the sense that they told me what I wanted to hear.

But with hindsight I can see that it would have been more useful to me if they'd said, 'You're behaving badly. It's not good for anybody else but, more to the point, it's not good for you.' I'm sure they felt as I feel now about my friend. I don't think they were badly motivated in not doing that. I think they were well motivated. They were kinder to me than I deserved but, rightly or not, I feel that these friendships will always be compromised by their having seen what a selfish, morally weak person I really am – or really was.

When the crunch came, I think, in the state that I was in, I was beyond friendship. I had isolated myself, physically as well as mentally. But I thought, No-one can reach me at the place I'm in. I was having a nervous breakdown really. So I think I was beyond friendship. I think that Isobel, on the level of soul to soul, would have been wonderful, but I didn't feel able to talk to her about the way I was thinking. It's not that kind of friendship.

More the sort of friendship where she'd come and look after your house and make sure there was food in the fridge?

Oh, she certainly would do that. But no, she's more . . . We laugh together, we'll get drunk together. It's a little bit more decadent, I think. *She's* more decadent. She's a sensualist and I love that about her. But the other thing I really love about her is that, on some very, very deep level I know she truly wishes me well. And I think that sometimes you wonder about that with your friendships.

Isobel came into my life when I was about ten. At that point, Fred and Lyn became very good friends with my parents, and Isobel and I became firm friends. Fred came to paint at this island that my parents had, Erith, in Bass Strait, and then, even when Fred and Lyn didn't come down, Isobel came with our family every summer. So Isobel was very much part of my family, very close to my parents as well as to me, so there was a sisterly aspect to it as well. I spent many weekends in their house in Hawthorn. When Fred died, that was a very significant experience for us both. And subsequently, when my father died. Those tragedies cemented our relationship.

If you met now, would you become friends?

Good question. I think that certain aspects of what attracted each of us to the other are not so visible any more. We were very spirited girls as teenagers. We were quite wild. Isobel now lives in this lovely house on the other side of town, her husband is an architect and if we met now at a party, I don't know that we would have tapped into our – I mean, I think we would have got on very well, but I think that aspects of ourselves have become camouflaged by other things. By behaving properly, basically, by behaving in a socially acceptable way.

The other thing is the fear or difficulty in making that leap of faith now when you meet someone with whom you feel a kindred spirit. I now have this life of absolute belonging with my husband and my child and my work. In my thirties these things have become the way in which I define myself. In a way I have less need for friendship. Now, if I met Isobel, I'd have to come home and say to Ray, 'They were lovely. What if we invite them to dinner? You know, should we reach out across the city and say to these people, Would you like to come out?' We might, but we don't take those kinds of risks so much now because we're all insulated by marriage. I think marriage has affected friendship.

Marriage is a much more detailed friendship, more absorbing, more exclusionary. It carries all the complexity of friendship, or potential friendship, along with all the complexity of a love affair. But, compared to my friends, I think my marriage is a bit unusual in that Ray is my best friend. With some of my friends, that's not the case. They love their husbands but they're not their best friends.

Do you and Ray have close friends whom you see only as couples – couple friends?

There are six of us who are very close friends as couples. We all have dinner as a regular thing and we see a lot of each other, but we don't really see each other individually. It is definitely a different dynamic from that of individual friends. We're very conscious when, through chance, that alters. For instance, when one of the men and I were in New York at the same time we didn't see each other but we had long conversations every night in our separate hotels, and I was very aware that there were the two of us and that this was different from the six of us. Occasionally Ray will take one of the women to the ballet or the opera or whatever, instead of me, and occasionally the three women will go out for lunch together. And that feels very different. They all feel like aberrations from the norm, because it works most often as a couples friendship. But they're definitely different kinds of friendships from those one-to-one friendships from long ago.

You've been exposed to friendship in a quite intense way, I would have thought, from your parents, who seem to have had a real gift for friendship.

Yes, they did. Yes, that's true. I think it gave me an enormous expectation of friendship. They had a great friendship with each other as well, which is perhaps why I know how to find friendship within my own marriage. But my mother, particularly, was also a very critical person, a *very* critical person. She criticised friends' ability to fulfil the demands of friendship. She was judgemental. And I think I have inherited that somewhat.

I was aware of her feeling that friends were capable of betrayal. These, of course, were not their closest friends. With their closest friends they had passionate, wonderful friendships, as my mother still does. I've just been at her house at Mt Eliza and I was amazed that the phone was ringing constantly, with friends of hers from university days who were ringing to say, 'Oh, we read this about Joanna and isn't it wonderful?' They would talk to me and say, 'Oh, that's funny that you're there because I'm just ringing up to talk about you with your mother.' And I thought, What wonderful friends they are, at this point in their lives to be ringing up congratulating her – I thought that was incredibly lovely.

I think they had an extraordinary number of really good friends. But because of my father's life in academic circles, and because of their early political roots, their friendships were formed out of great passions and shared ideologies and complicated times – the Second World War, the Cold War, literary modernism. So there were friends who failed as friends. It's getting back to themes in my writing: people who valued ideology above kindness or decency, or goodness or friendship. I think my parents felt that some old friends lost their humanity and their humour to political dogma. And as my parents became disenchanted by extreme politics, they left some friendships behind them. But our times are different. Sometimes there have been friends at dinner parties with whom I've had enormous disagreements on intellectual issues. And they've been terribly worried, but I say, I don't feel that the emotional or the spiritual connection is in any way jeopardised by intellectual or political issues. We can argue until the cows come home, it doesn't change my feelings for you.

The issue of loyalty is the most important thing in friendship to me. I feel very strongly about having the courage to remain loyal to your friends, particularly in difficult public situations. I think that, in our life as adults, that's a big test of friendship – the conflict between looking after yourself and being loyal to your friends.

What else do you think friends need to share? Apart from a moral sense, which, as you say, doesn't necessarily mean agreeing with one another.

Humour is very important. Humour was a big part of my parents' friendships as well. But difference is also important. I remember, as a child, going to bed on the island and hearing my parents with their friends in the little cabin – it was tiny, tiny – and going to sleep to the sounds of their voices. They would sit up boozing on and arguing, all night sometimes, and I think that that established in me a sense that friendship not only should and does tolerate certain differences, but it thrives on those differences as well. And sometimes those differences find a common ground in humour.

I find great pleasure in differentness with my friends. I hate that idea of all being like-minded, the idea of all agreeing about the same things, the feeling that we're all basically the same person but for a few tiny differences. I think difference is wonderful.

There's also a protective quality to friendship which is very important, particularly in down times. In difficult times, I've taken really great pleasure in thinking, Well, in a week or so, Paul and Margot and Ruth and Stieg [the couple friends] will come over and we're going to get back to the important things. We'll be able to laugh and talk and feel that we are insulating ourselves against whatever is going on out there, whatever darkness. Just the joy of camaraderie, and of knowing what's important. Friendship arms me against cynicism or despair.

So you would obviously be deeply appalled if you felt that any of those friendships fell away because you or Ray were having a rough time?

I would find that quite useful. I think I'm probably quite tough about that – I'd rather know now and not waste time. But I think I have a pretty good idea. Ray makes friends very sparingly. He gets on with everybody, but he is very careful about where he places his loyalty. I'm always the one who encourages making new links and he's the one who's somewhat wary of it. But when I was at university, and before we came together, he was the good-time Charlie of our generation at Melbourne University. He was just a laugh a minute. I think it's quite interesting that, as he's got older, he has tempered that.

Those close friends at university, are they still close friends?

Well, our closest friend we fell out with. We were a triumvirate. [Laughs] If you write a book on friendship you do need to know this kind of nitty-gritty detail, but it's so pathetic! Ray and I were living in New York and Ray was much more isolated than I was because he was at home with Sam. I was mainly at home with Sam and Ray, but I could venture out because I was at Columbia and going to a writers' group and so meeting people. Some of those people subsequently came to know Ray, but I was really the one who was leading that life out there in the city. And I felt very keenly aware that he was missing friendship, that he was having to make do with me and, vicariously, my friendships, but it wasn't the same as his own friendships. Ray's very extroverted in lots of ways, he enjoys social interaction.

Our friend was visiting New York for work. There's a strong sort of love that runs between the three of us still, I think, but the men are pretty competitive. Well, the friend is competitive. And he's utterly graceless. There are times when you forgive that, and there are times when it just irritates you. Ray would have hour-long conversations with him on the phone and fifty-five minutes would be about the friend and then in the last two minutes he might say, 'So how's work?' And Ray would say, 'Fine.' 'Well, I've got to go.' But there are lots of wonderful things about this friend that we adore and I think they're things that were particularly visible and accessible during our university days. When we were in New York, I thought he was cavalier about his friendship with Ray – I can't remember what it came down to, something petty, but I thought that in that situation, in that one week or so, I'd seen something. It gelled with all kinds of little incidents in the past and I thought, Well, enough is enough, and I finally said to him, 'You are not a good friend.'

He wrote us a letter, which was as close as he would come to an apology. He made an effort. But Ray can be very tough. Nonetheless I still think it is a very special friendship and cannot quite let it go. A few weeks ago, I rang him. A tragedy happened and I was in Sydney and Ray was frantic at work and couldn't talk, and I thought, I'll ring this friend. So we sort of vaguely started up again as friends.

When friends don't behave the way you think they should, do you usually tell them? Or do you let it drift?

I'm pretty forthright. I prefer it to sending little signals. I think good friendship deserves that forthrightness. In friendship you've got to show some courage. Friendship is not an abstract state.

I think that you do have to work at your friendships. That could mean you might not be able to see someone for six months, but you'll ring them and say, 'How are you?' Or you'll send them a card. Or whatever is feasible within that friendship. But I don't feel that friendship just perpetuates in an abstract way. I don't think one ought to allow it to do that.

I think friendship is quite practical, I think it *ought* to be practical as well. I think it ought to be renewed and kept alive. And
it doesn't take that much effort to do it.

I feel much more strongly about that now than I used to, but
I've come to feel that great friendships are very rare and I now
have a sense of how profoundly important they are. And for
those two reasons, one needs to look after them. I write reasonably diligently to friends overseas, and with friends here I'll write
or I'll just organise to meet. I tend not to have long phone conversations, although I do with friends who are interstate, like my
men friends. I have some good male friends, three straight men.
Two of them don't live in Melbourne but I talk on the phone, or
email. Some were potential lovers during the teenage years,
when everyone was a potential lover, but not since then.
Although I've always had good relationships with ex-lovers.
Maybe it's because I've always been the one who's broken up, so
perhaps it's been engendered through guilt. But I think I had
good taste in the sense that they were genuinely lovely people.

Do you think you are a good friend?

I don't think I've ever really been called on, which would be
a way of demonstrating my love for someone. I can't remember
being required in that way. I don't remember anyone saying,
Can you drop everything and come over now? I don't remember anyone saying, Can you lend me some money? I feel that
I've been supportive through difficult times for friends but
there haven't been those sort of overt, active statements of
friendship. I feel a very deep love for my close friends but I
don't know how well they know that.

*Is it, do you think, because people see you and Ray as such a
unit, and now you have a small child? One always tries to avoid asking people with a close partner and, especially, a small child to drop
everything because you know that, on the whole, it's impossible.*

It's probably partly that. And partly because people perceive me as being so busy. The only way I can reassure myself about that is that I know the extent of my love for them and I hope I declare it. I think I declare it more than Ray does, for instance. He is far less articulate about his affections. I think he's more steadfast in lots of ways than me, and more wonderful and more true a friend, but he articulates it less. I just hope that somehow the very truthful nature of my love for this handful of people is so real that it must communicate itself. I hope it does. But I don't know how to judge that myself. And, happily, most of my friends have led pretty tragedy-free lives. Isobel's father's dying was obviously an enormous event. In a few cases one parent has died, but all our children have been all right. I don't know anyone divorced or separated yet. [Laughs] But we got married late. I was twenty-nine. Ray and I had been together, on and off, for eight years or something. It was during that time, when I was twenty-six, that my father died.

I think a lot of the problems with yourself, which affect your relationships, are very significant in your twenties. But those of us who got through our twenties and then decided who we wanted to be with made those decisions with a much healthier backdrop, I think. I'm very glad I didn't marry Ray at twenty-five because our relationship would have had to have worn an awful lot of problems that were just inevitable.

Was that time of your breakdown, after your father died, the only time in your life when you felt friendless?

I think so. I did feel friendless during that time. Looking back, I think it was my own resistance to friendships. At the time I was utterly egocentric, in the way that desperate misery can make you. I suspect I was thinking, What can my friends do for me? And my answer to that was: nothing. So I think it was more my resisting them than their reluctance to involve themselves with my misery.

But I also grew up with a mother who had a very, very strong sense of the importance of – I could say discretion but I actually think secrecy. She had a very strong sense that you do not furnish people with information about your most private self.

Because they might use it against you at some point?

Yes. It may not be in any active way, but in some way their having information is going to make you more vulnerable. And I have tried to fight that in myself for years, since I first became aware of it, which was probably in my late twenties when I suddenly realised that my concept of friendship was really compromised by my reluctance to reveal innermost aspects of myself, even with very good friends. But I simply can't fight the power of that early training, those early messages that my mother sent me, her belief that blood is thicker than water. As a writer it is a real issue for me. It's about what one reveals, what one protects. Friendship is in some ways expressed as a mutual process of self-revelation. If you hide yourself, you sabotage the deepening of friendship.

I think the crisis in my twenties was very much to do with having false expectations of all kinds of things, including friendships. As a child I didn't see how different my life was from other people's lives. I didn't see what was special about that world. But now I can see that I was surrounded by people who had an enormous sense of social responsibility, an enormous creative ability, an enormous commitment to humanist values, and a sense of intellectual integrity. And it's really not prepared me very well for life. [Laughs]

Would you call your mother a friend?

Oh yes, we talk several times a day.

Is that a problem for Ray?

No, in fact the opposite. My mother has sort of become his mother. When she and I are having problems he is very loyal to me, so in that way he's quite separate, but in terms of support and encouragement, she's the one who rings him up and says, 'Ray, the pages [in the *Age*, where Ray is arts editor] looked wonderful today.' Or, 'So-and-so's review of that opera was just ridiculous, and this is what it was really.' She is engaged with him and what he does in a way that his own family is not, and he appreciates that.

I have a sister who is ten years older then me – big gap – and a brother who's nine years older. I'm closer to my sister now than I used to be, because of the children – again, children are the great connection. I have a lot of respect for her, but it's not an easy relationship. Along with other things I think there was the sense that I was the baby and I was the one who got all the benefits – I was the one who was taken to Europe, I was the one who had the piano lessons. I always felt very judged by her.

Do you have friends that you see on your own, without Ray?

A few, yes. The men friends, and a couple of good women friends. Ray thinks one of the men isn't trustworthy enough, and he's probably right about that. Ray has always had an excellent sense of the trustworthiness of people. It's interesting because in my family my mother did and my father was a bit naïve, I think. And in our relationship, Ray has a much better sense of that than I do. He knows the limits of a friendship, the extent to which that friendship will work and beyond which there is no point in his investing more deeply in it. We all do that to some degree but he seems to do it very well. With my other male friends he's not at all threatened. And I think that's a reflection of the substance of our love.

I think my close female friends really love Ray, although I

might choose to see them on my own for other reasons. On the other hand, there are women with whom I would like to be closer friends, and would if they were single, but feel that I can't because I don't like their partners or their husbands. I see them on their own to some extent, but I know that we can't go the next step because I can't stand the people they're with.

I think friendship does mean different things at different times in your life. During that horrible period when I was seeing two men, at one point I decided not to see either of them. So I was just on my own and I had nowhere to live. I was really broke and at my wits' end. I was staying in someone's house, house-sitting, and I remember thinking, Oh my God, I haven't looked after my friendships well enough. It was then, when I was on my own, that I was struck by the insulating effect of a sexual relationship and how destructive that can be, how blasé it can make you about your friendships. It was from then that I started to realise how important friendships are, and how fragile. I was vulnerable to the need for friends and that was because I had not been a good enough friend myself.

Another time when you really need friends, it seems to me, is when you have young children. Sometimes, when you're at the end of your tether, those friendships are lifesaving. They mightn't last forever but they're hugely valuable and can be quite intense.

Oh yes, and enormously comforting. Particularly as women shift into the first stages of motherhood. I felt that very, very keenly when I first had Sam – the first weeks really, where I just felt capsized by this love and also by the terror that it had created in me. I'd go to the Infant Welfare Centre in Fitzroy and most of the women I met there had first babies, and to sit in there when we were waiting to have our babies weighed and measured and all of that made me feel so cheered and so reassured.

It was obviously the magnitude of the experience we were going through that allowed us to be open. And that was the first time I had a really genuine sense of being a woman, being part of a sex. Instead of having a sense of myself as a human being, or as a young person, or as white or middle-class or university educated, or all the other things, I had a very strong sense of being a woman. And I had this incredible regard and respect for women, just women in general. The birth and those experiences after birth, and that sense of coming into yourself as a mother, and the fear, the anxiety and the extraordinary exhilaration, as well as having to deal on a practical level with the exhaustion and those things that make you feel as if you're in a torture chamber, which of course I'd never thought about. I remember sitting there breastfeeding in the middle of the night thinking, Women *forever* have been doing this. And what strength there is in womanliness, that it can adapt to this and be so quiet and good-natured about it. You don't see women out there screaming in the street, 'I haven't slept for fifteen months!'

Do you think that one of the greatest divisions in the world is between those with children and those without?

I do. I do. I'm afraid I do. That's the very, very big change in our lives, that recognition. I can't help it, but I have this terrible sense of superiority. Now I know what's important. And I have experienced depths of, well, misery, but also anxiety and pleasure and love and fear that I just don't think are available to people who haven't had a child. I look at women who have consciously made the decision that they don't want children – I know this is terribly politically incorrect and unfashionable – and I think, A child would actually be the making of them.

I feel appalled when people don't like children. When we came back from New York, we noticed an incredible difference in the way people treated Sam. New Yorkers treated him, all of seven months, as a human being. They were concerned for his welfare, they engaged with him, they were interested. And when we came back to Australia there was this sense that children are really not human beings yet. They're not human beings until they're adult. And it's very upsetting. As Paul Grabowsky said to me, 'Saying "I hate children" to me is like saying "I hate Jews" or "I hate Blacks".' It's as shocking, and yet people say it quite smugly.

I think of your mother's friends ringing up and saying, 'About Joanna . . .' I feel, with people I've known for a long time, that our children belong to all of us in a way.

That's right. It's a fantastic feeling. And that is the important stuff. When I talk to resolutely childless women at parties, I always have this sense of being outside of myself, thinking, This is her whole life and this is just one small part of my life, and thank God.

I wouldn't want to spend time around people who don't want to spend time with my child. I couldn't be bothered now. I think you have to make those decisions. It's interesting, because one of those male friends I mentioned lost a certain amount of interest in the friendship when I got married – that was sort of a sexual thing, I think. But he also lost a degree of interest when I had a child, and that made me feel a bit different. We're still good, good friends, but I'm aware that the friendship had ingredients to it which I was not always conscious of. It was the knowledge that a possibility we had once had was no longer there – and that possibility had made it more alive or energetic or something, certainly from his point of view. Once I'd removed myself from that possibility there was a lessening of interest. And having a child has sort of cemented that. It is – or I am – beyond the brink.

When you arrived in New York, brand new, with a new baby, how did you find making friends?

We had a very strong sense that we'd probably made all our good friends and that it wasn't going to happen for us in a new place. But we came out of that year with some very good friendships. I think a number of things contributed to that. One was that, as people in our thirties, we had a much truer sense of what it was in other human beings we gravitated towards, what was important to us, and what would furnish a real friendship, so we were much more discriminating in what we were looking for in people. I mean, this was all unconscious, but now I can see it. So when you're meeting people, you're sorting unconsciously and you're zeroing in on those with whom you feel a rare intimacy or affection. Often you come together because you have parallel intellectual ideas but ultimately that's not the most important thing. It gets down to much deeper issues, ethical issues, as well as humour and taking pleasure in how someone looks, all of that. I think you can look at a face and know whether that face houses the personality, the human characteristics that you admire. I do think you see people's deeper characteristics in their faces.

And there was also the new parenthood and being away from our own city and country as well. There was an honesty about us in what we were looking for and who we were, which I think was fired by going through this monumental life experience, this experience of parenthood. We were less camouflaged in our social personae. Sam was three months old when we went, so we were worn and tired and all of that, but also thrilled and excited. I think we were probably more open, certainly much more open than in our own home city where you're concerned about reputation, about who knows whom, about the incestuousness of the world you're living in. It was wonderful to feel free of that. It was just fantastic. It was such a liberation that I'm craving it as I speak.

I think friendship in New York takes a back seat to professional life, more so than for Australians. They just simply don't have time, Manhattanites anyway. So people would be enthusiastic – 'You must come to our house in the country' – and then not follow through. But there were a few people with whom we forged really deep and continuing bonds. And it was such happiness for us to leave that city with this handful of people as friends – it was like a slap in the face to mortality. It was as if life is always renewing itself. We felt this sense of renewal of all sorts of things, but this was a renewal of friendship, of being able to make new friends. And the zest that that gave us, just the injection of new people in our lives – new humour, new temperaments, new thoughts, new problems – all of that was a great pleasure.

We keep in touch, and when I was there for a week recently I saw most of them or spoke to them. So I feel that if we go back again, they're there. And even though the New York friendships are relatively new ones, in some ways we have more in common with these people than we do with our old friends, because we are more evolved into who we are and we made these friendships in that state. Some of those very old friendships are based on aspects of ourselves which we are now less in touch with.

So they're kept going by what? Bonds of affection? A sense of witness to the way you were?

Absolutely. Absolutely. Whereas the New York people are more to do with our lives now. I feel this more than Ray does because I've had the opportunity to, but I now am really split between friendships in New York and friendships here. I think, ultimately, friendships here are important because they're longer ones, they've been forged over a longer time. But in terms of sheer pleasure of interaction, I've now got such good friends in New York that it's painful for me to be separate from them.

Perhaps having close friends in two places will turn out to be your life.

I think that's true. Although some of our good friends here say, 'If you leave, we're coming with you. We're coming too.'

Chris MANFIELD ¶

A T THE 1999 *Sydney Good Food Guide* Awards, chef Chris Manfield and front-of-house supremo Margie Harris, best friends and partners in life and work, strode up to the platform to receive two hats for their restaurant Paramount, in Macleay Street, Potts Point. As they stepped up on stage, arm in arm, they turned the backs of their black leather jackets to the audience, revealing huge white letters which, when they stood as one, read 'NO GST'. The foodie audience roared its approval. It was a bold and irreverent gesture, very like Chris herself. ¶ CHRIS WAS ALREADY thirty-three and living in Adelaide when she gave up teaching for cooking in 1985. She and Margie came to Sydney in 1988, and two years later opened their first restaurant, Paragon, in the Paragon Hotel at Circular Quay. The next year they took over the dining room in the Phoenix Hotel in Woollahra, and in July 1993 they opened Paramount, their first completely independent venture. ¶ AT THE END OF 2000 – after we'd had this conversation – they sold Paramount to go freelancing around the world. Sydney will miss the pearly-walled Paramount, the room as elegant as the food, with Margie out front, a small, black-clad burst of pure energy with such a great welcoming grin that the first time I saw her I wanted to hug her, and in the kitchen Chris – tall, cool, blonde and handsome, with a killer smile. ¶ SOMEHOW CHRIS HAS found time to write three cookbooks – *Paramount Cooking, Paramount Desserts* and *Spice* – each so luscious-looking that you want to eat it. And there's another in the works. She is a self-confessed obsessive, a perfectionist: 'Mediocrity has no place in my world; it smacks of sloppiness, slackness, indifference and many weaknesses [. . .] My driving ambition has always been the pursuit of excellence, and that is what guides me in my work and in my life.' But it's a lively perfectionism sparked with great passion and generosity, integrity, a certain outrageousness, and what Chris accurately calls a wicked sense of humour. To Chris, friends are her family. As she says in *Paramount Cooking*, 'Life is too short to eat bad food.' And, she might have added, to have bad friends.

———

I'D SAY I HAVE a handful of best friends. Definitely a handful. Obviously my closest friend is Margie. There's a whole different element to that relationship, but we're best friends. That certainly helps to carry you through when you live together and work together. We don't tire of each other's company. And we both maintain our own independence.

We didn't start off as friends, we met and did the whole falling in love thing. And we've been living together now for twenty-two years. I think that whatever happens in the future – although I can't imagine us not being together – there's too much water under the bridge for us not always to be good friends.

The most difficult time of our relationship was opening this place [Paramount]. The first six months were – oooh. [Laughs]

If we could get through that, we could do anything. The other test of a good friendship is if you can travel together. When people say to me, 'We're going off travelling with our friends,' I always say, 'It'll test your friendship. If you can come back and still be good friends, then you've won it.' Margie and I travel a lot and we thrive on it. It's an essential element of our relationship. We have similar expectations and aims when we travel, so we're not at cross purposes. It's not like one of us wants to sit all day in an art gallery and the other wants to go shopping. We tend to get out there and do as much as we can.

I can't stand people who take all morning to get out the door. I'm up, out, on the street. And as soon as I arrive in a city, I don't care what time of the day or night it is, I drop my bag and I'm out. Get my bearings, suss it all out, and then get into the rhythm of it. And I don't think you can arrange that, it's something that just happens. You've got to get out there into the thick of it and be prepared to go anywhere – 'Okay, I'll go there.' [Laughs] I've got a bit of the old pioneering spirit.

When Margie and I have travelled with other people, it's usually been short-term – 'We'll meet up with you here and do such-and-such.' It's good fun, and often just that sharing makes the experience fantastic. We've been away for extended amounts of time, for a couple of months at a time and once for six months, and the thing you miss most is your friends. You think, I could live here if so-and-so came and lived here too.

That's part of the reason we moved to Sydney, because so many of our friends from Adelaide were moving up here. And we'd been travelling a lot – I used to teach and Margie was in the Public Service, so it gave us access to lots of holidays – and we fell in love with big cities. We both fell desperately in love with New York and just wanted to be in a faster-moving place.

I'm sure that's part of the reason why Adelaide has lost its spark – it's had a serious brain-drain. Even though it was a small city it had a very different feel to it ten or fifteen years ago. So yeah, we wanted to live in a place that felt as though it had a bit of energy pumping through it.

I came here to work with Philip [Searle, who had come to Sydney from Adelaide] at Oasis Seros [one of Sydney's star restaurants of the 1980s]. I'd just gotten into cooking and I thought, Right, I'm going to do this. I was very focused and I didn't want to do it with just anyone. I wasn't twenty years old so there was a much greater urgency about proving that I could do it. If I couldn't prove it in a couple of years, I was going to move on.

Margie started working on the floor at Macleay Street Bistro. We had a network of friends and contacts. When I first got here I was just hassling Philip. He'd said, 'There's nothing actually available,' so I said, 'I'm coming anyway. You're not getting rid of me that easily.' When we first arrived I worked at The Wharf for six or seven weeks, when Anders [Ousback] was running it, and I just persisted with Philip. I needed instant income. We'd lived in Adelaide extremely cheaply. We had this fantastic house in the hills that we used to have rent-free, and then we came to the harsh reality of Sydney.

Did that put a strain on yours and Margie's relationship?

No, not really. We were well organised and we were both fairly busy. And it was so new and it was fun mostly. There were pangs of homesickness, especially with Margie because she had her family in Adelaide. I don't come from Adelaide, I'd moved there when I was twenty, so I feel it's more my home than Brisbane is, where I was born – although that's not so true any more because I really think that feeling is people-directed. But then we'd go back regularly, a few times a year, so it took about nine months to really feel as though we belonged here. It was a bit disjointed at first.

But Sydney, like New York, is full of so many people from all over that you very soon feel as though you belong here as much as anyone else.

Exactly. And that's why I like it.

Does the intimacy and the longevity of your relationship with Margie affect the making of other close friendships?

We've both got other close friends. Both men and women, so it's not directed solely towards women. Although I find, just as a general comment, that women tend to make much stronger emotional bonds with each other, regardless of who they sleep with.

What is the difference between your relationship with Margie and another close female friend?

You always tell your best girlfriend everything, sometimes more than you would tell someone you're sleeping with. It's important to have that avenue as well, regardless of the sort of relationship you're in – to have other friends that are important in your life just so you're not too isolated in your expressions. And it stops you overloading that primary relationship too. I would hate to live in an isolated couple, I think it would be very destructive of your relationship.

A good example of that is when Barbara [a Canadian who ran the Paramount Stores] lived here. She was our best girlfriend, for both of us, but in different ways. She's probably our most treasured friend of anybody. Now that she's gone back to Canada it's a bit more difficult, but we communicate anyway. It's just that face-to-face contact is not there.

Margie and Barbara had a very close, emotional, let's-go-out-and-be-naughty-girls friendship. And they did all that chat, chat, chat. When either of them had the shits with me, they could have a good old bitch to each other. And they often went off on their own and cut loose. I did it a bit, but not as much. My relationship with Barbara was much more of a cerebral one. She's the only person I've ever worked with who got inside my head and understood it implicitly. So we had an extreme closeness and we still do. We talk about work she's doing, work I'm doing.

She came and applied for a job. Just walked in when she arrived from Canada. That was in 1993. In an instant, we just clicked. I just knew. It was, 'Yep, you can start next week.'

Was it difficult having somebody work for you whom you really liked as a close friend as well?

No. Didn't have a problem with it at all. It can be a problem if you operate in a fairly rigid way, but we have a level of closeness here anyway. We're all good mates. With our team it's not that really rigid, structured, I'm-at-work-and-I've-got-to-behave sort of thing because I don't set myself up in that way.

But your team has a very clear view of what you want. It seems to be very precise: This is what we're here to do.

Oh yes, I make that very clear. So you can't ever cross that line. But within that there's quite a lot of flexibility and a range of stuff you can get away with.

Is Barbara one of those really close friends to whom you would tell anything?

Anything. For instance, she was around at a very important time, when Margie's mother died a few years ago of a brain tumour, and that was very, very difficult because Margie was so close to her. Margie was going backwards and forwards to Adelaide for about six months. But Barbie was a really good anchor because she was someone else that Margie could talk to and just totally break down in front of, do whatever, as well as having the anchor of our relationship. Because sometimes that burden just gets too much, on both sides. And we weathered some of Barbie's emotional turmoils as well.

Have there ever been times when the making of a best friend outside the relationship became a threat? How do three women handle that?

Look, I'm sure it can be a threat. We're all jealous animals. There were certainly times, if I am really honest, when I was quite jealous of Margie's attention to Barbara. We always used to tease each other and say, 'She's jumped the fence, darl.' Because Barbie's so good with women and has great rapport and hung out with us all the time, everyone was convinced that it was a threesome anyway. And Barbie didn't help matters by saying she got the job by sleeping with me. [Laughs]

Do you think some women are hesitant about becoming close friends because they feel it's going to become tricky? Or are there women of whom you think, Uh-oh, better not get too close?

Not really. No. Not any more. I think that's part of the longevity thing, you just don't worry so much. In the first few years there was a bit of the 'Bloody bitch. How dare you!' sort of thing, in most cases over something quite innocent. But I think you're very protective in the beginning.

Have you come across that jealous possessiveness amongst close friends who aren't lovers? That excluding of each other that girls do in the schoolyard – 'You're not going to be my best friend any more.'

'You can't play with me today.' Yes, I know. People I consider my friends don't do that, but I know of women who are like that, who are incredibly undermining. I see them as being quite misogynist. And there are some women who are just outrightly anti-female; they only relate to men and see all other women as competition. I just have a private laugh. Because Margie's and my relationship is very well known in our peer group, I can be good friends with a lot of the boys around town.

Doesn't matter that some of them are married, some of them are gay, some of them live with girls, or whatever – you're not seen as a threat any more. You can be a friend or a confidante to these guys and it's not a problem for their partners because you're one of *them*. [Laughs] So they know that you're not going to do the big come-on. And we're quite honest about what we are. This is what we are, take us or leave us. It lays your cards on the table and everyone knows what's going on then, across all levels. Makes life a lot easier.

Have you ever had a close friendship that fell apart? When something happened that made you or the friend call it a day?

Yes, there are people we have been very close to in the past and aren't any more. But it's never been a spoken thing. It just dissolved. Quite strange too. Hard to know what happened. There were a couple of gay boys who were very close friends, and are again. The friendship was tested for a time, and that came about through feeling physically disconnected. They were living a totally different lifestyle in a different country and we were in our high-pressured urban environment. It was resolved eventually because we really loved each other and had an inherent closeness none of us could walk away from. We aired those feelings of being hurt and pissed off, and are now back to being girlfriends and boyfriends. That sense of connection is what you feel when you're really close to friends.

How much do you have to share with friends? Do you have to value the same things?

Oh, I think so. I think it certainly helps. The same sort of morality, whatever that is. You don't all have to agree. But personal politics are extremely important in terms of how you treat your friends and how you relate to each other and how you support each other. I also look for intelligence in a friend – you can't be vacuous.

Would your friends call you at two in the morning if they were in a crisis?

Yes, they've certainly done that, and it's been a two-way street.

One of the tests of friendship seems to be when one friend gets a new partner. How do you respond when one of your close friends takes up with somebody you don't like?

Well, we went through that with Barbie, you know. She took up with this absolute deadshit of a guy. At first we were quite noncommittal and for me that's a greater statement than saying anything. But she was just all over the place and went back home to Canada, after being here for five years, to sort her head out. It took quite a while to get it out of her system. Once she'd made that physical break it became a lot easier for us to say exactly what we thought. She's fallen in love with someone else now – we've just returned from the wedding. And we've made another really close friend. So yes, we're fairly opinionated about those things because we want the best for our friends, but we're also sensitive to their needs and try not to judge harshly because the important thing is that they're happy.

Are you ever torn between thinking that and thinking, Look, my job as a friend is to support her no matter what kind of idiotic things she does?

There's a bit of both. You have to do that. You can't just wade in saying, 'You're making a mistake here.' I certainly wouldn't do it initially. Everyone's her own person; you can't tell someone who she can like and who she can't.

Do you have any straight men as close friends?

Not really. Lots of gay men, though. I'm reasonably close to my three brothers. I'm the oldest, and we feel comfortable enough to ring each other for a heart-to-heart chat. And there are a few partners of girls we know that we're quite close to, but in terms of that real intimacy, spilling the beans about inner-most thoughts, no. With the innermost core you can talk about anything. And sometimes you just need to let off steam about something to someone independent. I think that's what good friends are for, because they put up with that sort of stuff. I guess that really separates your dearest friends from your good friends or not-so-good friends.

When you and Margie are going through a bad time, do you talk about that to other close friends?

Oh, yeah. I think that helps. It does give you a sense of objectivity, and sometimes they can set you straight. You may have overreacted about something, or been totally obstinate or stubborn, and they can put it into perspective, can say, 'Hang on, it's not as bad as you think.'

Do you keep contact with your friends on the phone or do you write notes?

I have almost daily phone contact with my closest friends. Margie's brilliant at that and thrives on physical contact with people. I tend to do the long-distance maintenance. I'm not all that good now at writing letters. If someone gets a letter from me, that's a serious treat. But email, faxing, yes. I'm very good at keeping up contact with people. Always have been.

I have to check the email twice a day anyway, so if someone has written I just respond straightaway before it goes out of my head. It's fantastic. The same with faxing, it's so easy because it's just right there.

Is it important for you to have old friends who knew you when you were a girl?

I don't have any connection with my childhood, apart from my family. I left school when I was fifteen, in Brisbane, and then I left Brisbane when I was twenty. And after I left school I moved to the other side of town. Left home, cut off. My parents had split up the year before and I was just a hell-child. When I was fifteen it was the sixties – God, look at what was going on. I didn't have a particularly close relationship with my mother at the time. In fairness to her, she'd had no experience of life herself and hadn't the tools to cope with the difficult times. We didn't really speak at all for ten years. I got married and divorced in that time. We speak now and it's developed into a more adult, more comfortable relationship, based on respect for each other. I was also fortunate enough to have an emotional relationship with Margie's mother, who treated me like a daughter.

My father is still alive but I saw him last when I was seventeen. He's disregarded and abandoned his past life totally, and I feel no responsibility or desire to seek him out. He obviously does not wish to confront his demons.

When I left home, and all through my teenage and adult years, I made sure I was surrounded by a close network of friends. Still do. To me that's my family. I couldn't live without my friends.

Do you think it's harder to make close friends as you get older?

No, I think it's probably easier because you cut through the crap. You can see things so much more clearly. When you're younger, it's quite hard because there are all sorts of other things at play – that whole sexual thing for a start. But by the time you're my age you've sorted out your own shit, you've got your place in the world and you feel much more confident. I wouldn't want to be twenty again for anything. I still *feel* like that, but the knowledge and the experience – you can't tell anyone that. They've got to go through the process themselves.

The other thing that's really important about a very close friend is that she's someone who doesn't judge you, who will accept you, who knows your foibles and knows when to leave you alone. Long-term friends are the ones who have accepted your growth as you have theirs, who haven't had this predetermined idea of 'this is the way you were and how dare you change'. I think this is where friendships often break down, because you've stepped outside the perceived boundary and the friend feels uncomfortable or threatened by that.

A very close friend, a best friend, will accept you and love you, faults and all, even though there are times when you give each other the absolute shits. [Laughs]

Mary VALLENTINE ¶

I N 1996 Mary Vallentine's friend, the writer David Marr, described their first meeting to Janet Hawley for an article on Mary in *Good Weekend* magazine. It was 'at a famously appalling party in Balmain in 1975. Jim McNeil, newly released prison playwright, was explosively drunk in the garden and threatening to murder a blowsy Wagnerian comedienne singing her way through the Ring Cycle at the top of her lungs, while the host tried to keep his chic party afloat. Mary sat at a 17th century spinet, observing the scene from a distance with a wonderfully quizzical eye and played on.' ¶ THAT TALENT FOR apparent serenity in the midst of chaos, combined with the wonderfully quizzical eye of the deeply, *fabulously* funny, are probably essential for anyone who spends her working life managing a large group of creative souls and has another sizeable band of them as her closest friends. On top of that, you have to love them – the mad, the bad, the dangerous and the difficult, who are also the inspired, the visionary, the passionate and the brave. Mary Vallentine, fifty-one in 2001, has been Managing Director of the Sydney Symphony Orchestra since 1986, and before that was General Manager of the State Theatre of South Australia (1982 to 1984), Administrator of the Adelaide Festival (1978 to 1982), and Assistant Manager of Musica Viva Australia (1974 to 1978). She is now responsible for one hundred and ten orchestra musicians, plus guest soloists and a chief conductor – more egos in a day than many people want to deal with in a lifetime, each prey to its own particular neuroses, obsessions and depressions – and her rather large circle of intimate friends includes some of the most interesting people in the arts in Australia. ¶ MARY APPOINTED Stuart Challender as the Sydney Symphony Orchestra's chief conductor in 1987. When he died of AIDS in 1991 she lost both a gifted colleague and a friend. David Marr speaks of her 'essential skill' as 'taking an indecisive, insecure great talent and helping them to mould and steer the creative process. She did it with Stuart and with Neil Armfield [theatre and opera director, Artistic Director of Company B Belvoir and one of Mary's intimate friends], both chronically indecisive near-geniuses. There's a whole scrum of people across the creative arts who rely on using Mary as a sounding board – myself included. Her advice is always so good.' ¶ AND SO HONEST. Mary is a straight talker. No bureauspeak, no bullshit. She is tough, ironic, amused and forthright, but also immensely loyal and generous. You feel you could trust her with anything, including ticking you off if she felt you needed it. She also has a luscious voice, deep, musical and warm, although what she says can be wickedly sharp, her delivery dry and her timing enviable. As in this story, told by another close friend, the playwright Nick Enright: 'A short, mean Adelaide critic had been unspeakably unfair about the South Australian Theatre Company while Mary was general manager there for Jim Sharman and Neil Armfield. One night

the little critic bowled up to the statuesque Mary at some function and announced, "Ah, Miss Vallentine, at last we meet face
to face." Mary peered down at him from her full height and
replied, "Not quite."'

———————

WHEN I TOLD David you were asking me about friendship
today, he said, 'Tell her that your idea of friendship is ringing
up a very good friend – me – and wheedling him out of his
ticket to the opening night of *The Boy From Oz* on the grounds
that this would be doing him a favour because he doesn't really
like musicals. So you go and of course it turns out to be terrific.'
[Laughs] Well, I thought I *was* doing him a favour. I didn't
expect to like it.

I'd said to him, 'You like musicals even less than I do, so why
don't I go?' He said, 'Oh, okay.' Then someone said to him,
'That's the hottest ticket in town.' And he thought, Hang on.
Have I just been had? [Laughs]

Your relationship with your dearest friend is obviously brutally
honest. David told me that when you were driving somewhere
together one day, he got into the car and you said, 'I hope you've
worked up some topics.'

I don't think we actually do have much more to say to
each other. [Laughs] But then he said to me this morning,
'I don't think talking is so necessary. One of the things about
friendship is that you don't actually have to talk to each
other.' And I said, 'Well, that's a bit difficult, seeing we have
mostly a telephone relationship.' He said, 'That's only
because you can't face seeing me.' I said, 'I'm a bit busy at the
moment.'

What do you do when you're so busy you just don't have time to see your friends?

I have periods when I'm so busy that I don't see them, but not when I don't speak to them. Often we're equally busy, and the phone is a really good vehicle of communication so it won't matter as much not having seen people. But my very good friends I usually see every week, and I'd speak to a couple of them daily – David, Neil Armfield, Jenny Coopes. But I also speak to my siblings each day: my sister Jane, my sister Kath, who's ill, and my brother John, who's older than me and whom I just adore.

I'm struck by how often it's those women who come from close, secure, loving families who are very good at making and maintaining friendships, who have a real capacity for friendship. Do you think there's a link between your family and the kinds of friendships you make?

I don't know. But I don't actually understand the expression 'the capacity for friendship'. It seems to me that it's something very, very fundamental that arises from a need in yourself, so to be good at something that you need doesn't seem to me to be a virtue or a skill. And it's obviously something I need. If I didn't need friends, I wouldn't rely on them, and I wouldn't have so many.

Why do you need friends?

To laugh at my jokes. [Laughs] And so I can offload and then get on with the things I enjoy doing. To have that long, sustained, shared life with. And also for the deep affection and love that one gets from them.

I suppose one of the reasons I'd say that you have a capacity, or gift, for friendship is because you have an unusually high number of very close, long-term friends.

I do have quite a few very close friends – eight, ten. A few straight women, a few gay women, and a few gay men and a few straight men. But the straight men who are friends are ex-lovers and were friends before that. And David, when I first knew him, was straight and was a friend. Then there was the affair, and we've stayed very close friends.

I think I'm probably a better friend than a partner. Lovers can be a nightmare. Fortunately there haven't been too many that have been too difficult, but a couple of times it's been the slough of despond. I think that absolutely wears you out more than just about anything else. Even though it would be nice to be in a relationship, I don't miss that terrible sense of loss and rejection when a relationship breaks up. Whereas I think friendship is probably less threatening to me to sustain. If I do have a gift, it's a gift for friendship rather than really sustained intimacy. At least that's what one friend says about me. She implies by that that I don't say everything, but I don't feel you should *have* to say everything. I think you should be able to leave certain things unsaid. There probably are things I don't say, but that's because I think that if things are bad, sometimes it's just not worth talking about them. I'd rather distract myself. So I assume that people will sense that you're either okay or not okay and if you want to talk about it you do, otherwise you don't.

Nonetheless your closest friendships seem to be capable of great intensity and great intimacy.

Oh yes, there's great intensity of feeling and we have intense conversations about things that are really close to the bone. But unless someone is having a particularly bad time, I don't think one always needs to do that. I couldn't sustain them on that level because that becomes far too enervating. You just can't do that and have a demanding professional life.

I rely on friends for a balance. I do what is often a really rewarding but also a really stretching job, and it's a great relief not to talk about it all the time but to break away from it. Talk about anything and nothing. Things theatrical, family, people.

Why do you think you have chosen these particular people as your closest friends?

You mean, why do they put up with me and I put up with them? [Laughs] I'm very attracted to that sustained, unswerving loyalty of long intimate friendships. So you can behave quite badly, or have your off times, and they won't irrevocably unbalance a friendship. I would find it really hard to have close friends who were super-sensitive or who were super-intolerant of me; they've got to be people who can sustain my own wavering, and at the same time can see the real point of me. Certainly I find it in long-term friends, but also in my newest friends – people like Jenny Coopes, the cartoonist, whom I met ten years ago through David when he was at the *National Times*.

I've known David since I started working at Musica Viva – I suppose it's twenty-five years. And I met Neil a couple of years after that. But Kim Williams has been a friend for the longest time. We were at university together. He and Jenny Vogel – my oldest girlfriend, who lives in Los Angeles – and I went to university together. Jenny and I did music together and we both, at different stages, had relationships with Kim. We'd been friends before and are still good friends since. They're probably the oldest close friends.

Jenny Vogel is a real grade-A friend. I feel very close to her family, in the way that she is to mine. Our friendship's developed since we were eighteen, so that's more than thirty years. We did our first European trip together and we pursued parallel careers, except that most of her life has been out of Australia and I stayed here. She felt, as I do, very close to her family, which wasn't such a common thing. Neil is the only other friend of mine who had that sense of being very close to the family. Mine only really came about when my youngest sister became ill. And my mother got sick. So it was crises that brought us together, although we were always very fond of each other.

David is close to his family now. He wasn't. He says I taught him to like them – I taught him to see them differently, I think that's what he said.

Is one of the great tests of close friendships when somebody acquires a new lover or partner?

Yes. But if you don't like the partner, you've just got to hang around and hope they will grow out of it.

David had a partner at one stage whom none of his friends liked at all, and I was the only one who had the courage, eventually, to tell him. He said, 'You're really awful about my lovers.' And I said, 'I'm just the one who tells you what we all think.' But that was afterwards. At the time I just thought, Back off, just back off a bit.

It didn't so much affect my relationship with David as make it settle into another pattern. Eventually David said to me, 'I'm not getting to see any of my friends.' And I said to him, 'Well, that's because you tie yourself up every weekend with your lover. And we're all working during the week so we see each other on weekends.' And I think he then made a decision that when he next got involved with somebody he wasn't going to let it override his other relationships. He'd cut off seeing everyone, and one friend in particular was really hurt by it because he felt as though he was just a foul-weather friend, only there when there was no-one else around. And there was a bit of that, but then I think we're probably all a bit like that. I was probably a bit more forgiving because I was more preoccupied with other things. I could still speak to David, I didn't actually need to see him. I was pretty overworked at the time, so I didn't have time to do much with anybody.

When you first met David, did you immediately like each other?

David was married when I met him. I used to go to their place for dinner parties. I always thought he was gay, but I thought he was a very jolly, smart, interesting person. I thought, Oh well, perhaps he and his wife have worked something out. Then suddenly she said to me, 'I'm going away for a while. David is going to sort himself out because he thinks he's gay.' Something like that.

Then he came on tour with us. I was working for Musica Viva and he came on tour with the Australian Chamber Orchestra, which we were taking to Indonesia. He came as a journalist and also just to help out a bit. We began an affair, which was not part of the plot, but it went on in a very intense way, in a very difficult way, for about a year or so. Then he was divorced, and there was all the other stuff, and it was just a bloody nightmare.

But David wanted, at whatever cost, to sustain the friendship. If it meant our not seeing each other for ages, he didn't mind that. It was really hard for me. I wished it hadn't happened. It was actually a factor in my making the decision to get out of Sydney for a while, to go to Adelaide so I could start another life, and let him have a life too. And it did work out pretty well.

I was twenty-four when we met and twenty-seven when I went to Adelaide, and he was thirty. I was in Adelaide for six years and we sustained a good friendship then. I became involved with somebody else in Adelaide, and then had a relationship with someone in Sydney. So I did a lot of toing and froing between Sydney and Adelaide. I would stay with David in Sydney, and we went through a few things together – me in hospital, my sister being ill, various dramas.

What does David do when you're going through a bad time?

David's very good. He's also very discreet. For a gossip he's very discreet. It is that loyalty thing and that understanding, not having to explain things. And he doesn't dwell on things. When my mother was sick, and now that my younger sister's sick, he doesn't ask about it in an intrusive way, he'll just throw it in.

It's also very important to me that I can level with him, that I can say, 'Look, I don't want to talk about it. It's driving me crazy. If she's going to die, I wish she'd die quickly.' I can say that to him and he won't be horrified. You can only say those things to really close friends. I don't feel guilty about saying it, but sometimes you're aware when you've said something terrible that people look a bit horrified, and you think, It's not really what I meant and I'm not really a completely heartless cow and I will be sorry when they're dead. But at the moment I'm very tired.

The first person I ring in moments of crisis is David, so when my mother died I rang up and said, 'Joan has just died.' And he came around and took me over there. Sat with the paper and read it, which was just the right kind of support.

Those close, sustaining friendships seem to provide many of the things that women long for in a lover or a partner but often don't find there – generosity, understanding, compassion.

You probably can't expect that response endlessly, but it's wonderful knowing that somebody knows exactly how to react. Again, David knew exactly what to do when Stuart Challender was dying in the hospice. He'd just come in every day and say, 'Want to go down to the Domain for a swim?' That and a cup of coffee, which was absolutely what I wanted and needed. It's that intuitive sense, knowing when to do something and what to do – often quite simple and uncomplicated sorts of things.

These long-term, major friendships in your life are pretty resilient. Would there be anything that could fracture them? Any limits on them?

I suppose if one became endlessly demanding for any reason, that could be a problem. I would worry if I were ill. I've never worried about it because I think I never will be [laughs], but if that were to happen I could imagine that you would become a burden, you wouldn't be able to keep your end up in any friendship. I suppose that's when the balance would change.

Did you feel that with Stuart?

No, I didn't. Mind you, there was an end to it. But I didn't feel that he was a burden. One of the curious ways in which Stuart was very thoughtful was that he decided to go to a hospice and die there, because he wanted to keep friendships separate. Stuart was such a dysfunctional human being. He had a really unbalanced upbringing, so he was a novice at experiencing what was nice about friendship because he basically didn't trust people. I think that is a major thing about friendship, that you have to trust your friends with your vulnerabilities.

Is there anything you don't share, things your closest friends wouldn't know about?

I'm not sure that you ever let go of absolutely everything, although there are not many things my friends and I don't share. When you're in a bad way you rely on their judgement, you rely on that level of sensitivity, that they'll know whether to swoop in with absolutely sure, quick-fire recipes to get you back on your feet again, or just a general sort of understanding that you want a bit of company and no demands.

Are your friendships your most important relationships?

Yes, because I don't have children, I don't have a long-term partnership relationship. Friends, my family, my nieces – they are it.

What are the other important things that you need to share in a friendship? Values?

Values, absolutely. You can have interesting relationships with people who are kind of off-centre in the way they look at the world, but I don't think you can be close friends. I find genuine amorality really difficult to deal with, more difficult to deal with than immorality. I find those things quite hard to put up with in other people, both in a business sense and a personal sense.

If you thought one of your friends was behaving really badly, would you say so?

Oh yeah, wouldn't you? Although I'd want to be pretty sure that it was actually what I thought it was before leaping in, otherwise the friend would be very justified in accusing me of misunderstanding a situation.

You've managed what I think is a very difficult thing to pull off – you've successfully lived with friends. You and Neil lived in David's house at one stage, I think, for just on four years.

Oh, that was a bit difficult, it got pretty close to being very . . . crowded. [Laughs] David and his partner were breaking up and I think they stayed together longer because we were having such a good time. But it probably wasn't healthy, ultimately, in the long term.

The holiday house is different. Penny Chapman [former head of drama for ABC TV, now head of her own production house] and Neil and I and Jenny Coopes own it. And that's really lovely, that's wonderful. But you've got to have the right mix of the flexible and the bossy.

In questions of domestic anything, Neil is unbelievably controlling. It's odd, because he seems such an easy-going person. You'll say, 'I'll cook dinner.' And he'll say, 'Oh, how are you going to cook that?' And you tell him and he'll say, 'Wouldn't you think you would do it this way?' And you say, 'No, I've decided to do it that way.' And there's silence. 'But don't you think it would be very nice to have it with that?' And you suddenly feel like throwing things on the floor. So I've decided it's easier to say, 'What would you like? Fine, we'll do it that way.' Because I'm on holiday and I don't want to have that sort of argument. Penny is pretty flexible too.

We've got this washing machine on the back verandah because Neil thinks it's a good idea. I voted against it, but he managed to get Penny in a really busy moment, so we've got this washing machine. And it looks like the house is owned by white trash. He's had second thoughts now but I said to Penny, 'No, I think we should leave it here until the house falls down.' And that is what we will do.

Whereas if David were there, he would be really bossy about that. I don't think he could have that at all. He's a real design queen about those sort of things. And he's big on 'This has got to be done and it's got to be done now' – generally a nightmare to live with. [Laughs] Neil calls him Basil Fawlty for more than one reason. David would say, 'We're going to have a bee today.' And we'd moan, 'Oh God, not another bee.' So we'd all have to get up and go outside and start digging. [Groans and laughs]

I would be very happy to spend weekends with David, but sharing a house full-time again would not be a good idea. Whereas I probably could with Neil. Neil is just a lot more relaxed, apart from cooking, but that's all right, he could just do it and I could be obsessive about other things. I couldn't live with David again, I don't think. I'm happy enough living on my own. Aren't you?

Oh yes. The mere thought of manoeuvring around somebody else in the morning is daunting.

Well, I did share with John Harding [violinist and concert master of the Sydney Symphony Orchestra], and that was fine because he's so incredibly chirpy to live with.

He's actually my oldest friend. We were fourteen when we met in Newcastle and we've pretty well been friends ever since. My mother heard that his accompanist, Sharon Raschke, was the best pianist in Newcastle, so she went and knocked on her door and said, 'Will you teach my daughter?' Sharon was so overcome that she did, and through her I met John. Then he moved to Sydney. When I was at university in Sydney, he and Nathan Waks [co-principal cellist in the orchestra] were sharing a house together and already working as musicians. They used to treat me and my boyfriend to restaurant meals. They'd say, 'Pay us back when you've got a job.'

Did you have a best friend at school?

Yes, I had those. I had a particularly good girlfriend in Newcastle. When I came back to Sydney I suppose the girl I was closest to was Kate Grenville, in the last year of school. We hardly see each other now. She went overseas and worked and wrote. I've seen her probably a couple of times at her book launches and things. But in that year, we were good friends.

Have you ever had a friend you thought you'd have forever, but something happened and the friendship fell apart?

I had something happen with Jenny and me which was terrible – Jenny Vogel, my friend in Los Angeles. We were going to share a house after university, and we'd both been looking. And my mother said, 'Why spend all this money on rent? What if I lend you some money to put a deposit on a house?' Which I did. And I couldn't, for some reason, bring myself to tell Jenny, because I thought it was going against the plan we'd made. It was really adolescent – I was only about twenty-two or twenty-three – but it was the biggest lesson I ever had. I let it go so far that I'd virtually bought the house before I told her, because I just couldn't face telling her that our plan wasn't going to happen. I don't know why she couldn't have come and lived in the house, but for some reason that wasn't what we were planning.

She was deeply hurt. Deeply hurt, although she didn't say very much. But because of that sense of having wounded somebody so much, I've never forgotten it. It has always made me quite conscious that I must be absolutely as straight as possible, as early as possible, about things like that. It was just my cowardice. I just couldn't face hurting her, but by not telling her it hurt her so much more. It was terrible. We put the friendship back together, but it took time.

Then there have been friendships that have become less intense when I've moved away, from Adelaide and things, but no other terrible catastrophes. Although the friend who thinks I don't have a talent for intimacy is sort of one. [Laughs] That's a very rocky friendship and one I find really difficult because she gets offended so easily. But she's still one of the most insightful, if irritating, people I know. Terrifically self-absorbed. Very needy on one hand, very giving on the other. I'd say I'm a close friend but not as close as some of her other friends. That's a very intense and testing friendship, one where you do lose points if you aren't regularly in touch or if you don't return a phone call. Whereas I think the general understanding in friendships is that you don't ring back because you can't, or something has come up that you really want to do and you feel you can at least put them on hold overnight. She gets *deeply* pissed off, and I find that inability to give me some leeway very difficult. She does forgive, but it takes a week. She doesn't forget, however, whereas I'm much lazier about those things. I just can't remember them. She is a wonderful test, though, of both my patience and making sure I don't behave too badly. She can incite me to really low-level, petty behaviour. [Laughs]

What about when you work very closely with someone – does that ever develop into a close friendship?

The relationship with conductors is a very interesting thing in my life, because working with them has become really involving. I get home and I don't want a lover, an intimate relationship, because my relationships with conductors are very close, in a very odd kind of way. They are really quite intense.

I can remember some of my early discussions with Edo [de Waart, Chief Conductor of the Sydney Symphony Orchestra]. I couldn't communicate directly with him and he would say the same of me. He said, 'I just can't function if I don't know what's going on.' I said, 'If I don't talk to you it's because I'm busy.' And he said, 'But when we do talk, you don't actually say what is bothering you, or what the issues are. You say everything is fine.' And I said, 'That is the way I work; I *have* to say that things are fine.' He said, 'I know you have stress in your life but you don't talk about it.' And I said, 'But we've just met. [Laughs] I'll talk to you about things as they come up.'

He's someone who's lived most of his emotional life on the phone, because he's always had girlfriends or wives who've been a long way away, so he's very good at completely unloading. Immediately you ask him how he is, he tells you. Whereas he asks me, 'How are you? How have you been?' And I say, 'Fine.' He just laughs now. He'll say, 'Oh, come on, apart from fine. How's your sister?' I'll say, 'I don't want to talk about it, all right?' 'Okay, what else is happening?'

It's a very intense relationship, and the thought of looking for a new chief conductor wears me out in advance because of the prospect of starting another one. You have to have all that honesty and trust and directness of communication, but at the same time you have to remember who's got the ego. You also have to be able to handle your own desire, and your need, to have your own views understood. You have to juggle your personal relation to the orchestra and deal with that person's relations with the orchestra, the audience and the public, and so on. We speak every day when he's in Sydney. It's quite an emotionally involved relationship, and pretty full-on.

Would you call it a friendship?

It is a friendship. It is. But if something went wrong, I wouldn't always think, I must tell Edo. On the other hand, when he has been around and there have been things to talk about, he's remarkably insightful. He's very interesting to talk to about relationships and partnerships because he spends a lot of time thinking about them. He's a very good listener if he's in a good mood.

Did your friendship with Stuart begin in that way?

Yes. I'd met him a couple of times, but I didn't know him until I really started working with him. It was a difficult relationship because he was so untrusting. He was both openly vulnerable and a real shit, and made things really hard for himself. Things need not have been so hard for him and I think he realised that when he was too sick to spend energy on self-loathing; he realised that you could actually have quite a good time without self-flagellation.

Why did you persist?

Oh well, I had great regard for him.

So you just adored him anyway, despite the difficulties?

No, no, I didn't adore him. I had a great regard for him as a musician, and I grew to like him and I did like him. But he wasn't someone you could adore in that way. He was a very irascible, difficult, cranky, gauche, prickly person who was just all out of step with everything. Well, you've seen the documentary [made for ABC TV by David Marr when Stuart was dying] and that, I think, is really the story. He was a hopelessly difficult person. You see some people who make life so incredibly hard for themselves, they can't win out of it, they're so dysfunctional. [David Marr says in the *Good Weekend* piece, 'Mary surrounded him with friends who made him see he was loved. It was a revelation he found amazing.']

Presumably, for you to be friends, he was giving you something back as well.

I suppose he must have. We used to have arguments a lot when we worked at the orchestra together, but ultimately I became quite protective of him. At the same time, I needed to push him to be a bit more open. It got to the point where he was incredibly selfish, I thought, regardless of whether he had AIDS or not, about the impact that his not being public about it was having on the orchestra. On the one hand, I understood his reasons, but when he said he didn't want to be public about it because his grandmother was still alive, actually he was just scared of being public about it.

But then, eventually, he did get enough courage, and I probably had a role in pushing him into doing that. Ultimately, I thought he was incredibly brave and courageous, and I admire that level of drive and that creativity. Even when he really got sick he'd wake up and study the bloody *Rosenkavalier* score in hospital while he was having blood transfusions. That was an extraordinary level of drive and I did admire that hugely.

Probably the hardest thing I ever had to do was after I sat through a performance of *Rosenkavalier* and it was really terrible; it was so slow I thought it was going to stop. And I said to him, 'Look, I don't think I can come to any more.' He said,

'I'll go and have a blood transfusion tomorrow.' Which he did, and then said, 'Will you come and hear it tomorrow night?' I said, 'Stuart, I don't think I can.' He said, 'What do you mean?' I said, 'I think you should stop.' And oh, how hard it was to say that because to him it meant, stop conducting and you will die. Which is, effectively, what happened. I said, 'It's your decision. You obviously have to think about it. But I won't be coming to hear it any more.'

I'd rung Moffatt [Oxenbould, then Artistic Director at the Australian Opera] before I said it and said to him, 'Look, I hope this is not going to throw you into a spin, but I think someone needs to tell him he should stop now.' And he said, 'Well, if you were to do that it wouldn't throw us into a spin.' So I did. And Stuart did decide the next day. He didn't say anything more to me but he rang Moffatt the next day and said, 'I've decided I have to stop.' Then about two days later he went into hospital and he never came out. Three months later he died. It was the right thing, I've absolutely no doubt about it. But it was probably the worst thing to have to do to him because as long as he could conduct, he was alive, and as soon as he couldn't conduct it meant that he was too weak to keep living, and that's exactly what it was. It was only spirit that had kept him going.

Do you admire all your friends?

Yes. Absolutely. With them all I can think, That's really what I do like about you. Not always professional things, but usually there's a capacity that translates to what they do professionally. I admire their personal qualities, but I can also say to them, 'I really regard very highly what you do – what you write, what you played,' or whatever.

And a sense of humour, which your friends have in abundance, is vital in a friend, don't you think?

A sense of humour is *unbelievably* important. Not a criterion that one would use to wipe someone off, but I tend to be attracted to people who make me laugh. I think it's really important, actually, not to take things too seriously. That gets you through the worst. Gets you through death. Not your own, but other people's. [Laughs] Well, probably your own as well.

Can you see yourself making another really intimate friend?

Probably not. Obviously if I met someone I really liked, I could spend the time, but it hasn't happened so far. New professional friends, perhaps. I've got very good colleagues at work. We don't socialise much or hang out together, but I feel immensely close to them. That's a different level of friendship, but it is equally caring and concerned. And of course there's the orchestra.

There's probably not a lot of time to meet new people. The people I meet tend to be people who are interested in the orchestra – new sponsors and government people. We're not likely ever to fall into socialising, or into bed. And if you're in a situation where you're working with a lot of people, the desire to go out and be with a lot more people is not really there. You can't wait to get home. Or you already have the ease of friendship to go to, the stimulation of being outside that world.

I would make the time and emotional space if I met some-one who was really nice for a partnership thing, but I've got plenty of very good friends. So if I met somebody who said that they didn't want a relationship, they just wanted a friendship, I'd say, 'I don't need that. You can fuck off. I've got much better friends than you.' Actually, it has happened, now that you mention it. 'I'd *really* like to be friends with you.' 'Well, I'd really *not* like to be friends with you. What makes you think you could be a friend? I'm only asking you to be a lover.' [Laughs]

POSTSCRIPT: *When David Marr was interviewed by Margaret Throsby on ABC Classic FM, he chose a piece of music which, he said, he'd first heard when travelling with a friend, Mary Vallentine. Margaret's ears pricked up: 'Not the Mary Vallentine?' Mary's best friend considered this for a moment, then said drily, 'Thankfully, there is only one.'*

Bettina ARNDT ¶

WHEN BETTINA ARNDT announced in October 1985 that she was going to marry again, Sydney's *Telegraph* announced it with a huge tabloid headline: 'Saucy Bettina, unlikely lawyer in love match'. No-one asked, Bettina who? There was only one Bettina – the woman who had given frank sex advice to Australians for more than a decade. Her first husband had called her 'Australia's ruling queen of sex and the country's sole sexologist'; the *Sydney Morning Herald* once referred to her as 'the Dr Seuss of heavy breathing'. ¶ THE CANBERRA-RAISED daughter of a professor of economics, Bettina is a clinical psychologist who used to specialise in sex therapy. Fame came when Clyde Packer hired her as an editor on *Forum* – the magazine that told you everything you wanted to know about sex but didn't know who to ask – and as a therapist at the magazine's sex clinic. She was lively and smart, good-natured and good-looking, with a ready laugh and the ability to say 'clitoris' and 'masturbation' without stumbling or blushing. The media couldn't get enough of her. ¶ HER RADIO PROGRAMS made her a celebrity by the time she was twenty-four, when she was banned from live broadcasting for two years by the Broadcasting Control Board, which couldn't cope with her explicit advice. That was 1973, the year that her first husband, *Age* journalist Dennis Minogue, interviewed her and fell in love. It was an intensely passionate 24-hours-a-day relationship. They bought *Forum*, which they co-published and Bettina continued to edit until Dennis's sudden death from a heart attack in 1981, at the unripe age of thirty-seven, leaving her with a five-month-old baby son, Jesse, and debts. Bettina closed the magazine down and began to write a syndicated column for Consolidated Press, mainly features for *Cleo* and the *Bulletin*. ❡ SHE WAS THIRTY-FIVE when she met her 'unlikely lawyer', Warren Scott, a New York corporate lawyer three years her junior and the son of a US general. Bettina had managed not to tell him what she did for a living until, on their second date, someone asked for her autograph and she had to spill the beans. They married in 1986 and went with Jesse to live in New York City. ❡ AFTER FIVE YEARS Bettina, Warren, Jesse, plus daughter Taylor, now thirteen, and son Cameron, now ten, returned to Sydney to live. Bettina is now a features writer with the *Age* and *Sydney Morning Herald*, where, not afraid to advocate an unpopular point of view, she writes on men, women, marriage, divorce, and the ways that families do or don't survive.

FRIENDSHIP IS QUITE a vexed area in some ways. I keep coming back to my experience of relocating to a new country. One of the worst things about having to start again is that you're totally missing your support system. To have to go into a new environment and find out who might be interested in befriending me was just extraordinary for me.

Did you feel like a child on your first day at a new school?

[Laughs] Yes, it was horrible. I was acutely conscious of the seduction element, the business of reaching out to people and always being nervous of whether they had room for you in their lives. There's the sniffing around each other like dogs, the initial stuff of 'Is this someone who interests me?' But then the big issue is, are they going to want just an acquaintance or have they got room for something more? Do they have room and time for the strong friendships you're looking for in that circumstance? Most of the people I ended up being close to had lived in New York for years and had lots of friendships. And you become very conscious of muscling in on that.

One of the great shocks of that process is trying to work out how much your self-image is linked into a particular environment and what you actually take with you. I found it really quite gruelling in my late thirties. I had always had such a strong sense of myself in friendships, so it was weird to have to go up and present that self to people who didn't know me.

So did it work? Did you make close friends?

Yes I did, and the sad thing for me now is that I feel closer to some of my friends in New York than to anybody else. I think there are issues around stages in your life. I had lots of friends in Australia who had been friends for fifteen years. Then I went through this dramatic new experience, and, inevitably, when I came back some of those friendships didn't work as well any more. There are lots of reasons for that. I'm sure one of them is changes in me. I had gone through a transformative experience, essentially. And that wasn't just living in a different country for five years, but also marrying someone that no-one really knew. Warren and I met only a few months before he had to go back to America, then he came back and we got married and went back to New York. So people barely knew us as a couple. Then, when I came back to Australia, I'd been Mrs Scott for five years and they didn't know Mrs Scott. And in some of those friendships it caused real problems.

Was it that you now had this partner and an established relationship that friends had to take on, so the whole dynamic of the friendships had shifted?

It was lots of things. When I left, I'd been through a five-year period as a single mother, and a single mother is often very dependent on friends, who tend to take a fairly protective role – my married friends were very nurturing to me. I was a widow with this baby and people took care of me. Then, I suppose, I came back not needing the same thing from them. So I think that was part of it.

The single-mother experience is such a different world. One couple, whom I would have certainly thought of as close friends, clearly had huge problems when I started to go out with other men after I was widowed. We just never connected after that. If I'd been a husband left in that position, I think they would have coped better. It's just assumed that a man left on his own will eventually make a new relationship.

The combination of individual friends and partners can be tricky, can't it? I suppose that's why couples tend to have couple friends.

It's all tricky [laughs] but the business of couple friendship has always intrigued me. It's so rare to find a couple where all four of you are equally close, and such a gift if you do find it. We met this couple in New York who are in their fifties and don't have any children and we became their family. They're extremely good friends to both of us and they love our children. We've gone on holidays with them and they're among the few friends who really know all the intricacies of the marriage and where the problems are. We'd talk it through with them, and Warren would talk to him too. So it's an extremely close relationship.

It's partly the age they are, but they were just heartbroken when we left. And they now say, about making new friends, 'It's just too heartbreaking when people leave.' So they've really done very little since we've left to fill the gap. We write and we call. They both have extremely busy lives and they're very close as a couple. They get invited to everything, but I know that they don't socialise much because we were very much their social life. It's interesting that they felt it as this huge loss, and you can only take it so many times.

Are all of your closest friends women? And how would you define that closeness?

Except for the man in that particular couple, whom I would call a very close friend, all my closest friends are women. And one of the defining things about that level of friendship is that we talk about really intimate things.

I was very conscious of not having that when I first went to New York. There was one notable occasion when I was newly arrived in New York and I knew nobody. I met a few people through Warren, including one particular woman whom he was very close to, a lawyer in his office. We'd only been there a couple of months and I was finding it so difficult and everything was going wrong – I can't remember what now, but there were various things that I was having real trouble with. Warren was involved with some deal somewhere interstate and I was in the depths of despair, so I rang this female lawyer and did this big emotional, not-coping thing with her. And she told Warren. She said to him that she was really shocked that I would let down my guard. I got a huge surprise when I heard that. So I certainly see friendships in terms of being able to talk about vulnerabilities and letting down the guard. And feeling that it's welcome, that the confidence will be kept and that it will be reciprocal. To have that flung back at me as a sign of weakness was a terrible experience. I really didn't have anybody then. Yet it gave me pause and made me think. I'm very inclined to just let down my guard very quickly with people, and I suddenly realised that maybe you can't do that. Fairly soon after that I did find people to whom I felt I could unburden myself a bit, but you also don't want to be a boring, pathetic creature.

To be in a situation where you're really under stress and depressed and struggling and yet have to try and make friends is very difficult, because you have to seduce people by being cheerful and interesting and charming. All the dreary, listen-to-my-woes-for-the-next-hour stuff is something you feel you can only impose on a relationship where you've got a certain degree of trust. New York was an extremely confronting place to be living, especially with a little child. And I was just married too. Poor man [laughs], he put up with it endlessly, all this.

How important are the intellectual connections in friendship, the shared values and ideas?

That depends. I think there are times in your life when you can be friends with people with whom you are unlikely to be friends forever. Particularly when you have small children, because you can just connect on the mother thing even when you have nothing else in common.

Some of my friends in New York were mother friends. There was one particular woman whom I would ring every night. We used to have this wonderful routine. I had two children under three, and Jesse, who was older, and hers were a bit older. We'd get home from collecting them from school and do all our household chores, cooking the dinner and everything, on the phone. [Laughs]

I have never filled that gap. That was very much two mums with the same routine, and it's different now; everyone's so busy and few of my really close friends have young children. You need lives fairly much in tune with each other to be able to fit in such constant intimacy. I really miss it. She and I were very close – she's a wonderful woman and a very interesting personality – but we wouldn't have that much in common other than that. We wouldn't talk about ideas much, we'd talk mainly about children and relationships. But she's just lovely and I think of her an awful lot. We're not very good at writing but we feel just as close when we see each other when I'm in New York.

What about women at work? Do you think women have particular problems in the workplace because their mode of operating is to want to make friends with people, yet they're often also in competition?

That doesn't relate so much to me because I've tended not to work in an office, but women talk to me about having been very close to someone who they then feel has betrayed them. Somebody becomes their boss and starts demanding things of them that they think are unreasonable.

Where I do have some direct experience was when I used to run *Forum*. I always had women working for me and I think it is extremely difficult. There was one woman I very deliberately employed because she had two young children, which was probably a big mistake because it made life very tough. I know you can't come to work if a child has measles, but we were a very small ship and it was extremely hard to keep managing in that circumstance.

So your feminist principles come up against the practicalities of the workplace. Women always talk to each other about their lives, so women will know what a hard time someone is having. That makes it extremely hard to say to somebody, 'You still have to be in tomorrow.' I've had that with endless nannies and other women I've employed. You always end up as friends and yet I'm so dependent on their being there to do the job. I constantly fall into holes over that one. You allow them to cut corners and cut more corners because you know what's happening in their personal lives, but then they're not doing what you need done.

I think that is a microcosm of the whole issue of the workplace, because even if you're exactly on a par with someone, inevitably you're competing at some level. And women handle that so much worse than men do. Men don't expect to have friendship – that's the essence of it.

There's a lot of research which shows that whether women like their work or not has a great deal to do with workplace relations, whereas men don't see it as a big issue in the same way. Some of that's to do with men being better able to compartmentalise, and not seeking to be friends at work. For us it's part of wanting to be liked and wanting to be nice, so we will make efforts at friendship with people just because we're working with them, even with people whom we wouldn't necessarily seek out as friends.

Is it partly that women have a need to confide, do you think? And that they like intimate friendships? The only intimate friendships many straight men seem to have are with women.

Yes. And one of the things I think is really interesting is that women being in the workforce next to men is dramatically changing men's friendships with women. It's providing an opportunity for men to have friendships with women, and for intimacy with women, which was never there before. Men are starting to talk to women in a way they've never talked to women, other than their wives, before. And they'll talk to women about things they would never even talk to their wives about.

It raises the issue: is the real man the man at work or the man at home? A lot of men, men who have careers that are really fulfilling, have said to me that probably the real man is the man at work, in the sense that that's where he's fighting the bears and proving himself and doing the things that really give him probably the biggest thrill in his life. And a woman who's there is seeing quite a different man from the man his wife knows.

Most of the time the wife spends with her husband, he's asleep. But the woman at work is sharing the thrill of meeting the deadline or solving the problem, and that sets up a real intimacy. It's got potential for revolutionising all sorts of relationships. And, of course, for causing chaos in marriages. Because that's where all the really sexy stuff starts.

How do wives or sexual partners compete with that? Or is it a hopeless task?

Wives not knowing what their husbands are doing when they're not at home is one of the biggest problems in lots of marriages. And saying to men, 'Well, you should come home and tell your wives about what's happening,' is not always realistic. When it's all over and done with, you don't necessarily want to regurgitate it all. You've had it, you've done it. You don't necessarily want to explain all the intricacies and the relationships. It's so different from being there and getting it. And some of it's really hard to explain. But women feel a huge sense of betrayal when another woman knows more about her husband than she does.

Do you think women have a completely different concept of relationships? Look at little girls – the way they form and break friendships is absolutely Byzantine.

Oh yes, and the *Cat's Eye* experience that Margaret Atwood writes about, of being a mother, seeing it all and trying to help – I've been through that. My daughter had a bad year a couple of years ago. At one stage I rang some of the other mothers and then it was worse for her. Girls are so horrible to each other. It's a totally different pattern of friendship from that of boys, and it's all about best friends. My daughter had had a really close friend for years who took up with someone else who was really jealous and quite nasty, and so excluding. It was just heart-breaking to watch. And that was all about that best friend issue.

I've had that too – I have two very close friends who get on quite badly and there has always been an element of who's really my best friend. There have been occasions when they have been terrible to each other, and each will run down the other to me. It's so peculiar because I love them both.

Do you think you learn how to make friends as a child? Is it then you learn about the value of friendship and some of the difficult things as well?

You are certainly very lucky as a little girl if you don't learn about being excluded and the huge loss when you're no longer a best friend. Whereas with boys, it's the pack that matters. Boys are very rarely exclusionary in that sort of way, they don't usually form pairs as such. Jesse has had the same really close three or four friends all through high school and there's none of that stuff. I don't think any of them ever thinks, Oh, he's over at Lenny's house tonight, why didn't he invite me? Whereas the girls are constantly obsessive about that sort of stuff: Does that mean you like me second? I don't think it would occur to Jesse to think in those terms – Am I her first best friend or her second best friend?

It's very competitive and very exclusionary. It's this pair and that pair. I'm very conscious of the fact that I don't handle it particularly well. Do you get any better at it as you get older?

I was hoping you'd have the answer to that! I don't think you do handle it any better as you get older. Men seem to handle it much more easily.

I don't think that for men there's the same emotional

dependence on friendships that we have, the worrying about them and fretting over them.

I've made a new friend since I got back to Australia, someone I really like a lot. But there's still that wondering, Does she like me as much as I like her? Worrying when I realise that I've rung her three times in a row and she hasn't rung me. It's all that putting yourself on the line and worrying, Am I showing myself as too needy? It's partly that you don't want to encroach and partly that you don't want to impose a degree of friendship that she might not want. So there's always this toing and froing going on of 'Where are we in this relationship?' And the obsessing over it. It's very like a lover – that whole business of 'Is she interested or is she not?' is exactly the same sort of thing. 'And if she hasn't rung me back does this mean . . . ?'

Are there real no-go areas amongst close friends?

One of the areas, and women do it to themselves all the time, is stealing each other's boyfriends. Poaching stuff, which is really dangerous territory. And I think there are really interesting areas in terms of honesty. Okay, you know that your best friend's husband is having an affair, do you tell her?

What would you do?

That's very difficult. I always feel one of the big issues is, would she want to know? In one sense you never want to know, you want it not to be happening. But then there comes a time when the worst thing for some people is the betrayal of everyone else knowing except you, the feeling that everyone is deceiving you. 'Why didn't you tell me?' Women hate that.

I think what gets very tricky is the couple versus the individual friendships. All of us have no time in our lives, and what spare time we have we have to save for others, so you have to try and look for couple friends. Individual friends are a total indulgence to me. It is the ultimate treat to organise to go for a walk with one of my female friends on the weekend, and I feel really guilty about that because I'm taking time from my kids, I'm taking from the family. I do it, but not as much as I'd like because it's extremely difficult to co-ordinate with anyone else.

I have a cousin in New York who is now one of my really close friends. She now has a child, but at the time I was there she was a single New York woman in her mid-thirties, classically living her life for herself. My other women friends – who were almost all married with kids – and I were constantly accommodating each other because we're so used to making an arrangement and having it fall apart when the husband suddenly has to do this and the kids suddenly have to do that. It was a miracle if plans ever worked out, and we were all eternally forgiving of each other. Whereas with my cousin – and during the time I knew her I was pregnant, and I ended up with these three kids – it was always still very much when she wanted to go for her run and when she wanted to do this, and she made no attempt to accommodate. And she'd be quite irritated if all the other stuff interfered with our arrangements.

It was just fascinating, that difference, because it highlighted to me the way my friendships with most other women are very much . . . well, we try to connect but actually our friends are fairly low down the priority list of what has to be done in the day. So we're lucky if we have a phone call, and if we actually get to see each other it's a miracle and a real treat. And, as I said, we're very understanding of that, whereas she wasn't nearly as understanding.

Is it for you a test of friendship that your friends will actually put themselves out for you, if they possibly can?

Oh yes. And I am very conscious that some of them are so endlessly giving, and that one or two in particular are much better at it than I am. They're always considerate, thinking of what is just the right thing for you.

Have friends got you through the really worst days of your life?

Oh definitely. When Dennis died, my parents were really hurt that I rather rejected them at the time. But there were one or two people who got me through it – friends, women. I'm now extremely close to my mother, but she just wasn't the person who could help me then.

Do you have sisters?

I don't have sisters, only brothers, and you grow up totally differently. Warren has six sisters, which makes him a most interesting man. He's very in tune with what matters to women. He has one sister in particular who is just wonderful. We're very close and that's as near as I've got to having sisters. It makes a difference when there's a family connection, because we're always going to be around for each other.

She came to visit a few years ago and we had this fabulous time. She came out for the *New York Times* to do a profile on Keating, but she arrived at Christmas and of course no-one was around. So she was stuck here for six weeks. Warren had to go somewhere in the middle of all of this, so she and I had about three weeks by ourselves, both working. Oh, it was the treat of my life. To have someone working in the same house, writing, was just fabulous. We talked and talked. [Laughs with pleasure]

Conversation is at the very heart of women's friendships, don't you think?

Oh yes. Women's conversation is central to their friendships. Thank God for the telephone. Women use the phone to sustain relationships with their friends, families, with adult children, and so on. But the male relationship with the phone is very interesting. When we were in New York I would have these long phone calls with my mother, but my father couldn't bear it because of the cost, even though it was me ringing them. So I'd be talking to her and he would make an excuse to get on the phone. He'd say hello to me, talk for one second, then say, 'Oh, all right, bye,' and hang up because he was so anxious about the cost of these calls. Then I wrote about him as The Terminator and now he's sort of on guard.

Someone told me this wonderful joke: How do you tell when a man in the office is having an affair? His voice drops two octaves and he spends hours on the telephone. It's the only time in their lives that men use the phone the way women do, when they first fall in love or are having affairs.

But men don't connect on the phone. That's all been written about endlessly. Men ring to arrange things. There are exceptions, of course. And in terms of the workplace there's the whole issue of whether you conduct personal phone calls at work, and how other people feel about that. And what you do when you're at work and someone rings in a big crisis – there's that whole issue of what you are prepared to walk out on to go and help a friend, especially when you have one of those big, important jobs. Women have tended not to have much to walk out on, but as they take on those jobs it's becoming more and more of an issue. What – and who – comes first?

Elizabeth Elliott ¶

Tʜᴇ ꜰɪʀꜱᴛ ᴛɪᴍᴇ I met Elizabeth I put my head on her table between the bouillabaisse and the orange cake and wept with laughter. 'Will,' she said to the friend who had invited me, cooked our dinner and was now in his rigid-with-mirth position, napkin pressed to his mouth, 'does she always put her head on the table?' John, the third adult member of the household and Elizabeth's soulmate, was in South-East Asia staging one of his spectaculars for the Disney Corporation, but his irreverent spirit was palpable. We had all gone too far. ¶ ᴇʟɪᴢᴀʙᴇᴛʜ ᴇʟʟɪᴏᴛᴛ ɪꜱ co-ordinator of creative arts at a performing arts college in Sydney. An only child, utterly adored by her parents who adopted her as a baby, she grew up in country New South Wales, went to art school in Sydney, became a teacher. She married, had Alexandra in 1980, and in 1982 bought a house in Sydney's Rozelle with her then husband and John. Husband and lovers have come and gone but Elizabeth, John and Alexandra have lived there as a family for eighteen years. For the past eight years, the household has also included John's partner Will, whose idea of relaxation from his hugely demanding job is to poach fifty peaches, make a year's supply of apricot jam, and cook dinner for ten while listening to a little something from *The Ring*. ¶ ᴊᴏʜɴ ɪꜱ ᴡɪᴄᴋᴇᴅʟʏ, outrageously funny. In his vicinity tea towels appear on heads, legs are bared, songs sung. He is also extraordinarily generous and affectionate. The relationship between him

and Elizabeth, both now fifty-two, is one of the closest and most
enduringly loving that I know, perhaps because they have never
been lovers. They are bound together not by ties of blood or
marriage, but by intimate, loving friendship. This is one of
Dorothy Rowe's happy families, one that values friendship, is
hospitable, kind, interested in other people, and treats them
with affection, respect and dignity. In this warm, welcoming
house you eat sensationally well and you can, and do, say anything. ¶ ELIZABETH RESISTS CALLING any of the important
people in her life, including John, best friends: 'I don't think I
believe in best friends.' Make of that what you will, but it seems to
me that a best friend by any other name is still a great thing, and
a life lived with friends, best or otherwise, a most fortunate one.

I HAVEN'T HAD a best friend since I was a child. [Laughs]
I went to boarding school, and you tend to have really intense
relationships at boarding school. But even then I had a number
of different friends rather than one best friend. I've always had
friends for different parts of my life, quite intense, close friendships that are about particular bits of my life. My friends are
quite diverse and they're all a bit odd, which I like about them.
They're not necessarily conventional people and they don't
belong to groups – I'm not a person who belongs to groups or
causes myself. So I have friends who are in all sorts of different
places doing quite different things, who might not even like
each other.

Toot and Chris are friends from school, so we go back to

when we were twelve years old. Those relationships have changed enormously. They have been really close at particular times and then changed as our lives changed. Chris lived overseas with her family when she was a kid and I didn't see her for years. Then Toot left school and we went off in different directions. And then at various stages we all got married and unmarried. We're like a group, now that we're older. Our friendship has survived marriages, changes, geographical relocation, and there's now an enormously satisfying bond between the three of us. Though initially I had a separate friendship with each of them, in the last twelve years it's become the three of us as a core friendship.

Surely you've just described your best female friends?

No. I don't have a best friend. [Laughs] They're just these incredibly important parts of my life. But I've got other people who are incredibly important parts of my life too. I don't have millions of friends, but I have a number of friends with whom I have a fairly intense relationship.

I talk to Chris and Toot about anything. I don't have a problem with that at all now – now that I'm older. I can tell anybody anything, whether they're friends or not – that can have its problems too. The real strength of these two particular friends is that feeling of absolute safety, because they knew me as a child. They knew my family, they know the other parts of my life. And as you get older, probably most of your friends don't know those parts of your life. And for me, it's like winning a lottery to have relationships like that. You can take all sorts of things for granted so there's this wonderful shorthand. You can just say, 'How's your father?' and everyone screams with laughter because you know the father and you know the family stories and you know what that actually means.

I remember meeting Chris for the first time in sixth class. And exactly the things that I liked about her when I first met her are the qualities I still like now. In women I like a range of things: I like women who are quiet and logical and calm and intelligent and incisive, and then I like women who really go over the top. And I think, looking back on it, that I've had this balance with friendships, because you don't necessarily get those all at the same time. And Chris, when she was twelve, had the going-over-the-top quality. I thought, Oh, Chris is heaven. I've met somebody who is a bit like me. Actually she's not like me at all, but she gurgles and gets excessive really quickly – she still does it. Sometimes I look at her and I know she's going to laugh at something that I'm going to laugh at. And I can see her swinging on her seat when we were in sixth class, at the back of the room, being naughty.

I met another old friend, Kath, in Newcastle when I first went teaching. I didn't have any friends there and I kept thinking, This is awful, I'm going to hate this job. I'd just gone out teaching for the first time, although I was twenty-seven, and I thought, Oh, God, this all looks a bit dull. I had no-one to play with. And then one day this funny woman arrived and she just sashayed into the room and started on with this rubbish coming out of her mouth, and I thought, I've found her, a playmate. I was so excited I almost jumped on her. I fell in love with her instantly. She was diabolical and I thought, Oh, thank God. It'll be all right.

I always get excited when I'm meeting a new friend. I love it. It's fantastic.

Is a shared sense of humour one of the key things in your friendships?

Humour is incredibly important. Though, thinking about it, humour is not something that all my friends have, especially.

But humour is something that draws me to other people. It's also important to have shared values, a shared sense of what's important. The women – perhaps everybody, but the women particularly – that I like have a really strong philosophical basis about the way they run their lives. How they have relationships, how they parent, how they view the world, social justice, all those sorts of issues. That's really important, although I wouldn't have known that when I was young. I think that's wisdom you get as you grow older, unless you're particularly clear about friendship and its role in your life.

I guess there has to be some shared interest, something that brings you together in the first place. Although some friendships are just based on how people look, too. I don't mean a sexual friendship, but sometimes you meet somebody and you think, I'm going to like you, even before you know anything about them at all. A lot of the women who have been, and are, really good friends in my life have a particular, distinctive style of their own that draws me to them. They may not be conventional beauties but I just find them fabulous to look at.

To me loyalty has always been the keystone of friendships. I expect it of my friends and I expect that I give unconditional loyalty.

Even if you think they're totally in the wrong?

Yeah, absolutely. I stick by them until either we talk about it or I say, 'Look I think you're behaving badly,' or whatever. Which is not to say that I haven't got failed friendships. I had one friendship that really fell apart in a dreadful, dramatic way, and I was so shocked I couldn't eat for weeks. I was also going through a difficult time personally and I didn't have the strength to repair that friendship. I realise now that I probably could have, but now I know something that I didn't know when I was younger and that is that some friendships have a time limit on them.

With some other friends it's been more a drifting apart, perhaps of interests. One of my friendships changed when I had a child. She was an incredibly close friend and somebody who made me laugh like a drain. It was a very, very intense relationship and she had wonderful qualities which she still has. But I changed and my needs changed, and with young children friendships get muddled for a while, and probably some friendships get lost forever at that point.

When I was first pregnant with Alexandra I didn't have any friends who'd had children or were having babies. Then I met somebody whom I liked enormously, who was pregnant too. We did all that early babying stuff together and that was wonderful. She kept me going because I would've been quite pathetic without her as a support system. Our kids were best friends when they were little. But then when I separated from David, some friendships changed because they weren't necessarily individual friendships, they were family friendships, and sometimes they can't go on because you're not that group any more.

Do you expect that you'll go on making new friends, or do you expect it to be more difficult as you get older?

I don't expect it to be more difficult, but I think as you get older you become less tolerant and therefore you probably limit your chances a bit. But I expect to keep on making friends. There are going to be women in the Zimmer frame shop who'll probably become friends. [Laughs] Can't you see it? In fact, when I go anywhere new – new work or new whatever – I'm always looking for that person who's going to be my playmate there, my friend.

I have friendships that have lasted and developed from all different periods in my life. And different jobs – I think I have maintained a friend from every job I've had. But then I've worked in small places, where people have a very specific common interest. You might work for a government insurance company, but it doesn't necessarily mean you're fascinated by insurance, and it's not a passion for insurance that got you there in the first place. Whereas being a visual arts teacher, I'm working with other people with whom I have that common interest, and they tend to be creative arts people. So as well as having a common work environment, you've got this core of things that you're interested in. And then there is this bonus that they make you laugh, or whatever it is.

I've always found women friends enormously easy to have, and essential – this thing that you absolutely need in your life. I like to know where people are at in their lives; it gives you a reference point. Women have enormous empathy with you and they're interested in your life, really interested in how you are, not that you've got a fabulous job and everything looks good on the surface; they want to know about what's going on inside you. It's one of the hugely valuable things about women's conversation.

So one of the requirements of a close friendship is that you reveal yourself, that you confide in people?

Absolutely. When I was younger I was a better listener than I was a confider. It took me a really long time to expose myself to my friends. I found it very difficult to tell people that I wasn't getting it together and things were not as they seemed. I was a great coper, you know, brought up as a coper, and it's probably the nature of whatever beast I am. I was very willing to listen to other people's stories but frequently not willing to reveal my own. Then, when bits of my life started to fall apart, I eventually told someone. And as soon as I did that, my friendships acquired much greater depth, as they do when you can reveal your vulnerabilities – that you aren't what you'd like to be, or that you're disappointed, or feel that you've failed at something.

I actually believe that friendship is not intuitive. I think people often have to be taught how to be good friends, and I was. My mum has a great capacity for friendship and I was brought up to understand that friendship isn't just something that happens, it's something you have to work hard at and it's something that you teach children – how to be a good friend. My mother instructed me quite carefully and thoughtfully and well.

My mother's sister, who's sort of a role model for me, is a great maker of good friends. She's eighty-eight and she's just been travelling again, and she's met another new person who's going to be her friend. She's kept making new friends, so I just assumed I always would.

Of course friendships have to be maintained. You have to give them attention. And that's one of the difficulties of this particular time that we live in, and of growing older. Women talk about it all the time, don't they? They've got kids growing up, homes that need to be contended with, work – everybody's work is infinitely more intense than it was ten years ago, and most people spend longer hours at work. So you get home and you're buggered. You need to replenish yourself. I find now that there are longer periods where I don't speak to my friends, but I've got this internal clock that will go off and I'll think, Oh God, I haven't spoken to X for a couple of weeks so I really need to phone, check in. And different relationships have different times. There are some friendships that are maybe thirty years old and we might only see each other once a year. And then there's a core of friends that I have to see a lot of, be in almost constant contact with.

I think one of the things about maintaining friendships over a very long period is to recognise that there are times when you must let your friends be, to let them get on with their life in a particular way. For example, when a friend remarries or gets a new partner, you just have to give them a longer rope for a while because their primary interest at that point is in maintaining this new thing.

Despite your best intentions, you don't feel hurt by that or see it as a failure of the friendship?

No, I don't see it as a failure of friendship, although I can be pissed off with it and think, Oh, Christ, get over it. One phone call wouldn't have killed you. But I think in maintaining friendships that leeway is really important.

And there are other times when your friends are going through a hard time and you know that you need to call them every day, even if you don't want to. Even if you're tired and only interested in yourself that day, you know you have to do that. The requirement of the friendship at that particular time is that they need you, whereas at other times friends actually don't need you. They need to know you're there, but they also need to be able to get on with that other aspect of their life. I think with my closest friendships that is an essential core. In a really good friendship, one that you want to maintain over the distance, there's an elasticity – although you can probably stretch it too far and then it will just fade away, so you have to do some maintenance on it.

I think maybe the first thing in friendship is that people know they've got somebody to talk to. I guess it's important that friends do things together, and that you know they would come at the drop of a hat if you really needed them to. But the kids I teach frequently tell me they don't have a friend to talk to, and that's the greatest lack in their life. They might have family but they don't have a peer to tell things to. It's not about advice, it's about listening, actually *listening.* You have to be a listener and you have to tell as well. A real friendship, I think, is to be able to tell people your vulnerabilities, or show that they exist, and to trust them enough to feel absolutely safe doing that. And to feel loved anyway. It's an ideal, isn't it? But not impossible.

A lot of straight men seem to survive without close friends. They replace friends with work. But women, however busy they are, on the whole don't do that. Women seem to need their friends.

I certainly do. Friendship is the core, it's absolutely essential for me. I would go mad without it. I couldn't exist, I'd be just a blob on the floor.

A lot of straight men say their best friend is the woman they're involved with, don't they? Whereas that's never enough for me, although I really do believe you need only one friend for a good life. But I think that a life without friends is no life at all, is a bereft life. There's got to be one person of whom you can say, 'This is my friend,' and know what friendship is. Maybe if you are best friends with your wife, then you would have other degrees of friendship with other people.

There is something that I never understood about men but have come to understand as I've got older, and that is that there is great comfort in being with people whom you like, who are friends, without necessarily having to talk all the time. Just being with somebody. Perhaps that's what men do. [Laughs] I don't know what men do – who knows? But maybe a lot of just being with each other and mucking about and doing something you're interested in, or talking about things other than the reality of your life, is friendship too; it's just at a different level, a different kind.

Gay men are among my closest friends, so I'm particularly interested in other women's experiences of that.

I think women who are close friends with gay men have the best of both worlds. Gay men have the perspective of an outsider, they have the vulnerabilities of the outsider. They *are* outsiders. They are outside their tribe, that masculine tribe, and they're outside the main social tribe – even now, although that's obviously changed a lot from when we were young. And women find that interesting because women are often outsiders – whether they recognise it or not – from the main culture. Gay men have a different sensibility from straight men, but they have the male sensibility as well. It's the daily double, isn't it?

How would you describe John?

I don't know how to describe what he is. For me, John's like a drug.

I knew him when I was twenty. We were kind of friends then, but it was at art school and I was in a different year. Then we met up again when we were twenty-seven. As soon as I saw him, we started to laugh about something idiotic and it was like coming home; it was coming to this incredibly safe place. That friendship developed and is, and has always been, a very, very intense relationship. If I don't see him for a while I get desperate to look at him and to feed on his energy and to be rude to him and laugh hysterically and talk about stuff, talk about how I feel.

How did you come to live together?

How *did* that happen? Oh I know, I'd just got married and I've always hated it when people say, 'My husband's my best friend.' I'm sure it's lovely for other people, but I've never been able to believe that any one person can be everything to you. And I knew that there was no man on earth with whom I could live totally alone without driving him insane. I've never, ever thought that your needs for friendship and intimacy and intellectual stimulation would come in one package – either in a sexual relationship or in friendship. So I got married thinking, God, I'll be stuck in a house with this man and whatever will we talk about?

I also had this rather odd view about nuclear families. I was an only child and I was brought up in a nuclear family that was very successful. As nuclear families go, it actually was a good, functioning one. I was happy and I was absolutely loved so I was very, very fortunate. I went away to school having no idea that people's parents didn't like each other. I thought everybody's family thought the sun shone out of them, and that mothers and fathers got on. It wasn't until I went to the city that I realised life was not like that.

But I had absolutely no interest in duplicating it. I don't know where that came from at all. Actually, I do know where part of it comes from. When I was little I was frightened to go away from my family for any length of time because I got incredibly homesick. And I always thought, If I ever have a child I'm going to make sure that child is loved at home but is able to go out into the world without feeling fearful she's going to lose home.

I also had a number of people who were extended family, who were like parents but just that little bit removed – especially aunts, who were just fabulous. When I was repulsive they could say to my mother, 'Oh, she's all right really.' They were always on your team. So there was this intensity of the nuclear family but there were all these backstops, particularly these terrific women, these aunts. I knew from a very early age that I was really lucky to have that and I always wanted my daughter Alexandra to have it. Being an only child myself, I wanted her to have that because it was really valuable for me, these older people who were on your team but weren't necessarily on your back all the time.

Then, when David and I were married it was the seventies, when people were living in extended houses and community houses and communes. I could never come at a commune, but I thought I would really love to experiment. I also thought it was a terrific idea in terms of economy, because by putting incomes together you were able to buy a bigger house.

John was actually married at that point but the marriage had fallen apart. As it happens, I did have things to talk to David about so I wasn't totally frightened, but I felt really committed to the idea of the shared house. I don't know now whether David really thought it was a great idea, but he went along with most of my ideas, which was gracious of him. And John thought it was a very good idea. So we did it – we just bought a house. I was making a cake one day and John came down and said, 'I've found this house.' I said, 'Hang on, I'll just put the cake in the oven,' and off we went and that was it.

I don't know that David was there, I think he had to come back later, but John and I walked in the door and just knew that this was the house. So we said, 'We'll have it. That's the one.' And that was this house. It was the only house we looked at.

So we pooled our money and bought it, and it was as simple as that. We just knew it was right. David went after a while but John and I have lived together ever since. Our families all thought it was very peculiar.

Do you regard yourselves as a family?

Oh yes. We are John's family absolutely. And so is Will now. To me, Will is family. I've always wanted an extended family and I guess I have it. Because I'm adopted I have this real sense that family is not only blood. It *can* be blood but you've also got choices, and I guess that was one of the very positive things about being adopted, that I knew very clearly, early on, that family could be whatever you wanted it to be, although I didn't know how to articulate that for some time. I felt that I was chosen by my parents to make up a family, so I could quite deliberately choose somebody else to become family.

But I don't know how you'd describe my relationship with John. He describes it as being soulmates, says he's always thought of us as soulmates. Somebody once told us that in a former life we'd lived together in Egypt. John had been an Egyptian princess and I had been a cockroach. [Laughs] That'd be right. He'd get all the good frocks and I'd be this cockroach on the floor in Egypt.

Does the fact that you are not in a sexual relationship make it easier?

Oh yes, because we're so gracious with each other. There's far less rudeness with each other. I would never take John for granted in the way that I would take a lover, or that I took David. We are very attentive to details of the other person's life. I think that we are extraordinarily considerate of each other. If it were a sexual relationship – I don't know what happens, but I was frequently careless with lovers. I *am* careless. But I'm not in friendship, I'm good at friendship.

I think respect is hugely important in friendships. You meet somebody and for whatever reasons – either they make you laugh or you're overwhelmed by their brain or something that they do – you respect them. Perhaps respect is the foundation of friendship. Whereas you can fall in love with somebody and just want to screw their brains out: you don't necessarily have to respect them, although you'd hope that all those other things would come up afterwards. I think respect is absolutely essential in all relationships, but because friendship isn't physically an intimate thing, respect is probably the bedrock of it.

We've done it now for eighteen years. We've had ups and downs like anybody else does, although I can't remember what the downs were. [Laughs] People say that, don't they, because they feel they should, but in fact it's all been ups. When one of us is a bit off the air or pathetic, you just let them be that for a while and then you tell them to pull their socks up. Perhaps you tolerate behaviour in friendships that you might never tolerate in a more intimate relationship.

You seem to offer each other great sympathy and understanding, as well as more laughter than I've ever heard in a house before.

Oh yeah. Empathy, sympathy, generosity of spirit, and enormous consideration. For Alexandra, a whole part of her childhood has been about being considerate of other people in the house because they're not her father. So it's, 'Don't do this now because John needs his own time out.' Or, 'Will needs a break.' I don't know whether she would think this, and it was certainly not the plan in bringing her up, but the result is that she's very respectful of other people now. I guess that's through living with them on a daily basis; you become considerate of other people's feelings, of other people's time, of not wearing people out continually.

Maybe that's what people in sexual relationships often do, just wear each other out?

And perhaps take each other for granted too. That's a question of respect too, isn't it? John and I have discussed this endlessly for years, because we could never understand why our sexual relationships were as they were. [Laughs] And I still don't have an answer, sorry.

How do your sexual relationships affect the central relationship between you and John? Oh how does that affect your sexual relationships?

Well, I suppose David was there in the beginning and that was an established relationship. Then after a couple of years David and I separated, and John and I have lived together ever since. I've had other relationships but they were never relationships in which I was going to live with someone. Because of the way that I live with John, I don't want a husband. I don't *need* a husband. The things that I really value enormously I have on a daily basis. I mean, some days it's so good I don't want to go to work, which is not to say that I don't want an intimate life as well. But at the moment I don't have to worry about it. [Laughs] Should it ever happen, I couldn't move anybody else into the house, that'd be just far too much trouble. [Since this conversation, Alexandra has moved into a house with her best friend and Elizabeth has a new relationship. She and her partner spend nights at each other's houses and Jude has been warmly welcomed into the Rozelle household.]

Did your relationship with John alter when Will moved into the house?

No, my relationship with John hasn't altered, it's this wonderfully constant thing. But we work really hard at it. Now that he's away during the week [John works in Melbourne or Asia during the week], we are very attentive about phoning each other. I don't phone daily, but we phone regularly. Sometimes he's overseas and busy, but I need to talk to him all the time.

We work very hard at considering each other's needs and John would be one of the most thoughtful and sensitive people I've come across in that way. He's very intuitive and he has a gift for understanding where other people are at, and he fine-tunes that all the time. He can be revolting [laughs], let's not think he's a saint, but he is extraordinarily good at that. He's extraordinarily considerate of me and of Alexandra.

We always check that it's all right with somebody to do something. I guess in some ways there's more of a formality when you live communally than when you live in a nuclear family. For instance, if somebody is going to come and stay in the house, does it suit everyone to have them here at the moment? And if someone says no, then that's it. Everybody's needs are primary in the house, everyone's needs are respected. That's the only way I think it can work.

It's about respect and love. Absolute love. I just love John and I now love Will. I suppose it could've been a disaster when we got Will, but it wasn't. It's been really wonderful. I can't speak for the others, but for me it's wonderful because I don't want to live alone and I love that companionship. I love coming home and sharing the day. And I always knew that I could never have brought up a child alone because it would've all been too intense. I'd be tragic as a solitary parent – you know, I'm not exactly your battling mother of eight. I'm probably the only woman in the world who's needed seven adults to bring up one child. [Laughs] I need three people to talk it through with, four people to help me do it. I think I knew that I was going to be pretty pathetic at it and I needed quite a lot of help early on. Now I think I'm actually a very good parent, but I can't say I've done it by myself. I won't be one of those fabulous headlines: 'My Mother Did Everything'.

But I also have an absolute horror of that single-mother-and-daughter enclave. A while back Alexandra was going through a black period and she decided she had no friends – you know how you do sometimes. I said, 'You've got friends, what's wrong with you?' And she said, 'Well, it's pretty embarrassing to have to say your mother's your best friend.' I said, 'Don't ever say that. I can't bear it. I'm your mother, I don't want to be your best friend.' The fact that you might be friendly, or you have the capacity for friendship with your child is an absolute bonus, but, oooh – I don't know why it makes me cringe but it does. I think it's a revolting idea.

Alexandra and I have a very good relationship, but I'm her mother. It's wonderful if you're fortunate to have a child you really like and respect and who likes you – well, most of the time – and whose company you enjoy. But I think it's a real privilege to be a mother.

When kids I work with tell me that their mother's their best friend, I think, Yes, I can see that you're missing things that need to be there in a proper parental, adult-to-child relationship. The mother is taking the easy option and going for the soft line of 'We're equals.' In fact, the first thing about being a mother is that you've got to draw boundaries and you've got to make kids safe. And you have to be able to say no, and put down limitations. You're *not* equals. You have to do things that friends don't do – maybe the best thing about friends is that they *don't* do those things for you. A mother has to be able to say, 'I actually know best in this case. When you are a parent, you can do it your way. But I'm your mother and this is what we're doing. End of conversation.'

You become best friends because you can't be a parent. It's tough being a parent. It's much tougher being a mother than it is being a friend.

Well, Alexandra not only has a mother but several fathers as well. John is a devoted father, isn't he?

Absolutely. I wanted Alexandra to have that thing I had in my childhood of these people who are on your team, so I did it. Although just about everybody I know thinks it's peculiar. And I suppose it is odd, but it does work and it suits us. My mother thinks I'm about the luckiest woman in the universe. It doesn't stop her thinking it's unusual because, really, I should have a lawyer husband on the North Shore. But she thinks if I can't have that, I've got something that's the next best thing.

Two husbands in the inner west.

One of whom cooks fabulously and regularly.

Anne Summers ¶

ANNE SUMMERS'S FIFTIETH birthday party in 1995 was packed with friends. Some of them appeared on the invitation, which featured an often hilarious collection of photographs that in charting Anne's life also charted a chunk of the history of the women's movement in Australia. Writer, activist and author of the now classic *Damned Whores and God's Police*, first published in 1975, Anne grew up in Adelaide before moving to Sydney as a postgraduate student. She was one of the original femocrats, that particularly Australian breed of feminist bureaucrats who went from protesting in the street to working within government to bring about much of the change they had advocated as activists. Anne worked with two prime ministers: she ran the Office for the Status of Women for Bob Hawke from 1983 to 1986 and was political advisor to Paul Keating from 1992 to 1993. ¶ IN BETWEEN SHE lived in New York, where she and Sandra Yates bought *Ms* and *Sassy* magazines and Anne was *Ms*'s editor-in-chief. Unfortunately, Australian outspokenness collided with American puritanism, and major advertisers boycotted *Sassy* in objection to what some of them saw as controversial material in it. Anne returned to Sydney to live in 1993, accompanied by her American partner Chip Rolley, who is nineteen years her junior. ¶ ANNE HAS WRITTEN for the *Australian Financial Review*, the *National Times* and the *Independent* and was for four years the editor of *Good*

Weekend magazine. She now writes a regular opinion column for the *Sydney Morning Herald*. In 1994 she revised *Damned Whores and God's Police*, adding a new introduction in which she challenged younger Australian feminists, and in 1999 she published the first volume of her autobiography, *Ducks on the Pond*.

———————

AT THE MOMENT I'd say there are maybe four people whom I would regard as *very* good friends, and then there are the others who are goodish friends. I've been friends with those four for probably twenty years. Dany Torsh and I met each other when we were students at university in the sixties, so we've been friends for more than thirty years. I was still in Adelaide when I met her and she was in Melbourne working for the National Union of Students, something like that. I was a late starter, so by the time I came to Sydney I was a postgraduate student in my twenties and Dany had finished.

There have been times when we've gone more than a year without seeing each other, particularly when I was living in the States, and have only exchanged a Christmas card or the occasional letter. But I think one of the characteristics of very good friends is that it doesn't matter how long since you've seen them, because you pick up immediately; you sit down and you start talking and it's as if the last conversation was only a few days earlier, even though it might have been a couple of years earlier. That's to do with the level of comfort you feel with that person, so there's no need for small talk, no need for all that ice-breaking stuff.

What are some of the qualities that those people share? Why these particular people and not the many others that you meet?

I'm not sure if I can answer that precisely. There's some sort of attraction between you, or some sort of empathy. You feel able to trust them and you feel able to confide in them. Being able to confide is a very important thing; you confess or confide things to close friends that you certainly wouldn't to other people, and you trust that they'll keep that confidence. You expect to be able to go to them if you're in trouble and, likewise, you'd expect them to come to you. Conversely, if you're very happy, like when I first got involved with Chip and it was wonderful – I'd found somebody after years of being alone – you can't wait to tell your friends, can't wait to show him off. It's your closest friends that you can't wait to talk to, to tell. And you have confidence that they're going to be *genuinely* pleased for your happiness – and also that they're not going to try to pinch him. [Laughs]

It's interesting about confiding, though. I have a very good friend, not one of my very closest friends, but a good friend whom I do confide in, and she confides in me a lot and trusts me not to talk about things, even though neither of us would say we're each other's best friend.

Are there some things you wouldn't tell an intimate friend? Any barriers?

I think one barrier is money. I'm still quite conscious of not talking about money. I'm not particularly interested in money and I don't have any. [Laughs] And I've had some periods in my life when I've been in an unbelievable fix, worse than broke, and not knowing how it's all going to work. I've felt very angry and embarrassed to be in that situation when it's happened, but I have talked to people about that. But on the whole I think it's tacky to sit down and talk about money.

What about that vexed question of whether you tell a close friend that her husband or partner is having an affair? Would you want your friends to tell you?

I *think* I would. In some ways you're better off not knowing. But I've never really been in that situation, as far as I know anyway. This is the longest relationship I've been in – we've been together ten years and I hadn't been with anybody for about ten years before Chip came along – but prior relationships tended to break up over stuff like that.

Are common values important in close friendships?

I can't really think that I would be best friends with somebody who was a racist or who was anti-abortion or opposed to other things that I think are important. I can imagine being friends with somebody and having a difference, something that we agree to disagree on, but it's not the case with any of my friends. We do tend to agree on core values, although there may be incidental things we don't agree on, and we might have different opinions of particular people. But having different opinions about someone is not usually a make-or-break issue.

Have you ever had a best friendship go sour?

Yes, it was quite a long time ago and I don't think it was over one particular thing. She and I still occasionally see each other; we're not close friends any more but we're kind of civil now. However, we probably went for five or six years not having any contact at all, and things were quite acrimonious. There were a few big scenes.

It was all brought to a head by jealousy, actually. This woman was a mentor and brought me on, if you like, in Sydney. I'd come here and not known anyone and she looked after me and used to introduce me, and then I'd started to overshadow her. My book [*Damned Whores and God's Police*] came out, and suddenly I was more famous than she was and she really hated that. And I wouldn't do what she wanted me to do. Even though we're only a few years apart in age, it was probably a bit like the daughter asserting herself against the controlling mother.

Have issues of jealousy come up at other times with your close friends?

Yes, although at the time I actually don't see it. I've had it pointed out to me by other people when I'm having a difficult time with somebody. It's tricky because I don't see any reason why anyone should be jealous of me. Whatever I have, I've worked for; it hasn't been bestowed on me. It's not as if I've inherited stuff or anything like that, which I can imagine some-one might well be jealous of.

Is it possible to work with close friends?

I have in the past, but I haven't for a long time. Dany and I made a film together once and that was pretty hassle-free. I guess most of my projects are solitary ones. Writing books and so on is a solitary occupation. Working in magazines, though, when Sandra and I were working in New York, placed a lot of strains on our friendship. We're still friends now, but we didn't really know each other beforehand. We met when she first came to New York and we were starting to become friends when it all suddenly happened – getting to know each other and becoming friendly and going into business together and having all those problems. It was a bit much to cope with.

Chris Ronalds is a very good friend of mine, and she and I worked together in the Office for the Status of Women when I was running that. She's a lawyer and had been engaged by the government to draft a green paper on affirmative action. We had to work together to get that into shape and I rejected the first draft. I think she had me around for lunch and we had quite a few drinks before we started to talk about it, and I broke the news to her that I thought that in the present climate we couldn't do X and Y. I was extremely nervous and thought she would probably kill me and never want to work with me again, and blame me all around town, but in fact she was fantastic and we worked closely and very successfully together for about eighteen months getting that through [*The Federal Affirmative Action (Equal Employment Opportunity for Women) Act*].

We're still very good friends and she's been fantastically helpful to me in lots of ways. For example, when I was in New York finishing the revised edition of *Damned Whores* I needed some help with the research back here, so she found a young student to do it for me and supervised it, which was extremely good of her. She's great at practical help, with documents or legal advice, or whatever it is that's within her ambit. I used to stay with her for long periods whenever I came back to Australia from New York, and Chip and I lived with her for three months while our house was being renovated. That's a real test of friendship, I think.

What about making new friends? Do you find that becomes harder as you get older?

Yes, I think it's much harder. Also, I've moved cities so many times – in the past fifteen years I've moved from Sydney to Canberra to New York to Canberra to Sydney – and one of the things I feel very lucky about is that my old friendships have survived.

It's hard to think of any new friends I made when I moved to New York that have endured. The good friends I have in New York are people I knew before. Going to a new city is very hard, I think. Particularly as I was forty-two when I went to New York, and I think it's very difficult to make new close friends at that age. I made a lot of acquaintances, and there was never any shortage of people to go out with or anything like that, but no close friends. I guess you're more likely to make friends when you're younger. And the other thing is, I met Chip in New York and being with him makes a big difference. We're incredibly self-contained – we spend weeks never going out, very happy with each other's company. We don't see people; in fact, we have to remind ourselves to be hospitable. Whereas if you're by yourself you do seek people out. I had a lot more friends, a lot wider range of contact with friends, and I was constantly making new friends and perhaps working harder on the friendships, when I was single. I've become quite conscious of that and have been thinking I should make more of an effort to see my friends by myself, rather than Chip always being there.

It's interesting that every single one of my close friends has become very good friends with Chip too. They all love him, they all think he's fantastic. I say to them that they all like him better than they like me. Some of them gang up on me. You know how, if there are three people, two of them always gang up on one? Well, Chip and one friend always gang up on me, and sometimes I've thought, Fuck this, I've known you longer. You were my friend first. [Laughs]

What was it like when you came back to Australia, bringing Chip to meet your old friends?

It was very funny. I remember the first time I introduced him to Chris Ronalds. I forget who else was there, but I was talking at some function at the Harold Park Hotel and this huge number of people turned out. At that stage Chip hardly used to drink, but he'd gone to lunch with Michael Skinner, who had taken him on a pub crawl around the Rocks. So Chip turned up and he was legless and I had to speak. I said to Chris, 'Don't let him have any more because he's legless.'

Chris looked at me and said, 'Bloody hypocrite.' And by the time the speech and the questions were over and we all went off somewhere to have dinner, the two of them were getting on famously. I'd say, 'Don't give him any more to drink.' And she'd say, 'Why not? Chippie, would you like a drink?' So they got on fabulously from the word go. Occasionally Chris reminds Chip, 'Remember when you didn't drink?' [Laughs]

And Chip was pretty amazing. He'd heard a lot about these people. He hadn't met Chris before, but he had met a few people who'd come through New York, he'd met a couple of them in small doses and then he came back here for the onslaught. And survived.

I've just thought about another two friends, too. Trying to define what's a good friend – I guess a very good friend is someone you can ring and ask for virtually anything. You could ring them and say, 'I'm in trouble. Can I come and stay with you?' I don't think I've ever asked for money but I know I could if I were really stuck. I've had friends offer me money, but I would prefer to try and get it from the bank. I think you can basically ask good friends for almost anything and know that if they possibly can, they will. And if you include that in your criteria I have a lot more very good friends – probably eight or nine people.

Do you think that's because you were single for so many years, so your friendships were very important to you and had a chance to become well and truly formed?

Yes. All those friendships had very solid foundations. And I guess they have lasted so long and keep going because they are able to be renewed in ways that continue to be satisfying on all sides.

Are they all women?

Only one is a man, a gay man in Los Angeles. He's been one of my very best friends for a very long time. We talk to each other virtually every day on email. He lives in La-La land where things are a bit superficial. Not that he's superficial, but he's got all the latest jokes and knows all the latest gossip, all the latest fashions, everything. His emails are very witty. He's a great deal of fun. He made me buy my first Armani suit. He took me shopping for it, takes me shopping all the time – you can imagine my credit card. He has no money at all, and I had no money either when we bought the suit. I was in New York and he took me to Barneys and said, 'Here you are. You buy that. You deserve it.' *You deserve it?* No-one had ever said that to me before and I thought, What a fantastic concept. *Okay*. [Laughs]

I still wear it. Ten years old and I still wear it. It was the most expensive thing I'd ever bought up until that point, although I hate to say I've exceeded that limit now.

Do you think women's friendships are different from men's?

Men don't have friends. It's very strange. Chip doesn't have many friends here. The other day we were talking about what we might do in the future and he said, 'Oh, you and your friends are always talking about the feminist nursing home, that you're going to get this house by the sea, near a pub and a good restaurant. That sounds fine to me. We'll move in there.' And I said, 'What are you going to do with all those ninety-year-old women?' But he would be quite happy.

I feel a bit worried that he hasn't made many friends here, apart from a lot of joint friends and the friends that I've had for years. We've met people together and have a circle of friends that we know as a couple, and that's fine, but it kind of worries me that he doesn't have any male friends he can go to the pub with. Not that he goes to the pub, but metaphorically. It doesn't seem to worry him though.

You're very good at keeping in contact with your friends, aren't you? Before email, when you were away from them, did you tend to write or ring them up?

I used to write. I've lived in America twice. The first time I went, in 1978, I went to Minneapolis on a fellowship and I used to do a group newsletter to my friends. I did that for about a year, and I've still got them. They're incredible to read now. Then when I went to live in New York in 1987 I did the same thing. I did a monthly newsletter which was about ten pages long and I sent it to about thirty people, and initially some people were a bit pissed off about that. But I sort of persuaded them that I wanted everyone to share this experience, and the really close friend would get something personal as well. I'm really glad I did it because it's such a fantastic document when I look at it now. And because I used to send that, everyone would write back to me so I used to get a phenomenal amount of mail.

[Laughs] It shows I had nothing to do in those first couple of years in New York. I used to miss all my friends and write them all these letters. When life became a bit busier I wasn't able to do that. I used to come back a fair bit, and whenever I'd come back there'd be lots of parties. And I would certainly ring my close friends.

Do you use the phone more now?

No, not much. I hate it. I really hate ringing people up, which is a bit odd for a journalist. I'll write or email or do up little cards. Email is incredible; it's transforming, particularly for friends in different countries. There are people that I now chat with on email who would normally have got a Christmas card, if that. I now talk daily, or at least a couple of times a week. For friendship it's a real boon.

It's interesting that technology has made us revert to old forms of communication, written forms of communication, even if it is in cyberspace. It's still something you can keep, you print it out and keep it if you want to. Whereas a telephone conversation is so ephemeral and you forget who said what. I used to get very nostalgic – this was pre-Chip – and maybe I'd had a few drinks and I'd get on the phone and I'd ring everybody I knew. I called it an attack of telephonitis. One time I rang wherever it was that everybody I knew was staying for

ANNE SUMMERS

Christmas or New Year, and I drank a whole bottle of wine while I was talking to about twenty different people, and by the time it was over I didn't remember who I'd talked to or what was said. You really have to take notes of these conversations to remember. [Laughs]

But of course I still look forward to seeing certain people. I've got several friends in Canberra and when I go down there I really can't wait to see them. I think that's another test of friendship. There's a couple, a male and a female, who have become very good friends of Chip's and mine. They're very good friends of a very good friend of mine, and this friend would not let me meet them, she wanted to keep all her friends separate. I don't know why. Anyway, eventually we met them and we've become friends independently, and whenever we go down there we stay with them and they come and stay with us in Sydney.

How does the friend who introduced you feel about that?

She feels a bit left out. There is a complex propriety about this – if you meet somebody through a friend, is it kosher to contact that person and not let the friend know? Is it kosher to see that person without the friend who introduced you being present? There are rituals there, although I'm not quite sure what they are. I've noticed that with other people too. And it's happened to me a few times and I've felt funny about it. There are a couple of people that I only see with each other, which probably isn't necessary but this is the way it's developed. It's too difficult to say to one that you want to see the other alone.

Do you think feminism made a difference to the way women have friends?

Feminism transformed friendship for women. We learned to appreciate each other in ways that we hadn't been taught. What we learned from the women's movement was that women friends weren't people you spent time with while you

141

were waiting for a man, you could actually have a good time. My thirtieth birthday party was all women, and my mother was horrified, absolutely horrified.

I'd just finished my book [*Damned Whores and God's Police*]. I don't know if you remember the cover, but the illustration included a whorish-looking woman, so I reproduced the picture of the whore on the invitation and wrote, 'You're invited to spend an evening with some of your fellow damned whores.' There were about fifty women and it was fantastic. That was 1975, the height of the women's movement, and we'd learned to enjoy ourselves, not to feel that we were somehow suffering or second best because there were no men there. A lot of my very good friends go back to that period. Regardless of what relationship they may have been in, or not, at the time, we learned to value our friendships intrinsically.

We still have these girls' nights out. A few of my friends and I are invited and they're something that Chip can't go to, even though they all say he's an honorary girl and they love him and he could come, but it's actually important that we maintain that as a separate thing.

Loving, sexual relationships are obviously important, but do you believe that friendship is the major relationship in your life?

I think it is. I guess what you aim for is to have both, to be best friends with your partner (I hate that word, I've been calling Chip my husband lately). I'm lucky that we are such good friends. Despite differences in age and country, our interests are pretty similar, and our values and so on that we talked about earlier – I can't *imagine* living with someone who votes Liberal, I just can't imagine it.

You hear of people living together who aren't friends, but I can't imagine that either. Every decision that either of us makes we talk through. Occasionally I've done something that Chip has disapproved of, but I can't imagine that you'd do anything significant in your life and not discuss it fully with the person you live with. And if you had a relationship where that wasn't possible you'd wonder what that relationship was all about.

Would you call Chip a best friend?

Yes, I think I would, without wanting to diminish the importance of best friends I've had for much longer. He is remarkably insightful and mature. He has quite extraordinary insights, which is rare in men and certainly in younger men. So much so that when Chip does something that's really male, I think, God, yes, you're one of those too.

Dale Spender ¶

D ALE SPENDER, feminist, writer of more than thirty
books, researcher, teacher, and now director of an
online content company, has had the same best friend for
over fifty years – her younger sister Lynne. Like Hannah
Arendt and Mary McCarthy's, their friendship is a dialogue,
sustained and developed in daily conversation, no matter
where in the world they happen to be living. For the fifteen
years that Dale lived in London, doing her PhD on the very
different ways that men and women talk, and teaching at
the University of London, the conversation was largely a
written one. Since Dale returned to Australia to live in
1987 with her long-term partner Ted, she and Lynne speak
or email at least once a day. ¶ LIKE LYNNE (whose version
of the friendship appears in the next conversation), Dale
has other close women friends in her life whom she values
dearly. Her long-time Brisbane neighbour and friend
Quentin Bryce says that Dale is herself a wonderful friend –
generous, kind and hospitable, and always intellectually
challenging. Not surprising then that she is exhilarating
company: direct, honest, passionate and very, very funny.
We laugh a great deal throughout our conversation of three
or four hours, which we have in Dale's Sydney apartment
overlooking Coogee Beach, within walking distance of her
sister Lynne's house. A small, slim gamine figure with short

fair hair, Dale is dressed, as always, in purple, the suffragists' colour.

————

FRIENDS IN MY life have been extended family. In today's world, where the unit has got down to mother and children – not that that has ever been my life – how do you survive except by picking each other's kids up from school and having someone you can ask, 'Can she stay overnight?' Women's friendships have become what in previous centuries would have been support provided by siblings and cousins and aunts, unmarried aunts living in the house. In order for society to function you have to have groups of women. Until recently it's been a family-based thing and now it's about choice. And that's a distinct improvement – you don't always like your family.

But I did. We were very lucky, although my friendship with Lynne says a lot about our mother, who constructed us as a unit. Mum says that by the time I was five or six – I'm three years older than Lynne – there was no way she could discipline one without the other, that we just linked totally against her. That's a bit difficult for a mother. I can remember my mother saying to me, 'You're so lucky you've got a sister. I always wanted one and I never had one.' I used to go to school and say, 'Anyway, I've got a sister.' And people would say, 'So what, everyone's got them.' And I'd say, 'No they haven't, my mother didn't have one.'

My father was a product of his time and he still has difficulty with Lynne's and my feminism in lots of ways. The two of us, together, changed his life, and changed Mum's life. People say to Mum, 'How is it you have daughters like this?' And we say,

'You should have seen Mum before we started on her.' Mum is as much a product of us as we are of her.

We have a brother too, but he's fifteen years younger than I am. He just thought he grew up with three mothers. He's very at ease in a woman's world. Graeme's one of the few males who wouldn't necessarily need to leave the room when women are chatting. Not that he'd interrupt in any way, he knows better than to do that.

My friendships and relationships have all been with women. It's just the one guy I live with. And I keep saying, How did that happen?

Would you say you are close friends, you and Ted?

Oh yes.

Do you think it's possible for women to have as a best friend a straight man, with no sex involved?

I think it's hard. Apart from Ted, I don't have many straight men as good friends, although I'm acquiring more as I get older. There are some gay men who can be good friends, the kind who value women, not the misogynist kind. The kind who like the gossip.

I wanted to do a book at one stage called *Talking Comfort*, because the origin of the word 'gossip' is the talking comforter who talked you through the birth. It was the notion of someone who would talk away pain, who would talk about women's lives. And, to some extent, talking comfort is still what gossip is. That's what women do. We make each other's lives easier. It's talk that's at the absolute centre of friendship. That's why I think the telephone is so important, because of the talk.

When I was a kid you had a single best friend, but nearly all of us today have clusters of best friends. I have some in Sydney, some in Brisbane, and some in England, where I lived, and a couple in the States, where I've spent so much time.

They're networks. Only one dial and I can conjure up the whole thing. And email's made an extraordinary difference to me and my overseas friendships. There are about five or six women with whom I'm in touch nearly every day, and that's probably more than when I lived there. I know what they're doing, what their problems are. I forward some of their emails to Lynne, who always wants filling in. The network continues, the gossip continues, but it's electronic and quick. I would never ring my friends in the States every day, even if the calls came down enormously in price. Besides, it takes longer. Every morning, first thing, you send emails. You think of a joke, you send things that might interest them, there are all sorts of things you can do. If someone's sick, you send virtual flowers.

Apart from Lynne, do you have old friends from childhood, from school?

My oldest friend is Eleanor Ramsey. I don't have any friends from school, though Lynne still does. I'm sure that was because I took off overseas for fifteen years at that period of my life. I don't know how to get in touch with anybody I went to school with. What happens to me now is that young women turn up whom I taught, and they claim a sort of friendship. I find that quite interesting. So I don't have any close friends that have known me since I was a little girl. But Eleanor Ramsey and I have known each other since I was a big girl, and that's the friendship. She knows most about my history, about the times when things went wrong or when things went right. And that's a special sort of friendship.

Anna Coote in England was probably my closest friend there. I had a lot of younger women friends, but in some ways I nurtured them. Anna was the one who was the equal. I have both sorts of friendships. I'm surrounded by young women whom I keep telling it costs me an awful lot of money for their

lunches and I want them to look after me in my old age. A lot
of them have worked for me, have done research for me, things
like that, and I've loved having them around, but it's not the
same as someone who's known you as an equal and you're nurturing each other. That's a different sort of friendship – the sort
of friendship Lynne provides.

Our lives are so different now too. By the time our mothers
were our age they almost seemed to be out of it. At fifty, it just
wasn't on that you would have the sort of active life we're having. We would think of them as old and they thought of
themselves as old. They'd be looking after the grandchildren.
That's changed too.

A very good friend of mine was here this morning. I love her
dearly, but I was asking her who nurtures her. She now has a
husband who's retired, her elderly mum lives with them, and
she also has her daughter and her daughter's husband living
with them at the moment because her daughter's just had a
baby. She cooks the meal every night, she's the breadwinner
and she does all the nurturing. She's the centre. Oh, and she's
doing a PhD as well. It's the first time I've seen her for about six
or eight months, and she told me, 'I just haven't got time for
social things.' And I said, 'It's not on. You don't have any
nurturing friendship. You'll crack up if you're not careful.' She
loves them all, but doesn't have someone in her life who looks
after her. That's the other side of being fifty-five and still working. When do we stop?

Do you think women and men have friends very differently?

Oh yes. Women bare their souls. And they negotiate social
change. That's women's lore: how to negotiate, how do you tell
him that, how do you say this, what do you reckon about that.
We've had this huge cultural transformation in the last twenty
years, and all those ways of doing things and conversation and

repertoire have to be worked out again. One of the things that's happened in the last twenty years is that women have retalked who we are. We've looked at what femininity is, decided there were parts that we didn't want, chosen what we think is useful for the next century. I'm quite consciously a person whom I choose to be, as distinct from how I was reared.

Mum told me all this stuff and I'd say, 'It doesn't work, I'm not doing it.' My mother now wonders how she could ever have given Lynne and me the advice that she did. Most of what she advised us is totally inappropriate for the lives we lead. She talks about 'the footbinding period', and about how she thought she had to make us into wives and mothers. And she tried really hard to do that: 'You'll never get a boyfriend if you talk to them like that.' That sort of stuff. She says, 'I look at the two of you now and see how ridiculous that was.' She's quite apologetic about some of it, but also able to say that the advice had been handed on for centuries and suddenly, in the space of one life-time, it doesn't work.

I grew up in a culture in which women were sneaky, where you 'managed' men. I don't think I've ever played that game. Maybe it's because I'm too lazy – I'm not necessarily claiming it as a virtue – but I just couldn't do that stuff. Mum would say, 'Don't tell your father how much you paid for your shoes.' And I'd say, 'Well, why wouldn't I?' 'Because it's too much.' I couldn't give a stuff, but that was the whole attitude of women then.

Women build up communities in which they trust each other to talk about what they do and how they do it, and how to renegotiate. All the boys have been able to do in the last twenty years is react. Men as a group haven't held up masculinity and asked which parts are good and which parts are bad, and they haven't got communities in which they're renegotiating the rules and the roles. Whereas women are feeling quite confident because, from our basic six or eight best friends, we know that this is what we're doing and how we're doing it.

As a schoolgirl, did you have friends who shared your view of the world?

I have to be really careful how I say this because it could sound quite pretentious, but I was a bright girl at school and bright girls didn't have many friends. People didn't like me; they called me Miss Bossy Boots. As an adult I've never had any sense of not having lots of good friends, but I certainly have memories as a child of thinking no-one liked me. But maybe this happens to all of us. Maybe our friendships come and go. I had friendships that lasted three months. I didn't have many friends in high school, then I changed schools after the intermediate year, and in fourth and fifth year I had two really good friends. But I haven't kept in touch with them. I was the only one who went on to university, so I wasn't with them. I even tried to change, to go to teacher's college at the last minute, because I was the only one going on to university and I didn't want to go.

Then at university I did arts, eight hours a week. And you know what that's like – I think there were only half a dozen people with whom I did the same combination of subjects and lectures. I had a couple of women friends, but that wasn't the place where I really made friends. I wasn't part of the brilliant group; I wasn't the clever girl at university which, in a way, was really good. That was people like Germaine Greer. I was too bourgeois to do some of the things that she did; my middle-class background got in the way.

I often wonder about Germaine because I think she's brilliant. Courageous and brilliant. I think about how we shared so many cultural assumptions and ways of being brought up, and to this day I can't work out how she knew all these things that I never did. How did she know? When she was writing *The Female Eunuch* in 1968, all I knew was that boys were driving me insane because I didn't think I ever got my way in things, and yet everybody told me that being married was the ultimate. I got married because my two friends from high school said to me, 'You're very unhappy and the only way you get to be happy is to be married. Happiness is having your own kitchen.' And Mum kept saying to me, when I was twenty-four, 'You won't find your place in the world, you have to settle down, get married, have children.' So I actually got married out of a sense of, Maybe this is the way. You wonder how you could have been so naïve.

It took me seven years to leave my marriage. My mother kept saying, 'It's the woman's fault if the marriage doesn't work.' But by the time I was divorced, my mother was my greatest ally, saying, 'You can't continue to live like this.' I remember when Lynne said she was getting a divorce, Mum said instantly, 'It'll halve your workload.' And she was absolutely right. But when I got married and was so miserable, my friends said, 'Oh yes, it's awful, isn't it?' And I thought, Why didn't you tell me? Why did you tell me to get married? Why did you persuade me?

And I realised that my continued existence as a single person threatened them enormously. I also felt that they had betrayed me. They hadn't told me about the problems. They saw that as something married women talk about, and as a single woman I couldn't be told. I don't think that happens now. We were part of a generation where women were encouraged to be sly and manipulative. And now women are very open.

But there is still envy and competitiveness between women, don't you think, that can damage friendships?

Well, I have trouble with that. I'm very conscious that some of the things I'm saying leave me very vulnerable but I don't have any sense of envy.

Do other women envy you, do you think?

It's not something I think about a great deal. But Lynne often talks to me about things like envy and jealousy. Maybe it's because there isn't any between us. We can share genuinely in each other's good fortune, and bad. That's really one of Lynne's greatest contributions to our relationship – as the younger sister, she was the one who had to make allowances to start with because, by definition, I did things first.

Susie Orbach writes in Between Women *of a woman who becomes more professionally qualified and whose friends then feel that she's betrayed them, that she's trying to prove herself better than they are.*

I've certainly seen lots of that. You see it in Britain in terms of class, the idea that you're betraying your origins and you're getting uppity. And you certainly see the tall poppy syndrome here all the time. But in my own life, I suppose since the age of about twenty-five, I've always seen myself as a resourced person, and even in terms of the women's movement there's no way I've ever argued that I'm a poor oppressed woman. I've always argued that women are oppressed the world over, and that women who have the resources should be working to ensure that things are improved. But I've never claimed a personal case because I think it borders on the obscene for white, Western, educated women, who are probably in the top 2 per cent of the world's population in terms of the resources at their disposal, to go around arguing that they're oppressed.

I've always said that it's not what resources or privileges you've got, it's how you use them. Yes, I've had emotional things in my life that have distressed me, though not that much – my parents are still alive, there have been no tragedies in my family – I'm incredibly lucky – and I have a sister and brother with whom you could count on one hand the fights we've had. So I see myself as resourced and I feel that what I should be doing with my life is finding a way to leave the world a better place than I found it. I know it may sound trite and ridiculous. My mother said it sounds like Christianity to her, which really annoys me. But I do believe that if you're going to be involved in a social movement, and I think the women's movement has been that, it is on the premise that you want life to be better, that people should want to improve conditions for women and children. That's been the last twenty-five years of my life, that's the context in which I've worked. So even if it's defined politically, when you are part of 2 per cent of the world's population in terms of the resources you're using up, to envy someone within that context is . . . I think it's tacky, actually.

Do you sometimes see friendships that fall apart and wonder what happened?

Because one suddenly marries someone who's really wealthy? I think that happens. I think friendships are about comparable resources and comparable views of the world, although some of my best friendships have been with people with entirely different views of the world. One of my closest friends is Lisa Bellear, an Aboriginal woman who causes me grief on a regular basis. We had to have this negotiation about time because I'm extremely punctual. I thought about it for a while, then I said to Lisa, 'It's not just that I haven't got an hour in my life to wait on the street corner for you, it is, in fact, that it takes a year off my life every time I have to do it because of my stress levels. So let's get it sorted out that from now on I'll wait a quarter of an hour. You can tell me if it's going to be blackfella time, in which case I'll arrive leisurely and I'll wait a quarter of an hour, or if it's going to be whitefella time, in which case I'll arrive on the dot and I'll wait a quarter of an hour. But a quarter of an hour is my maximum.' Because it was something that was really undermining our friendship.

Negotiation is a great skill and a lot of women feel they don't have it. I'm not very good at it, so I admire it and am intrigued by it.

I'm a very . . . 'independent' isn't the word, but . . .

Outspoken?

But I'm not in lots of ways. I'm incredibly careful with some people. I'd not hit back because it's very easy for me sometimes to see what their vulnerabilities are.

Actually, I am aware of it a lot with Lynne and Ted and physical space. Both of them have needs about personal space and they don't like to have their space invaded.

Mother and I have always had a hugging relationship. She puts her arms around me – until recently she was much taller – and my brother is quite good on hugs, as are his kids. But Lynne and Ted – well, Ted can't even go into certain restaurants because the chairs are too close together. Lynne is a bit like that too. And you can't just behave on the basis of your own values and habits; it's about seeing the world as others do, and respecting it, that helps to keep friendships. So even though it doesn't worry me in the slightest, I am always looking to see that they each have enough space.

When you think about your other really close friends, how is it different having a sister as a best friend?

In some ways it actually stops you from looking for other best friends. Lynne knows me so well and has been such a brilliant and comforting and resourcing friend over all those years, sometimes at her own expense. Lynne and I have never competed. The most competition is probably at the moment because we're in a similar sort of world. But even there, I'm the one who is zany and she's the intellectual property lawyer, so it's still shared space but completely different roles. Lynne was the one who developed physical prowess, she was the fantastic swimmer. I was the one who wouldn't stop reading books. That's changed now. Now we're a book club of two – we each read a book a day. But we've never interfered in each other's space.

When we were young we used to go to dramatic art together, and we did a huge number of dialogues and things in eisteddfods, with the two of us playing different roles. We were once Sir Peter and Lady Teasdale from *The School For Scandal*. Lynne was Sir Peter because, although she is younger, she was taller than me, and I was Lady Teasdale, and there were the two of us in Grandma's curtains and Mum down the front because we never learnt the scripts properly, prompting us every time, mouthing the words so that we could watch her and follow. That's such a shared history. And we have a shared history through husbands who gave us a raw deal in lots of ways, and each utilised the other's strengths a bit. Lynne has let me manage some of her personal life at times, in dealing with husbands and so on, and Lynne manages almost totally my professional life. I'm not allowed to sign anything. There's so much shared. Mum says Lynne and I finish each other's sentences. We're in contact once a day and we're in contact all the time with email. If I haven't spoken to her during the day, I'll ring before I go to bed or she'll ring me.

Is there any other friend who's quite like that?

I used to ring Renata every morning for years and years when we were in London. She was very stressed at one stage, and one morning she said to me, 'I could die during the night and no-one would know.' So from then on, for maybe five years, I rang at quarter to nine every morning, and sometimes it was for seconds and sometimes it was a five-minute chat.

The one time in my life when I felt the world was coming to an end, when I gave up smoking, I rang her one morning and burst into tears and said, 'I can't cope!' She was there within twenty minutes. She said she paid the taxi driver double to get across London to me as fast as possible. I was in a total mess after being a very heavy smoker. I'd given it up and was unable to work and had no real support. It would've been different if Mum or Lynne had been there.

It's more than a sense of support. For me, there have been certain times of my life when I've needed to let go, but there are only certain contexts in which I feel safe enough to let go and that's with women friends, and especially with Lynne. I don't know if they become closer because you let go, or you let go because they are already very good friends. But there have been a couple of times in my life when I've been close to despair and I've felt that I can let go because I know they'll look after everything. A couple of times with Lynne, and that once with Renata, I could abdicate for a couple of days, take time out. Then you get your resources together and come back and deal with the world.

And, again, I think that is what would've happened with extended families in the past, where your mother would take over for a bit, or the unmarried sister. It was a household. It was not necessarily the same in working-class households, but there was still the eldest kid to look after the youngest kids. But certainly in middle-class households, historically there was never just one woman in the house. There were always two or three adult women because women didn't do paid work, and if you didn't marry or you were widowed, you joined the married household or you all lived together. That's what really drives me mad today, when they talk about blended families as if they've just been invented. Families were just as blended last century, but it was death that brought them together – the husband would marry another young wife and there would be stepchildren and new children, and so on.

Now I think that's the role of friends. I would say that women's friendship is the cement of our society. And I think one of the reasons for the huge social breakdown we've got – and in Australia at the moment everybody has this extra-ordinary unease – is that women don't know how to explain the cultural transition to the information age, which is chang-ing all our jobs, our patterns of understanding, the way we make sense of the world. We haven't resourced women to do the talking to put that in place. Historically, societies have always depended on women's networks. That's what the social fabric is. Men don't make social fabric.

I think in lots of male friendships it's about bravado. Women's are about being able to be vulnerable with each other, and also about letting the real self show. With none of my friends who know me well do I have to hide that. I've presented myself here to you today, I'm sure, as this extremely nice and pleasant person [laughs], but I've got the most vicious streak and it's verbal and it's lethal. Now, most of my good women friends are very under-standing about that. None of them would think, God, Dale is a bitch. They just know that's my mental exercise for the day.

Given that love and sexual relationships are exciting to be in but they come and go, do you think friends are the most important rela-tionships we have?

Oh, I do think that, yes. There's no way that in my life love and true romance has ever been the only game. I live with the guy that I do because he is a very, very good friend and com-panion. We've been together twenty-five years and I think the longer you are together, the longer you're together – you share history and it's so companionable in lots of ways. It certainly resources my life enormously.

I think you wouldn't be human if you didn't, particularly at our age, start to ask, I wonder if I'd have done that differently? Though I must admit that I divide women of my age these days into two groups – those for whom it wasn't meant to turn out like this, and those who are reasonably at ease with their lives despite the fact that they've made mistakes and might've done things differently. It's about the ease in your life. I've got a couple of acquaintances, because I think they make very poor friends, the entire fabric of whose lives is 'It wasn't meant to be like this. I never thought that this is how I'd be living at fifty-five.' And, because there aren't many choices left and basically they're going to be living it out from now on, there's a bitter-ness and a grief and a self-flagellation there that I find very difficult. I think they make bad friends. If I have one skill, it's that I've chosen wonderful friends, including my sister. I've been hugely well served in friends.

Some people can't get over their bitterness that you have made choices that seem to have worked and they haven't. Lynne and I were among the first of both our groups to get divorced. We were hugely frowned on and seen as irresponsible. And there are a couple of women who did stay in their mar-riages, bitter marriages. One husband died and the other went off with a younger woman, and those women have a strong sense of betrayal – 'We did the right thing and set up our lives and they've left. You just pissed off and your life is rosy. It's all right for you.' I could no more be friends with women like that than I could jump off a cliff. This doesn't mean that I'm not resourcing or helpful. I make the occasional phone call to a couple of the women I know whose lives are very bitter and twisted, but that's not the sort of person you trust your psyche to, is it? I think I've always looked for very healthy friends.

The more you're in working order, the more people are attracted to you. And that's not necessarily about being nice. I'm not all that nice. I grew up being nice – bourgeois and nice – but it's not satisfying being nice all the time.

I look at you and Lynne and wonder, Was it because you had each other that you became so strong so early?

Having each other has been crucial to Lynne and me. In so many ways she is my security – heavens, she can know what I think before I do – and maybe it's because I haven't had children that she is my primary identification as 'family'. My brother is becoming more so, but it is Lynne and me making space for him, really.

I keep thinking about it as my parents age and as the prospect of being an orphan looms – which I think is a good description of who you are when they die. As I think of that loss I am also daily grateful that Lynne is there. We talk endlessly about it, about ageing, about reassurance, about how our generation has to legalise euthanasia. And she is always there, my beloved sister. It's how I cope really, and it is strength.

It's not just Mum and Dad. There's hardly a day that I don't seek her advice – sound her out on something, and laugh together. Personally and professionally she is the best possible counsel – what more can you have?

When you were growing up, did your mother say to you, as my mother certainly said to me, 'Boys aren't interested in bright girls'?

Mum now remembers saying those things and I think she's quite right to feel embarrassed about it. She gets cross with herself that she didn't think about what she was saying. And that's the difference between our mothers' generation and us. We are actually thinking about what we are saying, we are choosing, we are not simply fulfilling the expectations of our parents. We've made choices about our child-rearing habits, about whether or not we work, about what sort of relationships we have, whether or not we're going to be married, divorced. My mother just lived it out. She said you got married and the choices were over.

It says much about Ted's ability to maintain and support separate lives. His total failure to be male-threatened by anything I do is one reason we've been very good resources for each other. But I still can't explain how we've spent such good time together. [Laughs]

Every time you want to know who you are, ask your friends. I'm a firm believer that the only way you know who you are is from the feedback people give you. If ten people say to you in a day, 'You look really ill,' you'll be sick by the end of the day. So I choose very carefully the sort of feedback I get.

You've maintained a long-term relationship, which is a real achievement. How did you do it?

I woke up one day and it had happened. Extraordinary to think that I'm fifty-seven. How did I ever get here? And what were the years I lost? Because it's only yesterday I was thirty.

But you've been so prolific – all those books. Doesn't that give you a sense of, 'Oh yes, that's what I did'?

Of course, yes. And Ted, I would say, is one of the few men I've ever known who, if I didn't talk to him for two weeks, would assume I was busy. I have never had the role of supporting his lifestyle. Never. I've done completely my own thing and he thinks that's fine. I'm not much of a domestic person, but he likes to organise the household. My friends think I'm the tidiest person they know, but Ted thinks I'm untidy. [Laughs] I do a lot of organising for catering and takeaway and things like that, but I don't very often cook at home.

But when people say to me, 'What's your contribution?' I say, 'I'm brilliant at conversation. I'm absolutely superb at it.' And, in a way, what we're talking about with best friends is involved in this too. Because I maintain Ted's equilibrium, and sanity to some extent, by my talk. He says it's obscene that somebody wakes up every morning like I do, perfectly cheerful. I always do. Early, cheerful, positive. I get up at six o'clock to go and do my exercises and then swim for half an hour or so. I'm always at my desk by about eight, eight-thirty. I love my work. I love being in my study and won't come out. Sometimes I say, 'Oh, hello! How long have you been home?' 'About three hours.' My self-containment has never been a threat to Ted.

I think that's what I'm trying to say – that women are now getting a sense of self-containment, as distinct from the way I was brought up, which was to get male approval. I don't look for approval, I really don't, not from anybody. But I certainly look for positive feedback. If Ted stopped saying I was the best thing that happened in his life, I'd be very upset. And it's not approval, it's an affirmation of the relationship rather than my doing something to get his approval – 'Is this all right? Am I doing it properly? Should I try again?' It's an affirmation of my existence, on a regular basis, as a good thing. And I must say it makes me feel fairly smug. I feel quite at ease about being the best thing that ever happened to him. That's reasonable.

Is he the best thing that ever happened to you?

Oh . . . well. The greatest contribution he's made to my life is an intellectual one. Taking me seriously intellectually. Ted used to say that I had a very creative way of looking at things but what I then needed to do was to go off and actually back it up.

I can remember when we first went out together, in Townsville – I met him at James Cook University where I was teaching in 1974–75 – and the new Family Law Bill came in and they'd rung me up and asked me to appear on the telly to talk about it. Ted said, 'What do you know about the law?' I said, 'It's been changed so girls can now get divorces more easily.' He said, 'You can't go on television and say that, that's appalling.' I said, 'Of course I can.' And he was alarmed that I would think that was the basis on which to go and be interviewed on telly.

This sounds so trite in retrospect, but when we went to England the first major thing I did, which really made me known in some intellectual circles in England, was my critique of objectivity. I said that objectivity was men's subjectivity, that in fact it was the male way of looking at the world that had been validated. That was twenty-five years ago and it was just heresy. Heresy. And because Ted's whole background is science and engineering, and because he'd read everything that I wrote and all the research I had done, I had absolutely no qualms about standing up there and saying, 'There is this huge male bias in research.' Until that time, proof and objectivity were true. Positivism was true. So it was a bit of a shock to have this woman arrive in England and say, 'It's just that men have called what they do true, and what women do not true. It's a load of rubbish.' Basically what I was saying was as simple as that. And it was his confidence that gave me confidence. Sometimes he'd say to me, 'You can't say this.' We had some huge arguments with me saying, 'I can.' But that was huge male confidence in me.

I didn't get any training in my university days about intellectually challenging the establishment. But if I was going to challenge something, Ted was going to make sure I did it properly. To this day, he treats me as a very serious intellectual. And you respond to that. That's a revolution, for women to be taken seriously.

My husband wanted me to be fluffy. One night he said to me, 'What happened to the sweet, pretty little thing I married?' And I said, 'You know, I've been many things in my life but a sweet, pretty little thing is hardly one of them.' [Laughs]

You become a doormat in such a short space of time. That's one thing I didn't involve my friends in, the collapse of that, that was very much done on my own. Lynne knew, as much by observation as anything, because by that stage she was married too and we lived a hundred yards away from each other in Wollongong. We taught at the same school so she used to pick me up in the morning and we'd drive to school together. We were both English teachers so we worked together all day, came home and went shopping in the afternoon. We decided that both of us weren't going to cook a meal, so the boys had to work out where dinner was on that night. So we were very, very close.

Looking back, I suppose Lynne and I have been the nourishment for each other, and because we nourish each other so well we keep each other going, and maybe expanding a bit. And we are the products of our time. We were certainly born at a stage when women didn't have a voice and I think circumstances and sibling support – and lots of other forces – have helped each of us to find our own way of articulating and shaping our worlds.

And we have lots in common, as do so many women who have come of age in the last few decades. We have all found a new freedom to affirm each other, to *like* each other.

Do you remember Virginia Woolf's book, *A Room of One's Own*, and that amazing line 'Chloe liked Olivia'? She reckoned it was one of the first times in the history of English letters that such a sentence had been written, and there's no doubt that the world I entered was one where women were taught to compete with each other, not to like each other, and the last person you could trust as a female was your best friend.

We are more likely now to compete for jobs than for men, but more likely too, I think, to provide a network and support. Perhaps that's why women are doing so well in the world of paid work in the twenty-first century. If we can make the money and have women friends, we could well have achieved something valuable.

Lynne Spender ❡

LYNNE SPENDER IS as measured and even-tempered as her best friend and older sister Dale (see preceding conversation) is mercurial. Where Dale is tiny and almost birdlike, Lynne is tall, lean and athletic-looking, an ocean swimmer. Lynne became a lawyer after ten years as a school teacher, a marriage, two sons – Jay and Aaron, both now in their twenties – and the writing of her first book, *Intruders on the Rights of Man*. She is currently Chief Executive Officer of the Australian Interactive Multimedia Industry Association, after six years as the Managing Editor of Redfern Legal Centre Publishing, and several years as the Executive Director of the Australian Society of Authors. ❡ WE TALK IN her house on the beach at Coogee, a conversation permeated with her wonderfully dry, ironic sense of humour, especially apparent as she talks about her robust friendship with her sister.

On the phone when we were arranging this you said something that made me laugh: 'Being friends with my sister took its toll.'

Well, that's my view. [Laughs] I'm sure she would have a very different view. And I guess that's why a fifty-year friendship still works. There's not a sense that either one of us particularly manages or controls the relationship, although at various times we each have done that.

In 1978 I went to live in Canada for nearly four years. I was married and had two small children and I didn't have a work permit, so I began to write my first book, which kept me off the streets. But it was Dale who stopped the world from closing in. I was very isolated over there and it was Dale who sent me books, sent me articles. She wrote to me virtually every day. And it kept up my buoyancy so that I still felt part of the world. That's pretty good friendship.

Did you have another close friend who would have done that? Who perhaps would have done it had they known that Dale wasn't?

I don't think so. I kept contact by writing to a lot of my friends back in Australia, but they of course all had priorities in their own lives, whereas I was still a priority in Dale's. She could see me sinking into suburbia and she was going to rescue me, at whatever cost. At the time I used to become quite resentful of her forever pushing me. But within three months of leaving Canada, I could look back and recognise the way she supported me. And I think at various times I've done the same thing for her. At times when she's moved down into the trough a bit, I have been there saying, 'It's okay, it's fine, what about this, what about that.'

There's an enormous security that comes from having a sibling friendship. Dale once said to me, 'It's all right, sweetheart, I'll still love you when you're old and wrinkly.' And it's absolutely true that that bond between sisters doesn't just go away, even when you want it to sometimes. Of course, not everyone gets on with their sisters and I'm aware that ours is rather an idealised state. Our mother played an important role in that by saying how lucky we were to have sisters, because she didn't have a sister. She desperately wanted Dale and me to value each other, and I think we just took it on without really questioning it that much.

But I think friendship is about half good luck and half good management. I was thinking before you came about how enormously lucky I've been. I'm friendly with my parents – they have been major friends in my life – and with my children. So I've got the generation before and the next generation. And then, in my own generation, I have an enormous range of friends, including Dale and my brother Graeme.

It seems to me that people whose families made them feel loved and secure find it much easier to make and sustain close friendships and other intimate relationships.

Yes, I think to have that security where you don't feel you have to be self-protective gives you a capacity for friendship. Dale and I have spoken about how that sort of security allows you to go into the public world and how, if you haven't got that, it's much harder. If you have that, even if someone out there shoots you down, there's a net to catch you.

Look, I'm as boring as batshit about this because I don't think I've got anything terribly negative to say. [Laughs] Although I have shed friends. When I came back from Canada, got divorced and set out on my own, I deliberately discarded friends who had been part of my previous life. My politics had changed. My natural habitat had changed. I went off and did law, became far more political, and the people from the past, with the exception of about three or four, I quite deliberately discarded. I didn't want to spend time being nice. I didn't have time – two kids, the studying, working. So rather than feel guilty about letting the friends go, I thought, Bugger it, I'll make the decision and be accountable for it. I was very pleased I did that.

How many people would you regard as your really best friends?

I suppose I have half a dozen best friends that I make a real effort to keep in contact with and am conscious if I haven't seen for a week, or haven't heard from for two weeks. And they're the ones with whom you just pick up where you left off – the running thread, the bonded friends, the ones you retain somehow, regardless of what else happens in your life.

What creates those bonds, do you think? You meet lots of people; what is it that makes a few of them stick in that really close way?

I think it's about experiencing some sort of vulnerability, one with the other. Admitting needs, understanding something about another person that perhaps the rest of the world doesn't know. You keep secrets for that bonded friend. There's a high level of trust.

I can't think of any true close friend who has ever let me down. I've had a couple of acquaintances who were, at one level, friends – those people you identify with who come in and out of your life, and who, I ended up finding, used me in a way. You can walk together as friends for a little while and then you actually recognise that. That's happened a couple of times, I suppose. But I never had any trouble walking away from that sort of thing. I just ring Dale and tell her about it and she says, 'I know, I know.' That's so helpful because you don't feel so hurt. There's always the sister that you can go and talk to.

And till very recently I could talk to my mum in the same way. She's now eighty and a bit slower, though still sharp as a tack about some things. But I could always unload on Mum about things like that. And she always gave wise counsel, my mother, but then I think she must have been a social worker in another life. She's calm, non-judgemental. 'Take in the full picture. Stand back and have a look. It may not be anything personal, dear.' A nice way out, so that you can move round things rather than having to confront them. I think Dale and I both do that.

Are all your close friends women?

All my level-A friends are women. Level-B friends – there

are some men, mainly ones I've known for a long time and with whom I keep in touch. But essentially those good, strong bonds are with women.

Are they all women you've known for a long time? Do you think you get to the point where you don't acquire new friends?

I think if you don't go daily to a workplace, if you're not exposed on a regular basis to people so that you experience the ups and downs, the vicissitudes of life with them, it's hard to form friendships. In fact two of my good friends I had at school. And I guess that's because we did our growing up together and just know such an enormous amount about each other. We don't move in the same social circles, but certainly on birthdays and things like that there's always dinner, a card, a phone call. Those links are kept.

Some of my friends have started dying. When you look at a whole lifetime of friends, by the time you get to fifty you have to realise that this is going to happen. That made me take stock about friends and how valuable they are, and that you can't let them go when they've been an important part of your life, and you of theirs.

Dale has obviously got you through difficult times. Is that one of the key things about friendships?

I suppose if you need somebody in periods of crisis, that's exactly when they are there and they're most valuable. But I guess my recollection of friends is always about good times rather than bad times. About funny things and the bonding through hilarity rather than the depths of despair. Dale and I have done the depths stuff together. That's always been worked through with each other, which probably means that I've been freer with other friends to be more outgoing, more at ease.

Dale's the solid base; it's always there and we either email, talk or write daily. When we lived on different continents Dale wrote to me every day. Now, of course, I've got these reams of letters that I'm not allowed to get rid of, cluttering up my study. I imagine they'd be very valuable but they're also a responsibility. It's like having a bloody child. [Laughs] I think, What if the house burnt down? What are the most valuable things? Oh, Dale's bloody letters. We're in the process of getting them to the State Library – she's got quite a lot of them there already – but I've still got hundreds of them, just sitting there in enormous bundles.

You and Dale were always friends, weren't you? You didn't hate each other as children and become friends later.

No, we didn't. We used to fight when we were younger. I've got quite a few scratches – she used to scratch and I used to bite. But I think – and I don't know that our little brother would appreciate this, although I know he would understand it – that when he was born we not only took on Mum as the common enemy, but him too. Here we were, two girls who thought we were the be-all and end-all of the Spender family, and suddenly there was this boy, who got a middle name and we didn't. We just got monosyllabic 'Lynne' and 'Dale', and he was Graeme Frank Spender, named after his father and his grandfather. So I think that pushed us together as well. We worked out that here were the two of us and this small male person. Fortunately, my mother had the very good sense to keep him in a cardboard box for his early years, which we thought was entirely appropriate – out of the way. He's quite delightful, actually, so it hasn't done him any harm, and he developed an extremely healthy respect for strong women, which we think was quite good for him.

He is one of the people that I would also categorise as a friend. He and I still touch base regularly about the kids and that sort of stuff, but particularly if something comes up that's an ethical or moral sort of question – we pass that around amongst the three of us. I think you select friends not only on an emotional basis; there are politics involved too, particularly by the time you're our age. You discard those people you can't genuinely talk to. And with Graeme and Dale and me those politics are understood and that allows us to discuss morality and ethics, which I always find quite enjoyable.

Do you think that people outside the family find you and Dale a formidable pair? Perhaps some of them feel that, no matter how good they are as friends, they're never quite going to come up to scratch.

I don't think you can have that same sort of relationship with somebody else. But I think having that sort of relationship gives you a capacity to form other very strong relationships too. I don't think it precludes you from doing that.

The interesting thing about that sister–sibling–friend relationship is the interplay of sameness and difference. For instance, Dale and I work in the same area, the literary writing area, and she has done a lot of things before me, purely and simply because she was older. But then I did some really different things from her – shot through early and went overseas, got married, had kids and lived in suburbia – did a whole range of different things so that while there is this sameness about us, there were always very different aspects to us as well. I think she lives vicariously through me and my children, and I live vicariously through her and her partner Ted and their access to a more defined intellectual life than I live. Because that's virtually all they do, whereas I do four thousand other things as well. So that sameness and difference thing is quite interesting too.

Have Dale's partners or yours ever seen that friendship as a threat or a difficulty?

Oh yes. Not her partner, but that was because by the time

Dale had set up with Ted we were all grown-ups, whereas my husband thought Dale was evil and interfering and manipulative. She and I roar with laughter over her being an evil person, but as far as he was concerned she was. He used to say to me, 'You've been speaking to your sister again,' if ever I disagreed with him about anything. Because Dale and I theorised, we intellectualised things whenever we got together, we talked things through, talked round them, over them, under them, and I'd come back with a different view. So to him she was a bad influence. That chipped away at the marriage, but the other reason that the marriage eventually broke up was that I still had Dale. I still had a primary relationship, so it wasn't a case of walking away from a primary relationship and being totally alone. So I'm very secure. I've never felt totally on my own. Even when I lived on my own I always felt that enormous bond, with parents, with my brother, but with Dale particularly. When she lived in London and I was in Canada, she and Ted had a spare room which was known as Lynne's room. And when my marriage broke up they'd actually worked out how they could reorganise it if I needed to go there with these two poppets until I got my life back in order again. It was absolutely taken for granted that there was my room in London.

And that wasn't a problem for Ted?

I think it would have been a problem if I had stayed there for very long, but absolutely no problem at all about that space in their lives for me. That has always been there. Ted is an extremely self-contained person and has never been threatened by my relationship with Dale. I think he's almost relieved if I go there and stay and take her off his hands for a couple of days, because I cook and do normal sorts of things. Ted thinks that's pretty good because Dale does none of the above. So life assumes a normal sort of routine if I'm around.

Several women have told me that their friends are the most important thing they have – what do you think?

At the risk of sounding sentimental and more than beyond middle-age, I often think that the most valuable thing in life is about giving and receiving from friends, that ultimately it's not the worldly achievements – it's all been worthwhile if you've given and received something on a personal level. I haven't even got the words to talk about that yet – I might have by the time I'm eighty. But I am less and less impressed with worldly success, with wealth, with any of those things, and more and more impressed with enduring friendships and relationships. Especially those sorts of friendships that work on body language as much as actual words, the look across the room that's based on a long period of knowing and understanding someone else. Not the romantic look across the room, a much more knowing look and the sense that you have understood something fundamental with another person. That does sound a bit sentimental.

I don't think so. It echoes the feelings a lot of people have when they're young, that friends are the most important thing there is.

When you're young there is that notion of friends being everything, but that's the time when you're still growing, developing. They are your access to a range of experiences. But then, as you get older you see more and take more into account, get a bigger picture. And you can make the decisions that will take you away from that group. And of course that group is still growing in so many different directions – you don't all grow monolithically in the same direction.

That was a very interesting lesson for me. As a young married woman I thought the friends I had then would be friends forever because we had so much in common and spent so much time together. We went for camping trips and the perpetual dinners, that sort of thing, and the kids going from one house to another, the 'you take my kids this weekend and I'll take yours next'. You think that will bond you for life. But in five years that family and those kids have gone in an entirely different direction, and they're working overly hard to own a BMW while you have gone in this direction, and you find that there's just not much to talk about any more.

I was asked to do a talk a while back at a careers night at SCEGGS [Sydney Church of England Girls Grammar School]. And I said, 'Most women these days will have three careers. You can in fact retrain, and probably need to, in a lifetime.' I also said I thought it would be very wise for young girls of twenty to envisage having at least three partners. In the early stages, they'd want somebody to grow up with, have fun with. Didn't ever specify which sex of course. And then in their middle years, when they wanted to have kids, they should get a partner who was also interested in children and who would share the housework and do all those sorts of things. But that period being over, I would look for somebody very much younger to look after me when I got older. And preferably somebody with a very, very good income and earning capacity. There was this shocked silence, particularly amongst the fathers. A lot of the mothers were going, 'Hmm, yes, that's a good idea,' but I think there were fathers there who thought, We're being mocked. Which they were.

And I think there are friendships which do the same thing. There are some people with whom you bond who cut across all of that, but there are also periods when you need and can give different things to friends. First of all there's the passionate schoolgirl friend – I always had a best friend that I was in love with – and then there was that stage when you were doing a whole range of things and you needed a support group. Then, out of that, you start to find out who you are. And that was when I discarded those friends who no longer shared my politics and my values, and selected friends a lot more carefully. Most of them moved on geographically too, which happens in Australia, but one is only in Palm Beach and I hardly ever see her. I was godparent to one of her daughters and she to one of my kids, and of course that just disappeared as their lives changed and mine did too. I sometimes thought it was a shame that what was apparently so close and so intimate in those years dissipated and disappeared, but I would only be sad about it if it hadn't been replaced by something else that met my needs at the time.

What do you think goes wrong sometimes in women's close friendships? It always seems to be more horrendous than when men drift apart.

You can see why it seems more horrendous, because as women we do open up a lot more to each other than men do. Women can actually say things like 'I feel suicidal' and a woman friend will come in and support them. I'm not saying men can't do that or don't do that, but women are almost intuitive about that. However, I also think that women can be very competitive. I think our society encourages women to compete in all sorts of ways, and I've no doubt that under those circumstances rifts, when they develop, because the relationship has been deeper, can be really painful.

Some people are very clear about what they will and won't put up with, whereas other people, and certainly I would say I'm one of them, are mediators. I'm a mediator in my relationships with people and more or less completely non-judgemental. I can go a long, long way before I have to take a stand. I enjoy eccentricity in people, I don't mind how weird they are. I've got some most eccentric and weird friends and I like them. I really enjoy that difference, that opportunity to see things through somebody else's eyes that are so different from mine. When you have that relationship with someone who's entirely different, you recognise, if the relationship survives, that you've been something to them too. Quite often, in my case, I bring, I think, a lot of humour and non-judgemental information and ideas and personality to those of my friends who are otherwise quite intolerant, difficult people, and I think that works quite well too.

Aren't those kinds of friends tough going for somebody like you who essentially operates through humour and good nature? Don't you sometimes just want to shake them?

[Laughs] The relationships like this that were too difficult and didn't work didn't survive. But there are about three of them that have. One is a friend whom I've had twenty years, who is quite a lot older than I am and with whom I taught at one stage, and who is now virtually confined to bed and spends all day reading and listening to the radio. She thinks I get around the world just having a good time. She says that to me, and of course I berate her for being a cranky old lady and ask why she doesn't just relax a bit more and enjoy things and take up drinking. [Laughs] Her view of course is that I drink too much.

What I give her, and see reflected back, is a warmth and an acceptance. She quite likes me coming in and teasing her and pushing her. And I have no problem with her saying things to me such as, 'You haven't thought that through, Lynne. You need to do some research on that, my girl.' Because usually she's quite right. She spends all day in her head and has thought things through much more than I, who work full-time and am out three nights a week at launches and things and don't have a lot of reflective time. I insist on having some, but she spends her whole life doing that and so feeds me some interesting ideas, which I value enormously.

I see her every couple of weeks, spend a few hours with her.

But I also talk to her on the phone in between. I don't always agree with her, but I respect her judgement and her input. I value that little part of my life that's got nothing to do with any of my other friends or networks. I would say that she's a very close friend. I probably tell her some things because I know she's a safe place. Dale and I are brutally honest with each other, but Judith is the one person I can talk to about Dale.

Does one have to be able to disagree healthily with friends?

With some friends. And here we get into another dimension about level-A friends, bonding friends, identifying friends. There are some friends where the central part of the relationship is about provoking each other a little bit, challenging. And there are others where to do that would be somehow or other to break some of the fabric, where there's a law of acceptance, regardless. Where you don't have to argue or push or pull.

Dale and I push and pull at each other quite a bit. For example, when I had my second child I desperately wanted a daughter. That was, as far as I was concerned, what having children was about, as my sons remind me from time to time. And Dale sent me this bloody book called *No Mamma, No*. It was the story of a woman who desperately wanted girl children, had sons – this is a very shorthand version – and dressed them as girls in Victorian clothes. And 'No Mamma, no' was what the oldest child said as she put him into the Victorian frock. And Dale, instead of cheerfully, as one would expect, moving me through my disappointment, sent me this bloody book that had me in tears because the woman obviously went mad.

And here was the role model for me: *you will go mad*. And that's push, push. Before I did my Leaving Certificate, which Dale did two years before I did, I got a telegram from her – she was away somewhere – saying, 'Best wishes, honey, for aiming at half my pass.' Which is her saying, 'You bloody go and do some work. Stop fart-arsing around on a surfboard,' which I had a tendency to do. And that was push, push. There are other times when I've bailed Dale up in a corner and pushed her until she has acknowledged that, yes, that direction is wrong, and she really should withdraw and do something else. So we do that to each other. But we can also spend four days together away on holiday and spend time giggling and laughing without any of that.

I guess we are each other's yardstick for staying balanced. She tends to be much more up and down than I am. Whereas I've had kids and there's a way in which that, almost inevitably, makes you cope with things without overreacting. And you learn about what matters and what doesn't, because if you're going to focus on events that ultimately don't matter, you end up as a battleground. I think I've learnt to let things go and make a very quick assessment about whether something, in the long term, is going to matter. And I think Dale has never had to do that. She's never actually had to filter her behaviour on the basis of kids and the sorts of demands they make on you. And I think in some ways I provide that role – 'Come on, get real.'

And I don't ever harbour grudges, which I put down to having kids too. Simply from being a single parent, I suppose. All the things that went wrong yesterday, if I dwelt on them, I'd never get up today and go to work and organise them and go to university, and so on. So every day is a new day. And I think I'm a bit like that with friends as well. There may have been some rift that developed there yesterday, but let's start again tomorrow and give it another chance. But if it's really not working, then you let go of those friendships. I don't have any friendships now where I feel there's a burden or where I feel it's not an equal, give-and-take relationship, on whatever basis. And they're all quite different, all my friendships.

Do you have gay men friends? A lot of women, myself included, would say that gay men are very good close friends, in large part because they'll have those frank, intimate conversations that women have – girl talk, to reclaim a good phrase.

Yes. It is because they do girl talk and because they're, oh, I don't know – there's not that ego thing. They're not afraid to be vulnerable. There's a lot of tension in heterosexual relationships for women who've got a feminist consciousness, who see in heterosexual relationships, regardless of the individual person, those bloody power structures that are almost inevitable. With a gay man it's a different dynamic altogether.

Occasionally women say that their best friend is a straight man who's never been a lover or husband. I wonder if you think that's possible, or if there's always one of you who actually wants to go to bed with the other.

I have two straight male friends. One with whom I worked for a long time, and that was one of those friendships that developed from facing trials and tribulations together. He's gone off to New Zealand now and we're still in contact. Whenever he's in Sydney we meet and have dinner and so on, and pick up where we left off and have general concern for each other.

The other male friend I've known since I was sixteen, and his second wife thinks I'm an evil woman. So he and I have a relationship which is about lunches. We talk often – he's also a lawyer so I use him as a sounding board for lots of legal things – and we have long lunches every three months. That's a nice sustaining relationship. We enjoy each other's company, have a good time, and go home and don't think about each other again until three months later.

I suppose the danger would come if you went home and did think about each other. Or if one of you did. And there's always that risk, I suppose.

Well, if either of you loses a partner, there's a tendency perhaps to demand more from that other person. But both being partnered, it's a very healthy, nice relationship, although obviously not a level-A friendship. And I don't want that balance to change. If one of those partners disappears – well, I've never actually thought about it in relation to him, but I suppose if I had more time and wanted more contact with him it would be problematic rather than just a pleasure.

Do you have friendships that you sustain on the telephone?

I used to do that a lot more than I do now, but my job now is virtually being on the telephone all day, every day. I don't answer the phone at home a lot of the time, refuse to have an answering machine. And I would still rather write to people. I'm a night owl, a real night owl. I pad about at night and write letters and stuff on my computer. I have a relationship with my computer – that friend. That wonderful friend. [Laughs]

There's a classic story that I say is my story, Dale says is her story. It couldn't have been her story because I can remember it, can visualise it, can see me roaring with laughter. She says so can she. Anyway, there's a woman in the club lounge at the airport with a laptop on her knees, and she's looking at it in horror, saying, 'Don't go down on me now. Please don't go down on me now!' I keep thinking, If ever there's an intimate relationship, this is it. And she was very tense and couldn't understand why people were rolling around with laughter.

Are there any restrictions for you on being both sisters and friends? Are there ever times when you think, Dale's my sister, I can't talk to her about that?

I think there have been certain times. I suppose the things

that she hasn't spoken to me about and I haven't spoken to her about have been areas of enormous vulnerability, so we've been protecting the other. But as we've got older and more aware of our relationship, we've talked about the relationship – it's a thing, it's the third party, it's not just something we take for granted. We manage it; we consciously, from time to time, have to take control of the relationship and nurture it a little bit. But there have been tricky times, particularly when I've had a new partner or been going through major changes. Generally I think we managed those times really badly. [Laughs] But how we're managing it has always been a topic that we can talk about. It's never been something that we can't discuss. It's always been, 'You were bloody awful last night to so-and-so.' But the dynamic does change, and I think that's when you take real care and you talk things through and make explicit the things you do not like and do not wish to have happen again.

Do you actually say to Dale, 'You are not to do this'?

[Laughs] Oh yes. 'I *didn't* do that! That's not what I was doing.' 'You were!' 'Was I?' I think that would be really dangerous if you couldn't talk about it, if you couldn't bring it out into the open. But we consciously decided that that's how we would treat Mum and Dad too. We told them about our lives, who we were, even when they were absolutely horrified – they still are a lot of the time. But this is who we are and we're not going to pretend to be anything else. We've done that with each other as well, and with our brother. Bailed him up about things, as he bails us up.

I guess it is a family that gives you that healthy ability to move on and not to take things personally and not be cut to the quick. There are people who can't do that, who don't have a family history of 'It'll be okay; work it through, deal with it, and move on.' Otherwise you internalise everything. I think we all put things away until we can process them and deal with them healthily, but if you've got no ability to do that, or no background experience with that – there must be a hell of a lot of people who find friendship enormously difficult.

I think there are. Perhaps one of the reasons is not being able to say when something's upsetting you, so that it doesn't fade but festers.

I think there's a personality type involved in that as well, but yes, to retain and to build friendships, for them to continue to develop, you have to deal with things. If you let them go, the possibilities for misinterpretation and all that sort of festering stuff are all there. Whereas if you bring something out in the open, at least you can clear it up. It might mean you never see that person again, but that's probably the better way of dealing with it.

It's hard to do, particularly at work, because you're seen as stroppy and difficult, but I've acquired that skill I guess since I've been a boss person. I know it would be easy for me to smooth things over and to ignore certain things, but they almost always get worse. There's a time, and I think it's always earlier rather than later, to pull people up and deal with them face to face. But I've had to learn to do that, I don't think it came naturally at all.

Dale's quite good at it too. She will actually be quiet for a little while, which is a sign because she's always so talkative, always just so full of ideas. When she lived in Sydney full-time she used to come with me every morning when I went for a swim. And I used to have to say to her, 'Do not speak. I want four minutes without you speaking.' And she, oh, she found that excruciating because during the night she'd have changed the world, she'd have revolutionised universities, changed the curriculum, and she'd want to tell me about it all. But at six o'clock in the morning I want quiet.

But if she goes quiet for a little while, you can see that she's

working out what it is that's really upsetting her – 'Is it legiti-
mate?' – and then what she's going to say. And then *bang*! Over
a period of fifty years, you get to know that this is not a personal
attack and you're not going to fall apart and this is not the end
of the relationship. This is how she deals with what's happening and you know that out of this will come a solution.

Do you think it's possible to keep former partners as close friends?

My former husband has become kind of friendly, which
puzzles me, but he's not a close friend. I think it's hard to keep
former partners as friends. I've never wanted to do it – why
would you want to carry that baggage with you? I think that
when you've had that sort of intimacy and it's broken off and
you've moved on, you move on. You don't carry them with you.

*Some women seem to have all their former husbands, lovers,
everyone's children, in a sort of extended family. I confess that I'm
totally baffled by this.*

I think I've mainly come across that in fiction, and, as an
idealised state, it's quite fabulous. But it's very hard to start a
new relationship with somebody else, which is about exclusivity
when it's a sexual relationship, and still carry this other person
along with you. Because in sexual relationships there are all
those jealousies and space things: 'You're mine. I don't want to
share you with the seven-plus people who went before.' Remember that AIDS campaign on television where you saw all those
beds with all the people you'd slept with and the people who'd
slept with them? Who wants to be reminded of that all the time?
I think it's probably healthy and self-protective to leave that
behind. Imagine how hard you'd have to work to have all these
people together.

I don't even want close friends living with me. The older
you get, I think the more true it is about needing your own
space. The reason I am still friendly with my kids is that they

learnt territory stuff very early and very clearly: 'That's your space, this is my space, you do not enter this without permission.' I think that's allowed a healthy respect and quite a good friendship.

I know some women say that their child is their best friend, but I wouldn't want that sort of intense, close friendship with my sons. I think one still has a private life that the children are not party to and wouldn't want to be. But there's still that sheer joy and pleasure in each other's company, in the interesting things that happen to them and the recognition that, as they grow older, they know more about some things than you do. And I think growing old graciously is about acknowledging that and being genuinely delighted by it.

Quentin Bryce ❡

I MET QUENTIN BRYCE, and first admired her friendship with Wendy McCarthy, at the Australian Bicentennial Authority in 1988. There was the usual pre-meeting paper shuffling going on one morning when in walked a tall, good-looking, impeccably groomed blonde, slim as a whippet, full makeup, with bright cyclamen lipstick that exactly matched her miraculously uncrumpled linen suit. Her earrings were the size of small plates and her shoes had the highest heels I had ever seen on a woman in daylight. 'Who,' I murmured to someone, 'is *that*?' ❡ THAT WAS QUENTIN BRYCE, barrister, activist for the rights of women and children, newly appointed Federal Sex Discrimination Commissioner, and mother of five. Born in 1942, Quentin married architect Michael Bryce when she was twenty, and graduated while pregnant with her first child. She was one of the first women admitted to the Queensland Bar, and the first woman appointed to the University of Queensland's law school, where she lectured for thirteen years. The list of her services to women and social justice is long and impressive. Quentin was a foundation member of the National Women's Advisory Council and its convenor from 1982 to 1983. After five years as Australia's first Sex Discrimination Commissioner, from 1988 to 1993, she moved to another hot seat when she became chair and CEO of the National Childcare Accreditation Council. Since 1997 she has been Principal of Women's

College at the University of Sydney. ¶ QUENTIN HAS MANY strong friendships but her best friend is Wendy McCarthy (see following conversation). It's a relationship that is both personally and professionally nourishing, a five-star friendship which Quentin calls 'the most significant and influential friendship of my adult years'. Quentin is an energetic, witty, loyal and generous friend. Conversations with her are an effervescent mix of frock talk, gossip, ideas, jokes, exploration of complex issues and frank discussion of the most serious matters, accompanied always by a great deal of laughter.

I MET WENDY when I was appointed to the National Women's Advisory Council in 1978. I was lecturing in law at the University of Queensland at the time and she was then the head of Family Planning, and that's how I got involved in Family Planning. I went on to the board of Family Planning in Queensland and that opened up a new part of the world for me.

I found Wendy very impressive and I just clicked with her. The wonderful thing about that experience was that there were twelve women appointed to that council who all became friends. We were usually described as women from all walks of life, and that was absolutely true. We all keep in touch, some more than others. All of us were doing interesting things then and have since. There's a deep bond amongst us because of the challenges we faced together. For me they went on for five years. My closest friend from that experience is Wendy.

Our children are good friends too. Wendy's daughter Sophie was in Brisbane the other day to see my daughter Revy about a big event they were working on. A colleague told me that she had lunch with the two of them and I said, 'My God, you wouldn't have got a word in. They're such know-alls, and so *bossy*, and they talk *all* the time.' When I'm in a situation like that I say to the girls, 'I'm paying for this lunch, I want to get a word in.'

I think Sophie and Revy spend quite a bit of time complaining about their mothers, having a few jokes at our expense. They're both in their early thirties. Rupert [Bryce] and Hamish [McCarthy] are the same age and so are Tom [Bryce] and Sam [McCarthy]. They have an enormous amount in common. I used to think when I was living in Wendy's house that if I closed my eyes I could have been in my own home, because many of the family patterns and the kids were so similar.

How did you come to live with Wendy?

When I was appointed the Sex Discrimination Commissioner in 1988 and I came to Sydney to take up the job, I was living by myself in the Astor, in Macquarie Street. It had been an enormous decision to come from Brisbane and leave the family behind and I had a lot of angst about it – should I do it or not? I was going home at weekends because the children were all much younger then (Tom was fourteen), and that was the first time I'd ever lived by myself. As one of my sisters said, 'You've moved from cocoon to cocoon. This'll test you out.'

After I'd been at the Astor for a while I thought, Ooh, I don't like this. So I rang up Wendy and said, 'May I come and stay with you for a while?' And I stayed for four years.

How long had you stuck it out at the Astor?

Oh, about six months. And I could never go back. I had a floor of Wendy's house; she lived upstairs and I lived downstairs with Sam. The other McCarthy kids had gone but Sam was still at school then. He was about fifteen, sixteen, and he was lovely. He and Tom, who's the youngest in our family, are very much alike. Sam and I were very good companions. We had a little agreement that he wouldn't say anything about me and I wouldn't say anything about him. He never complained about how long I was in the shower.

How often do you talk to Wendy now?

At least four, five times a week: 'How are you going? What are you doing this week?' If I'm invited to something I'll ring and say, 'Are you going to this, what do you think?' And sometimes I ring her and say, 'I've got to do this job. Can I come to your place and talk it through with you?' And I just go over and do that.

What makes a friendship into an intimate friendship?

Sharing. I suppose a test for me is the significance and the depth of it. Part of that is knowing that you could call and say, 'Could you drive me to Goondiwindi?' And they would do it. They'd take it on trust that this was important, that you were desperate and you needed them to help you with something.

I think we have very few friends like that and they're very precious. You establish that sort of bond often in hard times, I think. For me, that was during the time when I had lots of little children and all those extraordinary ups and downs you have with that. One child was critically ill. I'd leave the hospital at two in the morning and go and knock on a friend's door on my way home. And somebody would come to the door . . . I can hardly talk about it even now. [All these years later her eyes fill with tears.] One of them would come to the door. I'd burst into tears and go in and sit there and talk and cry for two hours. That sort of support forges eternal friendship. And then we had five teenagers at once, with all the usual crises. Sometimes I leant on friends. When I go back to Queensland, which I plan to do sometime, I know that I will just pick those friendships up. You can do that once the friendship's really there and it's been tested and gone through particularly tough times.

Friendships amongst women who have children are quite different, I think. That's a big part of my friendship with Wendy, talking about our children. They are very special bonds that come through children. There's a huge difference between women who have children and women who don't. And men too. Because, usually, people who don't have children have never really had to give up thinking about themselves first. And when you have that first child, everything changes forever. It radically changes your life and what you can do. When you have children, especially if you're a woman, you embark on a road of compromises, in terms of your career and other parts of your life.

I think now that I have much more in common with many men who have children than with women who have no children. Increasingly men talk about their children and their families, rather than pretend they don't have any. And I think women are encouraging them to do that. We're helping men to be better fathers.

Do you think you can make new friends once you've passed fifty? Friends that are as close as old friends, if somewhat different?

Oh, I think so. I hope so. It's exciting making new friends. It's lovely to meet someone and just go *click, click, whiz* because you find them stimulating and intellectually challenging. You can pick up on a lot of your past very fast and it's fun finding out about their lives, talking about the background to what's made that person the way they are in their fifties.

There are very special things about old friendships, but you must be able to make new friends who become close, dear, intimate friends because you move around and you need them wherever you are. Well, I do. Although if you have to spend three years in South America, then three in New York and are then posted somewhere else, I think you must miss a lot.

I also think you miss out if you don't have sisters. My three sisters and I are very close friends. I've just been staying with my elder sister in Adelaide. I was there for four days and I don't think we stopped talking for one minute. I was sleeping in the room next to her daughter Susannah, who's the same age as my daughter Clothilde, and she left this big note under my door: 'No talking until ten in the morning.'

One of the things I love seeing in my children now is that they're all very good friends, they enjoy each other's company. They're all in Queensland at present. Over the last few years amongst their friends there's been a warning: 'Don't ask any of those Bryces anywhere because you get the whole lot.' And I like that. I hear them on Friday afternoons, on the phone to each other: 'What are you doing tonight?' My husband always says, 'If you marry one of those Strachan [Quentin's maiden name] girls, you marry the whole lot.' He's very attached to all my sisters too. I can't imagine what it must be like not to have sisters.

How does your relationship with your sisters differ from your friendship with Wendy? Are there things you can talk about with your sisters that you can't talk to her about?

There are family things of course. I read once that sisterhood is the closest relationship. I've reflected on that and I think there's an enormous amount of truth in it. Because you've shared so much for so long, you have so many intimate memories, jokes, experiences. And you can't get away with anything with them.

The position in the family is influential. I'm second. My elder sister is *such* an elder sister. I can pick women who are elder sisters – they can't help being bossy, and they worry. They put hotwater bottles in your bed, keep you warm. My elder sister bought my first bra for me, and gave me some beautiful things in my student years. She's five years older than I am, which, when you're a child, is quite a gap. She's not quite a surrogate mother but she's certainly done some mothering, especially when I was at boarding school. She'll do dreadful things to me. I'll be leaving her house all dressed up to go and give a speech or something and she'll say, 'Take off that jacket.' And she'll press it again. I've already pressed it, but she'll do it better.

Do sisters get away with things that other friends don't?

I suspect that they do. Although those very close, dear friends get away with murder too. You forgive them things. As you grow older, their friendship is so important to you and you share so much that you know to look after the relationship. You really do respect each other's point of view. I guess the friendship goes on for so long because you do share so many important values and views and ideas, so you can skip over a lot of things. With close friends there are some things where, early on in the friendship, you just quietly agree to disagree.

What are the unforgivable things in friendship? Have you ever had a close friendship that broke up?

Yes, I did have a friendship that broke up. It was in a political context and the friend did something unforgivable, it just had to be the end of the friendship. It really shocked me because I think that close, true friendships are more important than anything else – political issues and so on. And if you don't agree, there's a way to handle agreeing to disagree, so if you're going to do something that's going to be hurtful – professionally, personally, politically, anything – there's a code you should follow. You should tell the person you're going to do it. You say, 'Look, this is what I'm going to do and this is why I've got to do it.' And the friendship may or may not survive, but if you just do it without disclosing and your friend finds out, it's the end of it really. It was a shock to me to think that that person would do that.

Can you tell your friends everything? Or are there areas about which you think, I can't talk about this, this is off limits?

Yes, you can tell them everything. By the time you've been friends till you're ninety, say, you will have told them everything, even if you have to wait for some of the people involved in the whole story to die. There are some things that friends know about in your life that you don't talk about, and they respect the fact that you don't talk about them. There's an understanding about things that are left unsaid.

What effect do close friendships have on a spouse or partner?

That's an interesting one. There are some partners who get quite jealous, and there are even times when one of the relationships breaks up over it.

Has that ever been a tussle for you, between your friends and Michael – possibly the world's most understanding male?

[Laughs] Especially now that I don't see him all the time, I have no doubt that sometimes Michael will think, when he comes down here and I'm off doing yoga and this and that, that I'm not spending enough time with him. But it doesn't become an issue. He doesn't fester over it – he's not a festering sort of person – but I'm conscious of it, which is why, when I go and have breakfast with my pals after yoga, for instance, he sometimes comes too. And joins in.

Michael's a man who really likes women and is very comfortable with them. He loves a lot of my friends and has a very nice warm friendship with them. He doesn't do that lunching with men and going to the club. Our five children take up a lot of his time. Today he's taking the two girls to the exhibition, you know, the Brisbane Ekka. They both rang him and said they wanted to go with him. I bet they go on rides, buy fairy floss, all the childhood treats.

I was only twenty when I was married and I think it's true

to say Michael and I have grown up together. He certainly saw immediately that I had a very close family. His sister, who died three years ago, was already a bosom pal of mine. We had been friends since I was a little girl so I'd known Michael since then. He's six years older than I am; I didn't embark on a romance with him till I was nineteen or so, when I was at university.

His sister and I were very, very close friends. When she was dying I used to go to see her in the evenings and get into bed with her and massage her body with oil. She was so wasted and I thought it was very important for her to be touched. We'd tell each other funny stories and remind each other – Remember this? And remember that? We used to have the most wonderful giggles, we had so much in common. She was very much like a sister to me. We used to gang up against Michael and tease him, but he was her much loved brother.

Michael knew from the beginning that friendships were enormously important to me. And they are. I'm sure lots of times it annoys him, but that's part of me, a treasured part of my life.

Some people say that their friends are their family, but you have friends and family. And your family are your friends.

My family *are* my friends. But my friends are like a part of my family as well. Certainly Wendy is. We get together and complain about our families too. I'll give her a blast about what someone has done to me. The intimacy of our friendship is knowing so much about each other. Our families become intertwined, as our children are. Our kids talk about 'Wennie' and 'Quenny' and crack jokes about us. They rubbish us to pieces. [Laughs]

I think your point about the friendships amongst women and the effect on spouses is quite a critical one. It reminds me of when we were all mothers in the neighbourhood together.

The way we survived was getting together at the end of the day occasionally. A couple of times a week, when you'd been doing all that driving everywhere, to the ballet lessons and the bugle lessons and the this and the that – all that stuff – you'd drop the neighbour's kids off and stay and have a drink. It was the heyday of the frightful Coolabah cask. We used to drink this dreadful white wine and complain about our husbands. It would be getting dark and the husbands would come home looking for their dinner, and there'd be a great cacophony of noise and kids racing around.

The husbands would signal. Michael's signal of 'I'm home' was to open the dishwasher and bang the dishwasher shelves in and out. I was talking about that recently to one of my friends who's now a judge. We laughed about those days with all our littlies and our long-suffering husbands. How chaotic and what fun it was!

That's how you get through having children, don't you think?

Oh yes. The safety breaks and the laughter. Laughing instead of getting absolutely furious. We'd sit around and say things like, 'When you see Michael Bryce, don't speak to him because I'm going to kill him.' And that would get it off your chest so it didn't all get loaded onto your husband. That helped marriages survive.

It seems that friendship plays a very different role in the lives of men, straight men at least. Do you think that's so?

Absolutely. Huge difference. I think Michael is better in a lot of ways than most men, but he doesn't have friendships like I have. Although he has some good, close friends – Maurice, for example, in his late sixties, godfather to two of our children. When Maurice had heart surgery some years ago he put me down as his next of kin and I had to look after him. [Laughs]

I got to know him through Michael, and have now known

him for thirty-five years. In a way he's really Michael's friend. I do the mothering, the looking after him. When he's in hospital I go to see him, take the fruit and sit there worrying, do the washing and ask him what he needs, have the sessions with the doctor. Michael goes up and just cracks jokes. I get all the emotional trauma. The two friendships – mine with Maurice and Michael's with Maurice – are sex-stereotyped, I'm afraid.

Do you have any straight male friends that are close friends in the way that your women friends are?

Some good men friends, yes, but not in the same way as my women friends. When Maurice came out of heart surgery his doctor said to me, 'Does Maurice believe in life after death?' I said, '*What?*' And the doctor said, 'You've been friends for thirty years and you don't know whether he believes in life after death?' He was shocked. I said, 'Well, I don't. We haven't had that conversation.'

Conversation is at the heart of women's friendships, isn't it?

Yes. Intellectual discussion and debate are very important in friendship. It's not all about the babies. That's a very important part of it, but I'm also seeking someone who's vibrant and who can be quite rigorous intellectually – sharing ideas and talking about books and politics and everything.

Do conversations with close friends help you sort out what you're thinking?

Yes, they do. I get some very practical help when I'm writing speeches or doing a paper or taking on something new or facing a problem. If I say, 'I had this problem this week at college, what do you think?', you know that it just stays there, that it's absolutely in confidence. You don't need to say, 'Don't tell anybody,' because those friends would know that that's something you would never pass on. That's very important, especially when you're in some particular roles, because you can be quite isolated. When you're in a leadership role, whether it's a committee or a board or your work, you've got to be distanced from the group. You need someone with whom to talk things through.

Wendy is the friend who is interested in all the things that I do. I talk about a lot of things to her. The complete friend offers you an enormous amount of things.

What about your old friend and long-time Brisbane neighbour, Dale Spender?

Dale is a great friend, a wonderful friend. I miss her. She's a very affectionate, loving sort of friend, and enormously generous. And great to have serious arguments with. I've learned so much from her. Dale's particularly good at looking after her friends, and that matters. The key thing in friendships is giving time to them. It's about seeing them as important and not cancelling arrangements because something else comes along. It's giving them priority. But time, most of all. It's corny, perhaps, but that's the most precious thing you have to give.

Do you remember Anne Summers's fiftieth birthday invitation, with its collage of photographs, some of them from the height of the women's movement in the early seventies? I know this was serious activism, but it also looks like the best fun. Is that a strong element in those close friendships you made then?

[Laughs] The women's movement in the early seventies was exhilarating and, yes, the best fun. The hilarity, risk-taking, outrageous acts and boldness bonded us in lifelong friendships. Of course we love reminiscing: 'Remember the time . . .?' When we tell stories from those years I can see people thinking, My God, I can't imagine *her* doing that!

I've had some hilarious times with Anne Summers. I met her in the seventies and I used to see her quite a bit when I went to New York for UN meetings. She's a very good friend.

She's also very funny and takes the mickey out of me. We were at a little dinner party together recently where she just gave me heaps, as she always does, torments me and entertains people by doing it. And I give it back to her. That's important in friendships too – that you feel absolutely safe about being yourself. If you're in particular jobs, if you've got any kind of public profile really, you've got to be circumspect in public. So you need to be able to be yourself with friends.

Michael teases me about these sorts of things. I was planning a lunch party for Wendy's birthday and telling him who I was inviting – all the really close old friends – and he said, 'Oh God, don't have all those women together. Don't. You're too much for other people. I'm used to it, it's all right for me, but . . .' [Laughs] I suppose we make each other more outrageous.

What about envy in women's friendships? Do you come across much of that?

I think there's some of that. It's a very natural sort of emotion, especially as you're growing up – there's the competition and the peer-group pressure and you feel desperately jealous of the person who's got everything. I love Margaret Whitlam's reply when she was asked what she thought about the dress that Sonia McMahon wore to the White House – the famous split-to-the-hip white dress. She just smiled and said, 'I wish I had legs like that.' I love that. I remember thinking, I wish I could think of something like that. But it's also about *being* like that. It's just a superficial example, but it reflects an underlying attitude, an underlying generosity.

I hope that one of the things about growing up and becoming a mature, enriched, full human being is that you become more generous, more confident and at ease with yourself, so you don't get pricked by envy. Because there's a mean underpinning to it. I hope we all get better at disciplining some of that out of ourselves, and at striving to be good, fair and generous. That's part of the search to understand yourself.

I was brought up to do the right thing and I still think how important that is. I think that really top people behave in a top way. Those are personal ethical matters – how you handle the challenges through your life, the human frailties that you slay on the way. And I think envy's a thing like that.

Does that still have currency, that notion of doing the right thing?

I hope it does. It's about ethics and is a natural part of the human rights agenda that's so central to my life. It's also a very important issue in friendship. I admire it in people, and my friends are people whom I admire. Their good qualities are what I love in them, but I also admire them and respect them. My closest friends are people I look up to, for their ethics and for their values. The fun and all those things are a very important part of it, but the values underpin it. That's what matters when you have ideals and aspirations for the next generation in the world, and hope that world will be a worthwhile place for your children.

Wendy McCarthy ¶

I T'S LUNCHTIME ON a glorious autumn Monday and Wendy McCarthy's best friend Quentin Bryce [see preceding conversation] is launching Wendy's memoir, *Don't Fence Me In*, in front of a strikingly diverse crowd of two hundred and fifty people. A few are family – Gordon, Wendy's husband of thirty-five years, daughter Sophie and son Hamish – but the rest are friends, not all intimate friends but people Wendy has known or worked with in one of the many parts of her life, people she treasures and who have a lasting affection for her. Today they are palpably pleased for her. ¶ IT'S THIS GIFT for gathering people to her that Quentin so accurately describes in her launch speech as 'Wendy's unique ability to be inclusive . . . she welcomes you to her.' It is warmth combined with wisdom and generosity. If you ask her advice, you'll receive a thoughtful, understanding and honest response, a response you can trust. ¶ A GIRL FROM country New South Wales, Wendy began her career as a teacher, and in many ways she still is a teacher, a born teacher – passionate, persuasive and prodigiously well informed. She is, as Quentin says, a 'clever, pushy dame', working in the areas of women, work and politics; sex, fertility and reproductive rights; public health, childcare, reconciliation. Wendy was a founder of the Women's Electoral Lobby, a member of the original National Women's Advisory Council from 1978 to 1981, and the CEO of the Family

Planning Association of Australia from 1978 to 1984. She is an exemplar of the credo of second-wave feminism – for Wendy, the personal is definitely political. ¶ WENDY WENT ON to be General Manager of the Australian Bicentennial Authority, Deputy Chair of the Australian Broadcasting Corporation from 1983 to 1991, and Executive Director of the National Trust from 1990 to 1993. After a brief flirtation with a firm of lawyers, she set up her own business, consulting to major corporations on managing change and diversity. She is also the Chancellor of the University of Canberra, Chair of Plan International Australia, Chair of Wik Ed, and divides her time between weekends with Gordon at the farm and her inner-Sydney house. ¶ AT THE LAUNCH Quentin, who will be wearing high-heels when she's ninety, has discreetly taken off her shoes so that she doesn't have to alter the height of the mike. Wendy, persuaded by Quentin to abandon her usual flat shoes for the occasion, is candid as always: 'Quentin has to take her high-heels off so she can reach the microphone: I have to leave mine on. Sometimes it's difficult having a tall blonde as your best friend when you're a short brunette.'

———

What are the qualities that, for you, define a best friend, an intimate friend?

Trust is enormously high, I think. Trust and affection. It's partly confidence in the response – that you'll get an unconditionally truthful response that's a way of looking after you. Judgement is also really important. I've had friends, not intimate friends, who've felt obliged to say things I don't want to hear and that it was not necessary for me to hear. I value in a friendship someone with a little more wisdom than that.

But I think it's the affection that's primary. And common intellectual interests are also extremely important to me. So there are emotional bonds and intellectual bonds, and if you get both of them in one friend it's fantastic. But friends can survive on either one of them. The closer friendship will be when you've got both, but I have friends with whom I have limited intellectual interests who've been friends for a long time, where the trust is high, the judgement is high, the affection is high, and we've shared experiences. Shared experiences are fundamental to all of those things.

But would you call them your intimate friends?

I'd call them close, but not intimate. Of my intimate friends, I have maybe half a dozen, with whom I share different intimacies. Gordon's definitely one of them. Quentin is certainly one. And Sophie, my daughter, is in many ways a very good friend, although she's not my best friend, she's definitely my daughter.

I can move to an intimacy in a relationship reasonably quickly because I'm very open about a lot of things that other people might see as intimate. But they're not careless or capricious or shallow friendships, they're real. I'm selective, but there certainly would be at least half a dozen, up to a dozen people, with whom I've shared some intimate kind of relationship. That never goes away. Once it's shared, it's always there. But in terms of daily contact, I see more of Quentin than anyone else, and then other friends come and go. I talk to Gordon by phone every day because he doesn't live here, I see or talk to

Quentin almost every day, and I talk to Sophie every other day. I have to have that contact, I have to have someone with whom I'm sharing on a regular basis.

Is your friendship with Quentin one of your oldest as well as closest friendships?

Not as old as all that. Quentin and I met in 1978 when we were both on the National Women's Advisory Council. And though that's over twenty years, I've got other friends like Elsa Atkin [Director of the National Trust in Sydney] – we lived next door to each other when we both had babies. Those babies are twenty-six now and are still best friends. So even when we are poles apart on other things, there is always this bond and intimacy about that time in our lives, and a great affection.

The friendships that get you through those years of having small children are very important, aren't they? For everyone's survival.

They're very powerful. I don't think I was really available for those sorts of friendships until I was in my twenties and I was, for the first time, living in a community that happened to be a village, a suburb. Until then, I'd had friendships with people I worked with, good friends, women I'm still friendly with. I'd been married, I'd lived overseas. But you confront the reality and the paradigms of being female when you're birthing.

So suddenly there I was, living in a house at McMahons Point, and I met a whole lot of women at the Baby Health Centre through childbirth education classes. We shared really intimate experiences. Of course there's also a physical intimacy in those friendships that there isn't in any other. I don't normally take my tits out at functions, but with other mothers you thought nothing of it. You talked about your vaginas, you talked about your stitches. We were down to the common denominator of being female.

And we were all really interested in being female. That was the very heady beginning of the women's movement. Because we were educated and we'd been used to operating solo, we were more able to extend and reach out in those friendships. We were Resident Action, we were Childbirth Education Association, we were Women's Electoral Lobby, we were Family Planning, a whole range of different things. The shared intimacies and the emotional things got us through many of those intellectual pursuits, which were about change. We were bonded about changing the world. Even now, when we all do different things, that bond is still there.

I meet other interesting women and I think, Would I ever get to that level with you when I haven't shared those things? Quentin is probably one of the few women I've met since who has become a very close friend, but because we met on NWAC it was, again, the sharing of the advocacy and many of those things, including the hostility that we weathered in that group. And our children were all still little, so we were very involved with children and families as well.

Once, Quentin and I were sitting in an airport lounge and one of those puffed-up politicians came up and said, 'Oh, I suppose you two are just talking about how to get rid of all the men in Australia so women can rule the world.' And we said, 'Actually, we're talking about the girls' formal dresses.' He was furious. He said, 'I didn't know you talked about that.' And we said, 'Well we do.' [Laughs]

I hadn't thought about it before, but I can't think of any person with whom I've got to that level of friendship where there hasn't been a significant sharing of those family matters and values. That doesn't mean we're in the same circumstances, but the fundamentals are there so you can take an awful lot on trust. And finish each other's sentences.

Is there anything you don't share with a friend?

I've never shared my sex life. I'm just not interested. When I had a termination of an unplanned pregnancy, Gordon and I managed that. I didn't go and talk to any of my women friends. I did tell one of them about it afterwards, though, and she gave me her pills. I was twenty-two when the Pill first came out and they wouldn't give it to you if you weren't married. My friend used to go to the doctor every three months and say, 'I've lost my prescription again.' I was taking these mighty doses of hormones, you know, enough to kill an elephant.

I remember that very well – all that pretending and making up stories that nobody ever believed.

Ridiculous. But even then I wasn't looking for comfort about it. I didn't see it as an issue. I suppose it's not just about sex, it's about relationships. Quentin and I do very good workshops on Michael and Gordon, but that's in a very high level of trust. I don't go around talking about that. I think that's for me to manage.

Given that you've got this really strong primary relationship, are friendships still of vital importance to you?

Yes. But even as you say that about the primary relationship, I've worked professionally in these areas enough to know that even a strong primary relationship can change overnight.

Friendships are very important to me. I would not thrive without friends. They are extremely important to my sense of wellbeing. To have that network of trust and affection and shared memories and experience. And my children are part of that too. The boys are my friends at a different kind of level, but I think that the identity of my daughter probably makes that friendship stronger and also we're really interested in similar things.

Do you feel you can call your friends about anything, even if you're really low?

Absolutely. And no matter what, they won't mind; in fact, they'll be pleased. Even if I'm dumping something on them – and I do that, as you know, because when you arrived today you got it. [Laughs] But if I trust someone and I'm bothered by things, I will share it. That's the way I deal with those things.

Gordon's the opposite. In 1981 Gordon got leukaemia. I'd just finished an Elizabeth Kubler-Ross seminar on coping with grief so I asked Gordon, 'Do you want a grief counsellor?' And he said, 'If you want one, have one, but don't let her anywhere near me.' My way of dealing with it was to talk about it; Gordon's way was to do the necessary medical things and restructure his life.

You have great pragmatic strengths, don't you?

Yes I do. When I look back over my life, as I have when I've been writing my autobiography over the last six months or so, I recognise it much more. If we'd had this discussion a year ago, I probably wouldn't have been able to identify it in the same way. Whatever version of it I already had, I certainly got a whole new dose of it when Gordon got sick. A couple of days after he was diagnosed, one of my doctor friends at Family Planning said to me, 'Well, you just have to learn to take each day as it comes.' And I did. And I always have since. It's a cliché but that's what I do. It's very, very unusual to see me stressed. And I almost never get depressed. Even when I'm on things like the ABC Board, with some of the incredible stress that was in that area, I always feel calm in the centre. That is a mixture of pragmatism and acceptance, accepting that there are some things I can't control.

It was when Gordon became ill that I made the really big decision that, no matter what, I would always work. I had always worked, but I'd never made a decision to. But the children were all at primary school and I thought, I could easily be the sole income earner in this family, so it's not playtime any more. I'm seriously in the business of earning an income for this family, and that's going to be my responsibility from now on. I'm just going to learn to have a very good time every day. And I've always done that. If I drop dead tomorrow I want to have no regrets.

That must be extraordinarily reassuring. And peaceful. Can you teach me how to do it please, Wendy?

[Laughs] That's all you do. But yeah, it is peaceful, and reassuring. It's a good thing to be able to do. It's about compartmentalising your time as well as your life, and it's the reason I've always been able to do things simultaneously. And if I can't do it, I just say I can't do it.

Did your women friends help you get through those long hard years of Gordon's illness?

My women friends were incredibly powerful, reassuring, supportive and encouraging. The friends who couldn't cope with it, of whom there were some, we just lost. It was too big a thing. We just didn't see each other, or they just stopped coming. It was almost as though he was contagious.

I think that would be very hard to forgive in a friend. What are the other things that make you think, Okay, this friendship is over?

I particularly dislike the habit that some friends affect, which is to tell each other what their husbands are supposedly doing, or what the gossip is about you. So if anyone felt the need to tell me, for example, that my husband was having an affair, which is the cliché thing, apart from all the obvious stuff about smacking the messenger I would instantly think that person had no sense of judgement and couldn't know me the way I thought she did, because she would know that is something I don't need to be told by her. If I'm being publicly humiliated, I'll manage it, and if I'm being ratted on, I'll manage it, but that's not our friendship's role.

I don't know that that's quite the same with children, though, because with children sometimes you can save a child's life by intervening. So, at the cost of a personal friendship, I would sacrifice a friend for a child's life. I have done that, in fact, by telling someone that her child was a drug addict. She's never forgiven me, and she never will, but the child is a drug addict and it was better for the mother to know. However, I've looked after abortions for some young girls and I've never told any of their mothers if they've requested that.

I probably pushed some of my friends to the extreme, they would think, when I embraced feminism. Now it's interesting because I'm working quite closely on a Wik project and one of the people I'm working with is an old friend. We became friends when we were teachers, and we've always had a degree of intimacy in the friendship but she could never quite come on the ride to the women's movement, although she arrived at the same destination subsequently. She's now running the Wik group and I'm kind of the backroom person. That's a very nice development in a friendship that could easily have gone sour. I had other friends during that time where things did go sour.

I've had other friends where we lost it for a while, but it's picked up again because, in a way, we have all reached the same destination about women's issues and women's rights. It's just that they didn't want to be out front and vocal about it and it took them a lot of time to think it through. I was sure the minute I read my first feminist thing that this was it for me. They just took a different time.

Can close friendships have an adverse affect on a primary relationship, on a marriage?

Oh yes, I think they can easily intrude. But that hasn't been a problem for me. As much as any woman, a man is the prisoner of his gender and his conditioning, and men assume that women have friends. They probably see it as a bit strange if women don't. And I never let friends intrude on the primary relationship. I was very predatory, really, about that for a long time. I spend more time probably with my other friends now than I do with Gordon . . . No, I don't spend more time, I probably *talk* to them more, more mental time.

But we know when to drop in and out and when the primary relationship reasserts. There is a lot of understanding about that. I've always felt that if you've made a commitment in a primary relationship to a man, as I have, it's your responsibility as well as in your interest to nurture it. I've always felt that. I don't think any relationship will survive on sex. And it probably won't just on emotional bonds, so it has to have other dimensions to it. A lot of those other dimensions are the things that sustain it later in life, so you need them, and because I've made that commitment, I've always worked on it. And many of my friends have made that commitment too, so it's okay.

Wasn't that a conflict when you first were involved in the women's movement?

Oh, absolutely. You know, 'Why do you sleep with them?' 'Well, because I like it.' I've got two or three women friends who happen to be gay but I feel the same way about the primacy of their relationship, so it's not just about heterosexual relationships, it's that you recognise that in order to sustain what it is that you're trying to build, you need to expend a little more effort sometimes.

But if I've made a commitment to going out with a woman friend and Gordon suddenly turns up, I wouldn't automatically ditch it.

What about sisters as friends? Some women say they have an extraordinarily intense bond with their sisters: do you?

No, I don't. I've got one sister who's eight years younger. We don't have very much in common, we don't share experiences. We share being part of the same family, and that's it. I went away to boarding school at eleven, so she wasn't really a very big part of my life.

Sarah, my youngest sister, was born just as I was about to marry Gordon. I just adored her and she spent a bit of time with us growing up. I have a lot in common with her, especially over the last three or four years, since she's had children.

What about friends in the workplace: is it hard to have co-workers as close friends?

I think you share intimacies with whoever you work with because of the nature of the time you spend together. And in my case, where I've often been the boss and could select people I've worked with, I've probably selected people I'm likely to have a level of compatibility with. I think it's easy for friends to be engaged in the same pursuits, but I think it's difficult to share the workspace because it's only a variation of sleeping with the boss.

I think you have lateral friendships at work, but as you move towards the tops of organisations and major responsibilities, that's quite hard because there's an element of competition. One of the great things about real friendships is equality: there are no predators and no victims, it's a relationship between equals. They may not look like equals, and people might not be able to understand it, but true friends do have an equality in their exchange of friendship. And that's very difficult in a workplace. I've become friendly with people in the workplace with whom I've pursued a friendship subsequently, but not closer than that. There can be a very interesting and pleasing sort of friendliness, but I don't think it's a friendship.

As for mentors, they shouldn't be close friends; mentors should keep their distance. That's about wisdom and length of experience and being able to counsel. Friendships often grow out of mentoring relationships, but they're usually not the starting points.

Did you have a mentor?

Yes. Some quite interesting, very mature men. Jim Kirk [head of the Australian Bicentennial Authority] was a very generous mentor to me, gave me opportunities that people dream about. And a man called Colin Wendell-Smith, who was the chairman of Family Planning, a very wise Quaker and a professor of anatomy, was a very calming influence on me. When I arrived there [1976] I was still feisty and he helped smooth a lot of the edges.

There have been others, but you outgrow mentors – you grow past them or away from them – because they fulfil a need at the time. You think about them with affection, and you find yourself doing the same thing because you know you can be pivotal in someone's life. There'll be an opportunity, you're there at the right time and you can turn someone's life around. You might not see that person again, or they might turn up twenty years later and say, 'You were so good to me, you made such a difference in my life.' And you've forgotten, almost, how it happened.

Do you think you are less inclined to make very close friends as you grow older?

I think you're less inclined because you're busy doing things and you've got wraparounds from other pasts. But once the children have finally, really left home, suddenly there are huge, vacant, unprogrammed spaces in your life. When you get your weekends back, there's suddenly a lot of space. I can feel that I'm more independent of my children than I've been since I had them. More freedom, more space.

Because I live a more solo life now than I've ever lived, I

can see that there is time to explore new relationships in a way that I haven't till now. So, probably in the next twenty years, I will develop intimate friendships on different bases. I want to go travelling again, I want to go and live in other places, and I'm sure I'll meet people there with whom I'll develop the sorts of intimacies that you do when you're travelling.

Yes, the aphrodisiac of travel is not only sexual.

Oh no. It's about stripping away things and reinventing and re-presenting yourself. I like that idea of travelling and finding new relationships. And there will be new and different things to talk about. I can envisage that there will be new intimate friendships. A year or so ago I wouldn't have thought that.

Do you write to friends or are you totally dependent on the telephone?

I don't write any more although I wish I did. I yack. The phone is absolutely fundamental. It's every American sitcom you've ever seen, from Lily Tomlin on, about women, friendships and the telephone; because we trust it, we trust the response at the other end, we don't have to have the visual image. And the talk is so sustaining, so nourishing.

I don't know any men who treat the phone in the same way. Men don't, I think they just *don't*, have those emotional needs that women have.

Do you think that's why, on the whole, they don't have the kind of friendships that women have?

It must be. I don't know any men who have friends. Gordon doesn't need friends. Gordon likes women better than he likes men – I think actually a lot of men like women better than they like men – but I don't think he misses friends at all. I can't believe that he couldn't, but he says he doesn't so I have to believe it. But neither of my sons has particularly close male friends either. My brother was an exception. He was a Vietnam conscript and he had an extensive network of male friendships, unlike most men I know.

That difference has profound impacts in the workplace too, about how you manage people. The whole form of communication in the workplace is cross-cultural. Gender communication is cross-cultural, in my view. And a lot of it is about how women develop relationships and how men do, and how people give feedback, and men and women give it differently. How they correct or intervene – everything about the style is based on a kind of archetypal sexual relationship. And it's very difficult for the workplace because you can get layers of misunderstandings.

I talk about it a lot when I'm teaching business courses, because women will be absolutely shattered by a man's rejection of an idea. It's like a sexual rejection, whereas that's not what the man intended at all. 'I don't like it. It doesn't mean I don't like *you*, I just don't like *it*.' But she's already taken on the entire responsibility for being personally approved of or disapproved of. Deborah Tannen has done some interesting work on this – analysis on linguistics in the workplace and the very different way in which men and women relate to each other.

The differences show up early, don't they? Boys either push off or go and play in a group, but girls exclude each other: 'You're not my best friend any more.' What do you think that's about?

Well, they're learning language, and they're practising, and they already know that friendship is profoundly important. Men aren't bothered by it.

Girls use friendship as a weapon. You see it in primary schools, especially about ages nine and ten, and then at about thirteen and fifteen. Years nine and ten are horror years for girls, because they are so cruel about who will be in with them and who will be out. You'll see friendships of years dissolve overnight. You see it as a teacher, you see it as a mother of girls – the huge anxieties over 'I won't be your best friend.'

I think it has a lot to do with the onset of puberty and about girls working out what's important. They know at that stage that friendships are important, belonging is important. Men are already learning to play team games and they are learning to relate at a more superficial level from a woman's perspective, but not necessarily from their perspective. They're learning to relate in a functionally useful way, whereas women are learning to relate in an emotionally nourishing way. Different strokes, really. And they're both limited as a result of it, because we've got 50 per cent of the world doing this and 50 per cent doing that. What we actually want, in the normal curve, is 80 per cent doing the same thing, and you can have 10 per cent of gender-specific, if that's what you need.

Do you think there are real disadvantages in the ways women relate to others? Do they over-invest themselves, or perhaps set themselves up for disappointment?

I think women have to learn to manage a lot of that stuff more effectively in the workplace because they still confuse friendship with professionalism, or friendship with authority, or friendship with approval. And they're not necessarily the same in the workplace. That's where you do have to develop that pragmatic sense of self. You have to learn to function more effectively. And that can be very hard.

Quentin told me that she came to live with you after she'd been living in Sydney on her own for a minute and a half.

[Laughs] She did, yes. That's an amazing friendship, to endure that. Quentin rang up and said, 'I've taken this job in Sydney and I feel really scared about it now. May I come and stay with you for a few days?' And I said, 'Sure.' Five years later, she left.

It was fantastically successful. Quentin lived downstairs in the house and shared a bathroom with Sam. There was nothing in the life cycle of our family that was going to disturb her, she'd seen worse or better and it didn't matter. She was undemanding – she just wanted a decent bedroom, she eats like a sparrow anyway, and she really just wanted a surrogate family. Gordon had moved to the farm and was away at least five nights a week. So I was there with Sam, and Gordon was there at the weekends, and she was mostly away at the weekends, back in Brisbane. Or I could be at the farm and she was in the house.

It was very companionable. And because we had so many intellectual interests and professional interests, we'd sit there like an old married couple talking about that, or we'd workshop our families. It was a very, very nice period of life. Very comforting and a very good growth period. We've done a lot of wise counsel.

Michael came and stayed occasionally but that didn't work as well, even though they're very comfortable together – we were all too cooped up. Quentin and I were far more able to do that without the men around.

And she knew when to scat. She could see when I was about to set to for a good fight or something; she could sniff it and disappear. We used to swim and walk and do all those things, it was great. It was very, very comfortable. And when I was travelling it was fantastic having her there to mind Sam – not that he thought he needed minding, but he liked having her there. He adored her.

There'd be nights when I'd be asleep in bed and Quentin would come in and sit at the end of the bed and say, 'I don't want to burden you with this, but . . .' And she'd go, 'Yip-yip-yip.' I sleep like a log, so half the time I wouldn't even hear her come in. It was terribly comfortable. It was like having a sister. Whatever you imagine a perfect relationship with a sister could be, it was.

Barbara BLACKMAN ¶

A S AN ONLY CHILD of a widowed mother, living in Brisbane boarding houses and shared flats, Barbara Blackman grew up with both 'a quiet addiction' to solitude and a gift for friendship. In 1951 the 22-year-old Barbara left Brisbane for Melbourne to begin a life with the young painter Charles Blackman in a tin shed with an outside loo and no bathroom. A writer and poet, future essayist, broadcaster, librettist, and soon to become an artist's model, Barbara had not long before been certified blind, 'a life sentence for a crime I had not committed'. ¶ IN MELBOURNE SHE and Charles found a central berth on 'the good ship Mora', Barbara's affectionate name for the unique entity that was urbane restaurateur and art dealer Georges and his dazzling young artist wife Mirka, newly arrived from war-devastated Paris, and their home and studio at 9 Collins Street where artists and friends such as Clifton Pugh, John Perceval, Joy Hester and Arthur Boyd gathered. (For more on the good ship Mora see the following conversation.) ¶ THE PAINTER JOY HESTER became one of Barbara's best friends. Joy had by then been diagnosed with Hodgkin's disease, had left her marriage to the painter Albert Tucker, given her son Sweeney to John and Sunday Reed to raise, and was living with Gray Smith. 'It was singularly Joy who gave me the courage to have children,' wrote Barbara in her 1997 memoir *Glass After Glass*. 'Blind people were not expected to take that step.' 'Big-sistered' by Joy, who had had two more children with Gray, Barbara had her first baby, August, in April 1957. ¶ AFTER TWO MORE children and three decades as an artist's wife, in May 1978 Barbara wrote a letter of resignation from her marriage. She went to Perth, made a new life, found new work, new friends. Barbara, now seventy-two, lives in the bush with Marcel Veldhoven, whom she married in 1992, and when she comes to Sydney she shares an apartment with a friend, where on the wall of the sitting room hangs a Blackman Alice, looking remarkably like a young Barbara.

———

In Glass After Glass, *you write about Joy, but also many of your other friends. You seem to have a great capacity for friendship.*

My mother did also. My mother was a very good-humoured lady and she had an immense capacity for friendship. It was something I grew up with and imbibed, and it's been a major part of my life. You see, I wear the Cladagh ring, the crowning love of friendship. And that, for me, probably outrides all other loves. That's a big statement, isn't it? Husbands and family are friends *à point*. Friendship is something very special and very important, a great sustenance in my life.

I have lots of intimate friends. Lots. You see, my friendship with Joy Hester was only over ten years and I've got friendships much longer. I have friends as close as sisters, and I really mean that, in Sydney, Melbourne, Brisbane, Perth, Adelaide. I can just walk in on any of them, saying, 'I'm coming.' And they'll say, 'Come. There's your bed. How long can you stay?' It's won-derful to have that friendship.

How would you define those friendships? What makes them inti-mate friends, as opposed to a lot of perfectly nice people whom you quite like?

Oh, you don't have to go through the shenanigans of polite-ness and putting on face. You walk straight into the middle of the conversation you left. You can be totally uninhibited, spontaneous, confiding, confessional, all those things. And it doesn't give out. You don't run out of things to say or ideas to exchange. That connection through ideas is particularly impor-tant when friends don't move in the same circles as you do, when there are parts of their lives that you don't enter, or need to enter. They're not antagonistic areas, they're just not areas of common interest.

How important is common ground, do you think? How much of it do you need to have?

I think common ground is part of it. I think just having found and sparking off from each other is very important. I've just been away to a conference on women's spirituality with my friend Margaret, who lives in this flat. We see an enormous amount of each other and we drove up together. Then another friend I haven't seen much of for years came down from Brisbane and the three of us shared a room. And although this third person didn't know my friend from here, the moment they met they hit it off together. We laughed so much. We kept up a constant patter of fun and repartee and silliness that was really wonderful. Silliness is a very important ingredient of friendship. You can go into musical comedy sequences with friends, and then you can come straight back into something that's really close to the heart, and tears, and 'What *am* I going to do with this situation in my life?' So it goes from those extremes.

Is that free-wheeling, all-embracing range of conversation a particular characteristic of women's friendships, or do you have that with men too?

I have a lot of very good friendships with men because I don't have affairs with men. That gives me the privilege of having great male friendships, but they're quite different. I think male friendships are much more on particular ground, they're much more territorial. I like to have men friends, and my good men friends I do hug, there's a lot of hugging. But there is a mutual reservation, and there are things that you don't confide.

But there is genderisation also. With women, there's a quality of womanhood that is always in the foreground. At this women's conference the whole feeling of being with a hundred and fifty women for five days was just wonderful. There are things you can take for granted. Not just dressing more casually, but the sense of flow, the allusions you can make. There are things that women will talk about that couldn't be talked about among men. This conference was not avowedly feminist, it was not anti-men in any way – most of the women there were in marriages or relationships with men, they were of that age – but it was about things that were not relevant to men's company.

There was a lot of talk about women's roles, women reclaiming roles, not only in birthing but in laying out of the dead – that's something that's been institutionalised but it is women's work. Women questioning and making changes in male authority. Oh, and there was a lot of singing and hugging and dancing about. There was a spontaneous concert put on and those who could belly dance did a belly dance. And there was nothing reserved – all the hip and bum movement was even more pronounced. It was not for men's flirtation, it was for women's joy, and it was even more joyous in the presence of other women. There was a great sense of freedom away from being looked at by men, and in using the body to the utmost, and if you overdid it a bit, that was wonderful. However, if done before men, it would have other connotations.

What are some of the other qualities of your most intimate friendships with women – loyalty, for instance, can you take that for granted?

If you can go without contact for a couple of years and go back and it's exactly there, that's loyalty. Some people are good letter writers and good telephoners, some people are not. So I think that's loyalty in the long-distance friendship.

Honesty's utterly important. Honesty is the basis of loyalty. And tact is the grace of it. For example, when people have areas that you're not interested in, I think you need to be very tactful about that. I've got a very good friend who is finding her life's meaning and her way of life within a particular sect. I let her talk about it and then move on. I think that's tact.

And presumably the same thing would apply if one of your close friends became involved with somebody that you thought wasn't right for her?

That's tact again. You know that part of her life is with this person whom you don't think is right for her, as you put it, so you try to amplify the other part of her life that is her friendship.

[Phone rings] That's me mate. [Answers phone, chats for a bit and returns]

Is a mate different from an intimate friend?

[Laughs] Oh yes, she's me mate. We're knockabouts. She's my theatre mate. She's much younger, about thirty years younger, and we've been going to theatres for about fifteen, sixteen years. And we tread on each other's toes and kick each other's bums. We're going to the theatre tonight. And all the spare time we've got we spend together.

What's the difference between this mate and your intimate friendships?

Oh, we feel like being together. My friend Margaret, who went to the conference with me, and Andy, the one who rang up, we're a great threesome. Any two of us are good together, and a threesome is even better. Then we've got others who join in and it becomes a foursome. It's a rolling thing. If I'm in the country, they tell me what I've missed so I'm present with them even when I'm not there. I think there's a lot of that in friendship, that including of you – 'Oh Barb, you would have loved this.' I think that's a quality of friendship.

Would you confide in the mate?

Oh yes. And we've been through bad times. For a while we lost common ground, lost touch. But with close friends, sometimes you move out of each other's orbit and it's just, 'I love you. I miss you. I'm here,' and that's all. And you wait till whatever's happening to them brings them back. Or whatever's happening to you. I cut off a lot from friends while I was intensively writing the book [*Glass After Glass*]. I had to. And people have been ringing up saying, 'Where are you? We've missed you. We're waiting for you to come back.' And I think that's part of friendship – they understand that I was doing something where I couldn't be in touch.

My mate and I went to a lot of theatre together. In London we went to thirty-two theatres in twenty-one days. Our husbands were there and we off-routed them back, changed their tickets and sent them back to Australia because they couldn't keep up the pace. [Laughs]

Barbara, I still can't quite see how your mate is different from your intimate friends, except in age, and maybe that's the key.

She's – what do we call ourselves? – she's a thumper, we bring out the aggressive in each other. We're both up and at it and into you and we've had a few fisties. We're bouncers, we're pushers and bouncers. But we're movers and organisers too, and get things done. But we're theatre mates, that's how our friendship was based. We started a little theatre together, the Lookout Theatre in Woollahra. Her role in it was very much the active role and mine was that of the back-seat driver.

Because she has two stepchildren and two children, there are times when the family demands are very great. I'm the godmother of her youngest, and we live close to each other here in the city. In our friendship there is a big difference in age, and there are still big territories we don't occupy together but we're a resource for each other. She's a wonderful loving friend to me and at the drop of a hat she'll pick me up from the dentist and take me to the bus. Feel like a coffee? She's outside in two minutes, that sort of thing. And we do talk deeply about our other relationships.

Being older, I've brought her into things like the Jung Society, and into areas of reading that she wouldn't have got into. Someone said to her once at the theatre, while I was in the loo, 'Aren't you kind to bring that old blind lady to the theatre.' And she said, 'She's my mate. She's taught me more about the theatre . . .' She says it's amazing to go to a theatre with someone who goes to sleep all the way through the play and then comes out and discusses it. Because there's no reason to keep my eyes open, I often just sit there with my eyes shut. She brings a lot to me in what she sees in theatre. She's a very intelligent woman who hasn't had any formal education but has done an enormous amount of work on herself in reading and studying.

How important are shared ethics, values, ways of doing things?

Spirit and values, pathways of compassion – very important. But I've got a lot of friends who wouldn't see eye to eye with each other at all on a lot of things. I seem to have a broad base in that I accommodate a lot of people – that's their way of doing it and I accept that. Astrologically I have an unaspected Venus in Aquarius – gregarious. But a lot of people are more defined and therefore have less of a range of friends. People have criticised me as being too indiscriminate in my friends, but I rather like the wide range. There are parts of my life that certain friends wouldn't know about – they'd be amazed if they saw other aspects of me. And I think that's nice. They colour in different areas.

What are the things that put the greatest strain on friendships in your experience, the things that really stretch and in some cases finish a friendship?

One of the things that puts strains on friendship is, as we said before, when one of the friends deeply, deeply needs to go into a private, solitary, exclusive place of her own for a period – either she's having a really bad time and has to get through it in her own way or she has to give all her time and space and thought to something she's doing.

I've just had a close friendship flounder because she was writing something that I realised was a total misinterpretation of me that she was about to make public. I confronted her about it and said that I was deeply hurt and that I felt she'd really misunderstood and trivialised the friendship. She said I'd lost my sense of humour, so it was a stalemate. I suppose the friendship is suspended. She's decided not to publish what she was going to publish, but she thinks I was wrong in my reaction to the manuscript.

Do you think that has put a permanent blight on the friendship?

I think there's a balance within oneself of extrovert and introvert, and sometimes one can have a happy extrovert relationship with someone, assuming that there is an inner or spiritual or profound side of the person. But if you suddenly find that that person says, 'I'm an atheist, I don't believe in your values, I think spiritual values are an illusion,' then the strings are cut in a way, because, to various degrees, my friends do have a sense of the spiritual value and the profundity of life and the poem of life, however different their views of it might be. (I'm not talking religion, by the way, because I think that's a very dangerous area.)

But sometimes a friendship is simply a shared history, where we've been through a lot together, we've seen a lot, we've been through a lot of hard times together. I think women form friendships if they have babies at the same time, or have common paths. You make friendships by taking your kids to the same school and being parents at the same functions, and things like that. You've got to be able to laugh at some of those terrible times when you have small children, or you wonder how you would've got through it. You wonder how you would have got through many of the things you get through in your life without friends to say, 'Well, it's happened before and it'll happen again, and we'll all live on to the next whisky bar.'

When you met Marcel, how did that affect your long-standing, very close friends? Were they pleased for you?

Well, there was a great change in my life when I left Charles. It was not just him that I left, I left a network, a whole area of friends; I left people, I left what is loosely called 'the art world'. The world of art as having a monetary value became more and more alien to me – a world where people owned a Blackman and it was valuable and they had a life that went with having an art collection. That gave me the creeps and I had to get out.

I found that, in a lot of cases, the people who had values about having a rich art collection had the same values about having a rich-looking house and rich-looking clothes and all that. And I just found that irrelevant to my life. So what I did, as I describe in my book, was jump in the opposite direction. I went bush. I went where people owned nothing, had nothing – had no walls to hang a painting on and didn't know a painting from a bar of soap because they did their paintings on bark. And I just started from there.

I got into the world of inner values, did a lot of work with the Jung Society. Then I went to Karnak, Diane Cilento's school of Sufi studies, in the early eighties and in one fell swoop I got an understanding of God, I got the things in my life to fit together – a workable attitude to life – and I got a whole pack of new friends. Marcel was one of them. The friend that I share this flat with was there, not actually at the course but around and about. I made a whole lot of new and intensely interesting friends who came out of quite different backgrounds, and with that I started a new kind of life.

What about the old friends? I'm thinking of, say, Judith Wright [the poet, whom Barbara had known since her Brisbane days], Mirka Mora.

Oh, Judith was always there for me. There are people who were always there for me. And Marcel was very fine by her because it so happened that Marcel is one of the few people who picked up [her husband] Jack McKinney's book and understood him immediately. So he was a great gift because of that. Jack McKinney, a philosopher, is not nearly as well known as he should be, so Marcel and Judith had a very remarkable, immediate contact. And Mirka had that French contact with Marcel, so at various points Marcel *did* fit in with people in my life. At other points, of course, he didn't.

But I think while I turned myself around and went bush, I did get out of contact with friends. And that's what I was talking about earlier – they simply didn't know what I was doing but they waited till I reappeared, knowing that it was important. Like Betty Churcher [retired director of the National Gallery of Australia]. I just showed up again after some years. I was doing oral histories for the National Library and I went to interview Roy [Churcher, Betty's husband, a painter]. I like them both very much but I chose to interview Roy because of his story. Betty got a lot of public profile anyway. So I went off and interviewed him. At about eleven o'clock at night they said, 'Can we ring you a taxi?' I said, 'No, I'm not going anywhere, I'll stay here.' So I stayed and the next day Betty said, 'I hadn't realised how much we'd missed you and how much I value your friendship. And how much your last years of struggle with Charles had taken you away from us.' And that's one sort of friendship. Betty and I have a great understanding. We have long telephone calls, but of course she gets caught up in things. But whenever we get the chance we ring each other up and then we're likely to talk for an hour.

We had our babies together, that threw us together. But Betty and I know each other from our school days – you don't know many people from your school days. We went to Crusader schoolgirl camps together. And when we were young women feeling our way into the art world, there was a particular woman who gave us great encouragement, so we always have that reference point – I think you do have reference points in friendships. Then Betty became so involved in the art world that I'd been in with Charles, and she has kept me in touch with that world.

When you're back in contact with friends, are regular doses of women's conversation important? You've mentioned the telephone – are you a great phoner?

I'm a great phone friend. I have huge bills, but without any qualms because that's my friendship. I think of it like this: if I ring my friend in Perth and we talk for an hour, how does that compare with shouting each other to lunch? You see, Perth's another area of my life where I've got a lot of wonderful friends, who don't even know my eastern friends exist. They say, 'Do you know a lot of people over east?' And I say [laconically], 'Oh, yeah.' And my friends in the west are diverse too. I used to give a lot of parties and at one of my parties in Perth some-one said to me, 'You come to this party and look at these people and you wonder why on earth they would be in a room together. Then you realise that they're all Barbara's friends because they're all talkers.'

Talk is *very* important. I suppose I regard shyness as negative aggression. Yet I have some friends who say, 'You have to under-stand, Barbara, I can't bear to pick up a telephone.' I don't understand, but I forgive it. It's a forgivable sin, but . . . [Laughs]

I've just got a new friendship with a woman who read my book and really entered into it. She lives quite close to me in the country, but because of her domestic situation she's fairly house-bound. She doesn't ring me up, she writes to me. And although it means someone else has to read the letters to me, she is able to say things by letter that she couldn't say on the telephone. Some people do this on tape. Now, on the tele-phone you're at a spontaneous, to-and-fro level, whereas in a letter or tape you can consider something – consider it, formu-late it and think, This is something I'd like to share with Barbara. So there are friendships also of that nature.

I have another friend, a very good friend whom I've known since I changed my life; she's a woman involved in incredible research in prehistory and we have a great friendship at that level. We make an appointment to ring each other up because it's too hard to visit each other – she's now eighty. So we'll say, 'What about Wednesday morning at ten-thirty?' And we'll sit down with a cup of coffee and we'll talk for maybe two hours. And that's a particular friendship.

Are there restrictions or boundaries with your closest friends? Things that you wouldn't talk about, or feel you can't raise?

It's all a matter of projecting onto a screen. If you know this person's screen cannot take this projection, you don't put it on them. I know some of my friends would be very embarrassed if I projected onto them certain confessions or problems that I'm dealing with. So one doesn't.

I can't stand droppers-in. I think it's a trespass, so I always ring first.

You've lived and travelled with an extraordinary range of people. Does that put a strain on friendship? Can close proximity to close friends be disappointing?

Travelling and staying with friends is wonderful. I don't find it puts a strain on friendship at all. I've always found it enlarging to stay with a friend for any length of time, just to be around the house.

I have a friend in Brisbane whom I've known since our 'child-having' days, so I've known her for forty years. She's one of the people I'd regard as a sister. There were about five years in my life in the eighties where I had my mother either living by herself or in a nursing home, and my beloved cousin Olive also on her own, and I used to spend one week in five in Brisbane, going to nursing homes. My friend's house was a home away from home and we just became closer. They used to say, 'Oh, gee, I wish you could stay here longer.' There was always that feeling, rather than, 'Time you went.'

I think it's a wonderful feeling to become a house familiar, where I'll cook the dinner or you'll cook the dinner, that sort of thing. I'm at home in a lot of people's houses and I know my way round. I'm a very domestic person.

Speaking of domesticity, I was very struck when I read the chapter on Joy Hester in your book to find you saying 'art was not uppermost on her list of life's pursuits. Mothering and domesticity enthralled her.'

They did enthral her. And I think this is what people haven't seen, or haven't wanted to see. They think art is something different. They think the artist does housework grudgingly. It's not true. Joy could hardly tear herself away to go and do her art. 'Oh, shut up, Joy, and go and do some art,' that was more like it. A lot of people have said that after reading my book they felt much warmer towards Joy, or understood her much better than they did from the *Dear Sun* letters, and things like that.

There was also that documentary about Joy, The Good Looker, which I thought was rather reverential and solemn. The only real sense of her as a warm, living, laughing person came when you were interviewed and you talked about having the babies and doing the painting and –

– and the chooks. And all that. [Laughs] Yes, Barrie Reid was laying it on thick and being pompous and pretentious and poncey, in his way. He was an old friend of mine but Joy couldn't stand him. He's just one of the people who have become possessive of this inflated memory image of Joy. So I had a great desire to reinstate Joy, to bring her to life as she really was.

Joy died just as we were going to England in 1960. Forty years ago, another part of my life. Mirka danced on the table at our farewell.

Your book is also an overdue corrective to the hagiography of Sunday Reed. You've said that you were 'a Heide reject', that being part of the Reed circle was too much like being a courtier for your taste. You don't say a lot about Sunday Reed, but what you do say makes it clear that she was a difficult and demanding woman.

She was. Sunday declared that 'artists shouldn't have wives' and when I became pregnant she sent Charles the fare to Sydney to escape.

Although Mirka has a rather warmer view of Sunday, as you doubtless know.

Oh yes, because Mirka has that wonderful quality of creeping under everybody's skirt. [Laughs] It's this wonderful playfulness, she reduces people to a play level. Charles used to call Mirka's salon a therapeutic kindergarten for adults, and Mirka does have that quality.

Is that playfulness an important part of your friendship with Mirka?

I suppose that's a part of my friendship with Mirka, but I wouldn't say it was dominant. Mirka's one of those people with whom I sat and talked about the most profound things. And when I was writing the chapter on Melbourne in the fifties, she would say, 'But Barbara, you must remember how we talked all night about the profound things, the deep things and the meaning of life. You must tell that that was what we were doing with each other and using each other for – to find how deep we could go.' And I think that was very much part of it.

I'll tell you another thing about Mirka. When I was writing that chapter I said, 'Well, Mirka, what did I look like? What did people think of me being blind?' 'Oh,' she said, 'you were very funny. I used to wet my pants from giggling because you bumped into this, and you went the wrong way. It was very funny. And people said I was very naughty to laugh but I said, Well, you had courage. None of us knew if we had courage but we could see that you did.' I thought that was lovely. Deeply honest. A deeply honest reflection.

She said this very generous thing to me about you: 'Barbara is such a woman. And this is a very difficult thing to be.'

Ah yes. Well, that's what I'm saying when I say our friendship wasn't predominantly playful. It was very womanly.

We had some schemes too. There was that mad time when
we were going to start a school of living arts. Then Joy and I
were going to start a child-minding service. We were going to
look after the children of the rich for a year, while they went to
Europe. We were quite serious about it. It was quite mad. But
the thing is, you envisage a new life.

Do you think women are better at intimate friendships than men?

Oh, I think so. But Marcel is very good at male friendships.
There are a lot of men who say that he changed their lives, that
he brought out the feminine in them. Marcel showed men that
it's all right to embrace and show your emotions. As a heterosexual man, he showed other men how to nurture babies,
because he nurtured his two babies, did a lot of the nappying
and feeding and nurturing. He is very well liked by men. I don't
think he understands women very well and he makes rather
flamboyant attempts to flirt with them that don't quite come
off. But he has very warm friendships with men, which is a very
nice quality.

Whereas Charles had a lot of mateships with men, which is
a very different thing. Mateship is sparring. With a mate you
spar.

*What are some of the great acts of friendship that you've
experienced?*

Oh, so many. You can say of some of the periods in your life,
I wonder how I got through it. When I had my first baby – it
was a Caesarean and he had a lot of rashes and things – I had a
metabolic reaction which gave me carbuncles, and then my
mother gave me a cup of tea when I wasn't awake and I spilled
it down my front and got burnt all over my breast. Judith
Wright said, 'You'd better come up here and let me look after

you.' So I went up there and she did. She had had a Caesarean and she knew what it was like. In Judith's not taciturn but very low-key way, she really looked after me with absolute care. She dressed my wounds, fed me in the right way. She just knew; she just did it. And I think perhaps we did something like that for her some years later when she was in a very bad physical state.

Another great act of friendship was the way my women friends just embraced me at the time in Perth when I made that huge decision I felt I'd never make, to leave Charles. Friends fairly recently met, who've now become close, close friends, just took me in.

Did any of them help you to come to that decision?

Oh no. I didn't know many people in Perth. It just hit me, an incident that I don't want to put on record. It just happened and I said, 'That's the last straw. I have to get out of here to survive.'

In Perth I was pioneering Radio for the Print Handicapped programs and meeting a lot of women. They were day programs and there were many more women volunteers than men. I met a lot of interesting new women, including Mary Durack, who is a great woman. Mary was wonderful to me. I didn't know her all that well but she hugged me and said, 'Oh my dear Barbara. We all go through big moments in our lives,' and saw me through.

I think women find it easy to flow into each other's lives in a way that men do not. And that's why men do it so clumsily over beer, at the pub.

Clearly you haven't found it harder to make intimate friends as you grow older. Can you imagine ever stopping making friends?

Oh no. I've recently been given a friend. Since the break in my life, my friends have mostly been in their forties, hitting fifties. I'm twenty years ahead and sometimes I get a sense that they're reading road maps of territory I've been through. So a friend of mine who's in this age group said to me, 'I'm going to introduce you to Rita because she's your age and she's singing your song: where are all the other late-sixties women who are still vitally interested in philosophy and doing things and having interesting friendships? So I'm going to give you to each other.' And she has. Now Rita and I both feel we've got a new friend.

I've recently met a woman whom I like very much. She's Dutch but exactly my age, so when she talks about her childhood, vastly different from mine, somehow because we are the same age it makes friendship accessible. I've enjoyed those friendships made in my sixties with people also in their sixties. We might not have known each other when we were young, but we share a lot of territory on a global scale.

On the other hand, when Marcel was away [a two-year separation], I had young people living with me who were turning thirty. That was a marvellous passage in my life because they brought a lot of people through and I feel I've now made friends in that young age group. The age difference is not insurmountable and we find each other's worlds interesting.

I also have little friends, five-, six-, seven-year-olds, who know Barbara as a person, who come and have things to tell me or show me. And I feel they're friends, not just offspring of my friends.

The friends who are turning fifty – do you feel that they are looking to you to show them the way?

In some ways, yes. I don't believe in the menopause. Well, I and a lot of my friends didn't have a menopause, we just sort of sailed through it, although I recognise that not all women do. Certainly I changed my life at fifty and I suppose that was a kind of menopause. But I do say to people, 'Look, when you're fifty, if there's something you really want to do and you haven't done it, go for it.' Which is what I did. That advice – 'Do as I do' – isn't necessarily the best advice, but that's what I did at fifty. I thought, If I don't do it now, I'll be a coward. I won't have done it.

So courage, the quality that Mirka commented on, is a thread that runs through your life. Of necessity, one might say, but necessity doesn't always produce courage.

I'm the sort of person who'd rather have a problem in front of me than behind me. I don't like to pretend it isn't happening. And I suppose in a deep sense I do trust myself.

You trust your judgement?

I don't know about my judgement. I trust . . . I suppose it's also that God loves me. God loves me if I make a mess of things. And if I get it right, God still loves me. I do feel that to be alive is a blessing, to live is holy. I do feel that very deeply, *very* deeply. I feel that there is something so much greater, so much beyond any life that we can receive, that we are part of. If God forgives you, you can forgive yourself and forgive other people.

Do you ever get depressed?

Oh yes, I get depressed. Blindness is ultimately frustrating and depressing. And sometimes one's courage and optimism and humility all seem to give out at the same point. There was a woman at the conference talking about goddesses. She said there's a goddess called 'The Goddess Who Falls Flat on Her Face'. Well, I'm often into that goddess archetype, the goddess who falls flat on her face. And you just say, This too will pass, we've been here before. Seems worse this time, but I've been here before.

And that gets you through? Even though, at the time, you can't believe that it's ever been this bad, that nothing before was a patch on this?

I think that's very true of writing. You think, Yes, I'm a good writer but I'll never get this done. This is a worse impasse than any bit of writing I've ever done. This time I'm totally finished. And then, two days later, oooh. But it's very hard to remember that it's been this bad before, that it's even been worse before.

When I was in that vacant space, post-husband, I knew there were three dangers. One was being sexually promiscuous, as a sort of self-evaluation. The second was getting drunk – I'll get out of here, I'll get into the bottle. And the third one, and I think the most tempting, was to become the Ancient Mariner, tell your story to everybody.

I tried to be very aware of not getting into those three apparent rescue zones. And in fact I made friendships with people to whom I *didn't* have to tell my story, both when I was in Perth and then when Marcel left. That time I made friends with a whole lot of young people who'd never met Marcel and who just saw me as some old chook there by myself. That Ancient Mariner archetype was, for me, the most tempting. I know promiscuity and drinking are tempting for other people, but I have to be careful drinking because, being blind, I can lose co-ordination and become physically accident-prone. So I'm almost prohibited from that one.

The friends that I made in Perth saw me without all that baggage. Because I was working in radio, because I was working in spoken word, they tended to be readers. And, God help them, a lot of them had never heard of Charles Blackman and they weren't involved in the 'art world'. Occasionally one might say vaguely, 'Are you any relation to Charles Blackman?' [Laughs] But they were friends in another world, and another world that was more my world.

When I was making a new life for myself in Perth, I joined five groups. I joined the Public Broadcasting Group, which was just beginning. I took up oral history, which was just starting then. I joined Jazz Action because I love jazz. I joined the Jung Society and I joined the Fellowship of Writers. So there I had a life, because by the time I went to all their meetings, I had somewhere to go and I was meeting people with common tastes who were not in the 'art world'. And that gave me buoyancy. In all of those areas I met new friends, as well as a man with whom I had a wonderful affair.

So, suddenly, I found there were worlds of other people who weren't concerned with the fame and fortune of the 'art world', and who weren't visual. So I escaped from fame and fortune and visual orientation. And maybe I should never have been there, maybe I was a trespasser, maybe I read the wrong road signs to get in there. So I sprang out to a world elsewhere.

I changed wardrobes completely at fifty. It was then I made my Aboriginal friends, when I went off on my bush trip with a man I'd never met. Mary Durack had spurred me on to do all this. She said, 'Oh, you'll be right once you get out on the road. You'll meet people.'

People said to me, 'Are you actually going off alone with a man you've never met?' I said, 'Yeah.' And they said, 'Well, you'd better check him out.' So I checked him out. I said to him on the telephone, 'We've never met, we don't know much about each other. Is it going to be all right?' He said, 'I like people. Don't you like people?' I said, 'Yes, I like people.' He said, 'Well, why wouldn't you like me?' And I said, 'Oh, yes, I like you.' So there we were. And he brought his little daughter who was three, and his girlfriend who was one of the Wik people of Aurukun.

The other thing I would like to say is that of all my women friends, my mother and my daughter are two of my greatest friends, with all the qualities that friendship has, apart from kin attachments. But then, we are all kin.

Mirka MORA ¶

M IRKA AND GEORGES MORA arrived in Melbourne from
Paris in 1951, bringing such an invigorating gust of
elsewhere with them that, as Bails Myers once observed, they
transformed that grey town into a real city. Mirka, artist and
dressmaker, was twenty-three, an absolute original and
enchantingly beautiful: tiny, olive-skinned, with a mass of black
hair, huge dark eyes alive with invention and mischief, and a
wide expressive mouth much given to laughter. ¶ THE MORAS
HAD deliberately come as far as possible from wartime France.
Paris-born and Jewish, Mirka had been detained in a concentration camp in France when she was thirteen. Unlike her
friends, she was inexplicably released and with her family hid
from the Nazis in occupied France for the remaining three years
of the war. At eighteen she married Georges, who was thirty-
four and a former member of the French Resistance. ¶ IN
MELBOURNE THEY rented the basement studio at 9 Collins
Street. Here Mirka raised three sons, made dresses, painted,
and showed the work of new artists such as Charles Blackman
and Joy Hester. The Collins Street studio became the home of
the revived Contemporary Art Society and a home away from
home for the circle of friends and artists that included the
Blackmans, Arthur Boyd and John Perceval. The patrician art
patrons John and Sunday Reed wielded their considerable
influence from Heide, their house outside Melbourne which is

now the Museum of Modern Art. ¶ THE MORAS OPENED the Mirka Café in Exhibition Street in 1954, with Mirka operating Melbourne's first espresso machine, followed by the Balzac, Melbourne's first real (and licensed) French restaurant, in 1958. In 1966 they acquired the Tolarno, a residential hotel and bistro in St Kilda, with space for Georges' first separate art gallery. They said goodbye to Collins Street and went to live above the new shop. ¶ IN 1970, AT his request, Mirka left Georges and her two sons, William and Tiriel (Philippe was already in London), to live alone, although the boys often came to visit. The man who became her lover then is still her lover thirty years on, although they do not live together. When I had this conversation with her, Mirka lived alone with her cat in her house of many years, a tiny, single-storey Victorian house in Barkly Street, St Kilda, its corridor stacked with books on either side, leaving a narrow alley just wide enough for one person to walk from the front door to the kitchen. The rooms were like magic caves, lined with columns of books, thousands of books on history, philosophy, poetry, French theory, art, on top of which sat paintings, Mirka's dolls and fabulous creatures – the painted-cloth incarnations of her figures – and all kinds of found objects. She has recently moved to a studio custom built for her by her son William in a new building that also houses his gallery and his family. It's a very contemporary space, but I am not surprised to hear that inside her studio Mirka has recreated her Barkly Street house. ¶ MIRKA'S TWO BEST friends – this is the most accurate description I can find, although Mirka questions it – were Sunday Reed, who died in 1981, and the artist Joy Hester, who died of Hodgkin's disease in 1960. Joy and Sunday were themselves intimate friends, and by the time Mirka arrived in Melbourne Joy had left Albert Tucker for Gray Smith, who suffered from *grand mal* epilepsy, and had given her son Sweeney to the childless Sunday. Mirka and Georges soon became regulars at Heide, and Mirka wrote to John and Sunday almost daily. ¶ AT SEVENTY-TWO Mirka is still intensely, *irresistibly* charming. Even in repose her mouth smiles, and as she talks – her voice warm, throaty and musical, her accent still very French with the occasional Australian vowel – she frequently chuckles. She's playful and irreverent and quick, but she is driven by an acute and constantly curious intelligence and works ceaselessly, obsessively. Mirka's generosity of heart and spirit are rare, her profound understanding of human frailty entirely untainted by cynicism or bitterness. And she has courage. She has come through the Holocaust, the death of a marriage, a breakdown and, most recently, uterine cancer, with the relish for life of those who know that it is essentially a tragedy, so laughter, love, art, and a passion for whatever other joys life can offer are the only responses worth having.

I DON'T THINK I've ever had a real friend. Truly. I'm quite ashamed to say that because I always call myself a friend. I *am* a friend. If something happens you can call me in the middle of the night, anytime, I'm here to help you. But I would not do it to my friends. I don't think you can inflict yourself upon someone else. You can't inflict yourself upon a lover or husband or your children, and your friends are the same thing. And yet I expect my friends to inflict themselves upon me. I ask them, and some do.

The last two months I had a really splendid flu. I could've had twenty people in this room to help me, but I couldn't inflict myself on people so I just fared by myself. I still went out every day to buy the paper, to test myself, and straight to bed again. I like to push myself.

So when friends offered, and they genuinely offered to come and do things –

Oh, they did, sure. Yes.

– why wouldn't you let them?

Well, they should have ideas themselves, they should leave me fruits and things at my door, in baskets, you know. They want me to say what I need but I'm not the kind of person to say, 'Oh, I need five apples and six oranges.' They should think of it. That's what I call a friend.

So if somebody had suddenly arrived on your doorstep –

– with a basket full of things? I let them in. But if they ring me to say, 'What do you need?' I don't have time to tell them what I need, and I might be extravagant. Do you think it's not fair?

It seems perfectly fair to me. But then you and I would just arrive with the basket of goodies.

Absolutely, yes. You have to think like the other person. Maybe it's demanding too much, I don't know.

I don't want to be too intimate with a friend. I think I'm a failure towards friendship. When I was younger I thought you were a friend if you went to bed with a man, or a woman. I haven't been to bed with a woman yet, but one day . . .

You're saving this up?

[Chuckles] Yes. But it is hard to be a friend. It's a terrible thing, the same as it is terribly hard to be a lover or a mother or a wife or anything.

I had friends. I had Mary Perceval, Lady Nolan, Sunday Reed, Barbara [Blackman] very much, and Joy Hester. Joy Hester was extraordinary. She was a true friend. Joy could read my mind. I think a friend must read your mind, and be interested in you. Joy was like that. She would go right into my heart in such a way that my heart was outside my chest and open and bleeding. That's how it was with her. Really, I can't give a better example. I call that friendship.

Joy cared about my thinking and it's the thinking that counts really. That's what I love. It's only when you think that you progress, even a little bit. Joy made me think. In France after the war, you were an existentialist – you *had* to be an existentialist. You had to have read Sartre and de Beauvoir, Camus. You had to read Flaubert, you had to read everybody, all the Russian classics. And Joy Hester was like that.

Sunday Reed would wait for me to say things. She wouldn't really ask. She cried all the time with me. She cried a lot, Sunday. Some days Mary Perceval and I, we used to cry too. And Joy. We cried an entire summertime. There was always something to cry about. First, because it was such a beautiful day, and then because of some man or because of Sweeney or because of . . . Mostly because it was such a beautiful day. It was terrible. It was torture. [Laughs]

What kind of friend was Sunday?

Sunday? She was more like a lover. She was very demanding too, like Joy Hester. But Sunday always said to me, 'It's funny, Mirka, I can't have any power over you.' And I would think, What does that mean? What do you mean, you want to have power over me? I really didn't understand what she meant, and I don't to this day. Because I adored her. I gave her so many drawings and paintings because it was so lovely to be with Sunday. The quality of her presence was just sublime, really. I don't want to use a word like this but with her we were in the presence of such good taste, and such knowledge.

Sunday was very well read. Extraordinarily widely read. When I was fifty, she gave me her most cherished book, the correspondence of Rimbaud in French. She had had the book for fifty years – it was printed in 1928, when I was born. See, this is what I call a great quality. She also gave me a book of her mother's, of Eloise and Abelard. *En Français.* I can't even describe the quality of this gesture, it's just too beautiful. She knew exactly what I liked.

How did you meet Sunday?

That was fabulous. It goes back to Georges [the department store], in Collins Street. I used to go there every week to buy beautiful cloth because I liked to make my own clothes in those days. There was a charming English man, Mr Allan Blake, a buyer for Georges, for materials. Very elegant young man. One day he invited me with my husband to a party that one of his customers was giving, a Mrs Ruddock. Mrs Ruddock and her husband had a big party in their big mansion in big St Kilda Road. So I went with my husband there. I think the party was for Irene Mitchell, so she was there with all her actors. It was 1952, something like that.

I wore a beautiful French hat that my husband had bought me. It was the last thing that I worshipped – I'd already thrown out gloves and things because in Melbourne you didn't wear anything like that, it was all different. I made a grand gesture and threw the hat into the fire. My beautiful French hat. I cried for it but everybody loved it. And a charming man came and sat next to me on the sofa and spoke to me right through the evening. Mrs Ruddock said to me, 'Ah Mirka, what have you done? This man is a very grumpy man and he never talks to anybody.' And I said, 'Well, he knows Paris inside out and he has never been to Paris.' This man was John Sinclair, the music critic at the *Herald* and a great friend of Sidney Nolan.

Next morning I had a phone call from Sunday: 'I hear that you're making clothes.' I said yes, because I always say yes to everything. And she said, 'I would like to have a dress made.' A tiny little voice. I said, 'Well, here's my address: 9 Collins Street.' And she came in three days. She had very white linen, very fine, very white, and she wanted a beautiful dress. I made her the dress and it was such a beautiful dress she never wore it, she hung it on the wall as a work of art.

That first time I met her she kept coming right up next to me. And I thought, That's funny. But she eventually told me, 'You know I can't hear very well, that's why I'm coming close to you.' She also didn't wear a brassière, which I thought was terrific, although I thought, You should really wear a brassière. But she didn't. Then John came to pick up the dress, with a cheque, and John looked magnificent, really beautiful.

At nearly the same time I met another French girl, Edith, and I spoke to her about a painting I'd seen that I loved. She said, 'Oh I know the painter, he's my friend.' That was Charles Blackman, so we met Barbara and Charles. They came to the studio one day with Barrie Reid and the three of them – [chuckles] I'll never forget them – they were like three silly little grapes sitting together. They said, 'We are very interested in art.' And I said, 'Oh yes, me too.' That French girl was a girl-friend of John Yule, who was a painter, and I'd said to her, 'You can bring paintings and I'll put them in my studio because so many people come.' Because I used to make dresses and collars and cuffs and things like that.

This was your dressmaking studio?

At the time, yes, but I was painting as well, and babies as well. Always painting – I never stopped. It was chaotic. Anyway, I began to show paintings there and the rest is history, as they say.

Then you began to go to Heide.

Every week. Every weekend we had these beautiful dinners and lunches. I had Christmas at Heide and it was a bit like this provincial, beautiful home in France, in the Loire. Like Flaubert's house. Sunday had a beautiful McCubbin painting and a beautiful Streeton. The grand piano. You existed when you were with John and Sunday, you were real because John and Sunday knew who you were. They could assess who you were straight away.

Did they like Georges as well?

Enormously. Without Georges there would be no Museum of Modern Art, let's face it. And Georges adored them because their style was impeccable. It's a quality – the way the table was set, or the way the fresh cream came to the table. Asparagus from the garden, chervil. Nobody knew in Melbourne what chervil was, or asparagus for that matter. Everything was perfect.

All that perfection didn't put a strain on the rest of you?

No. No. Because Sunday spoke French very well and I think – how should I say this? – she was more French than Australian. It was the Frenchness which probably seduced us. And also all the books. She had all the French books published in Paris, from Gallimard, that my husband and I had read because we were very ardent readers. And there they were on the shelves; we couldn't believe it. And the style of the house – in the *bibliothèque*, the room where we sat, three walls were covered with books. Everything was simple and homely, perfect. And Sunday and John were very beautiful too. Everything was agreeable. It was like being at home, really, in our own home, in my husband's and my case. Your brain was feeding and your eyes – everything was being fed.

I've put John Reed there [a portrait of John sits on a bookcase above us] because I miss him terribly. That's his portrait I did many, many years ago. Sunday always made me paint John.

And Joy?

Joy was a different person. She thought it was all a bit . . . Joy was a real Australian girl, with all its beauty. Don't misunderstand me; she was a larrikin and had a lot of cachet all the same, because she was an artist and she was so intelligent and electric. Joy was electric. Always picked the wrong men but she was electric.

The wrong men?

Well, she married Bert Tucker. Not the best of men. A great artist but a difficult man. And Gray Smith was very difficult. He was epileptic and difficult. A beautiful painter too. She probably was like me and didn't know what it was all about, to love a man – it's a difficult thing.

Did you talk about that? You and Joy?

The entire summer. That's why we cried. [Laughs]

Was Sunday part of that conversation?

Oh yes.

You make Sunday sound much warmer than anyone else has made her sound – including herself in her letters – and much more human than my brief experience of her in Melbourne in the sixties.

Well, Sunday, you could see that she was suffering all the time. She was a woman who loved and lost. So that's it, you can see that. You knew that she was still pining for her great love. And John Reed was just enduring everything and knowing everything. [Sunday's great love was the artist Sidney Nolan.

After eight years as Sunday's lover and John's friend and business partner, Nolan left the ménage at Heide in July 1947 when Sunday refused, yet again, to divorce John and marry him. The following year Nolan married Cynthia Reed, John's much loved younger sister, after a ten-week romance. John remained a champion of Nolan's work. Sunday was inconsolable at his loss and was still pining for him decades later. See Janine Burke's introduction to *Dear Sun: The Letters of Joy Hester and Sunday Reed*. Heinemann, 1995.] It was very dramatic. But when you're young you love the dramas. Now we are a bit more blasé. Mind you, if I go in a room and I feel something, I feel it there [hand on her heart]. But I think when I was young I would have felt it much more.

It sounds as though there were days at Heide when you could have cut the air with a knife.

Oh yes. Particularly at Christmas time. That was very tense because you had to be hypersensitive not to upset anybody. Particularly when Gray Smith was there because we were always scared he would turn into a typhoon, become violent or have an epilepsy. So you had to be careful not to annoy him. That was very unpleasant. I didn't like that. And you had to be careful Sunday wouldn't cry. She was easily upset. John Reed was all right but John Reed was a judge. A good balance. Very secure was John.

Did your friendship with Joy continue until her death?

Yes. She died in December 1960. I didn't see her so much the year before she died, but whenever I went to see her she always showed me her blue hands and she always said, 'What will happen to my children?' But Gray was always by her and that was beautiful. In the end she chose the right man, perhaps, because he was always by her. But if you are an epileptic you shouldn't inflict yourself on another person. He was very ill.

So when you say you haven't had, or been, a true friend, what would you call your relationships with Joy and Sunday? You wouldn't call either of those a true friendship?

Not really. No. It was something else. I don't know what it was. I don't know what friendship is, really. I don't mean to be – what's the word? – flippant. I don't mean to be like that.

So when you think about your relationships with Sunday and Joy . . .

Couldn't be nicer, couldn't be more elevating, but I still don't call it friendship because I didn't push it too far. Probably I didn't make enough demands on any of my friends to be able to regard them as friends, but then I don't think you should exploit your friendship or your friends. It was communication. It was a dialogue. Most people don't have a dialogue with each other.

And did you feel it was a dialogue of equals?

I was a bit younger than Sunday. Sunday died in 1981 but she would be ninety now, so I was twenty years younger than her, and five or six years younger than Joy, I think. [Sunday was born in 1905, Joy in 1920 and Mirka in 1928.] That's probably why I had the courage to talk.

Do you ever get in such a sad state that you think, I have to talk to someone, I have to ring somebody up?

I do get very distressed. The world is a very difficult place. And that's when I say, 'This is very funny, Mirka Mora. You'd better look in the mirror and smile.' I think it was Jacques Lacan who described this experiment: he put a little baby of two or three months in front of a mirror and if the baby smiles in the mirror his persona is okay and everything will be well.

Or I think, This is going a bit too far. Got to do something. So I'll go to a restaurant and eat. Or I'll go and have a shower. Or when things are really terrible I go to a hotel for one or two days, the best hotel in town. I used to do that even when I was married. I wouldn't tell my husband but I would tell my sons: 'Mummy will be there. If you need me, that's where I am.' The children loved to go to the hotel. [Laughs]

Has a friend ever let you down badly?

I've never made demands, so . . . But you know they will let you down, you don't have to search for it, because human beings are fragile. And it's very rare that a person will not let you down. But maybe I demand too much, maybe I want too much. Maybe if I said friend-all, friend-everything, I would go for it.

Do you wish that you had that?

No, I'm my own friend.

Tell me how you do that.

Well, I just told you. If things are too difficult I go to a hotel and pamper myself, because I do live in a kind of garret. [Laughs] But of course I like to live like that. I don't like it easy, I don't like comfort. But being a friend to yourself is also realising that you have not enough knowledge on different things. You have to have knowledge. You have to read.

[Laughs] But I'm an optimist. I might still one day find a friend.

And what would that be like?

Probably marvellous. But I think I would have to give up a lot of freedom, which I'm not prepared to do. It would interfere in my space, in my thinking. You know, if I'm alone and suffering, I might have an extraordinary *pensée*, an extraordinary idea. And if I have a friend, I can't think, or I can't work.

You see, I have to work all the time because I still have so much to learn. I'm always thinking about painting. It sounds corny but it isn't, because painting is really very difficult, as you know. As soon as you progress a bit, a tiny bit, you think, Oh, I've got it. But you haven't. In painting if you think you're getting somewhere, if you stop thinking about it, you might lose days going back to where you were. So you have to sacrifice time with people who could become your friends. If somebody rings I won't take the phone because I can't just go and talk. At the end of the day I might talk. Or sometimes I just like to be dissipated, that's nice.

Do you think that being a painter necessarily makes you solitary? Writers are solitary while they're writing, but generally their relationships with other people feed what they do, so most writers need to go out and talk to other people at some point. But perhaps that's not essential for painters?

That's right, yes. Painters have to go and look at other paintings but there's not really a dialogue, there's only an abstract dialogue. Although you have to read and when you read it's a dialogue, but the other person isn't there so it's not the same. It does isolate you a bit. Maybe that's why I don't let friends in. I never thought of it.

So you have to discipline yourself.

Yes. You have to, because you've only got one life. One life is not enough, although one life was lucky. Afterwards, that's it. So you have to make it fabulous. Every minute. Every day.

Have you done that, do you think?

Oh, if you look at my house, it's like looking inside my brain. I'm pretty happy, yes, but I'm aware of the long journey. And if I didn't paint I would die, so it's as simple as that. It's a bit of a prison really, but there's no other way.

I like what you say about my discipline though, because – nobody will believe it – I'm very disciplined in my work and my learning. I have to learn a lot still. And time is very limited – there [moves her hand through the air], it's running away. But I've always had a sense of urgency, because when you're born in France, by the time you're fourteen, fifteen, you've read lots of poetry. And once you've read Baudelaire and Rimbaud you know everything is fragile and your time is disappearing fast. So you have a sense of urgency from a very young age.

Let's talk about growing up in France. Were you very close to your family?

I left my family when I was sixteen. I put my age up to get a job, straight after the war. I didn't want to stay with my family, they were not letting me grow. I found myself a job but my mother still wouldn't let me loose. I married at eighteen to get away from my family, which wasn't very smart but it was my only escape. In those days there was no other way, unless I would have money and go to another country. But I didn't. Women with money were probably more free, but not happier, necessarily. I could have saved, but with the money I earned I straight away bought books and paint and canvas and perfume. I love perfume. Very important to have perfume. Sometimes I have no dinner, but I have perfume – and coffee. [Laughs]

Did your parents love you?

Yes, my parents adored me. And I had two mothers. They both adored me.

How did you have two mothers?

Oh, I'm clever. I don't have friends but I have two mothers. [Laughs]

Perhaps with two mothers you don't need friends.

[Chuckles] Very good. That's very good. Thank you.

So how did you come to have two mothers?

Well, one is my biological *mère*, my Jewish mother. And the other one was a beautiful journalist, Paulette. When I was four years old, she used to wave to me from her apartment. We lived on the other side of the street in Paris and she fell in love with me. Madly. My mother was extraordinary because she was what you call in French *une mère poule*, a mother hen. She loved her children but she lent me to Paulette until I was thirteen, until the war. With Paulette I had a double life because with Paulette I had different clothes, beautiful clothes, and we went to the opera, went to the south of France. I think I replaced a lover she couldn't get, on the weekends and summer holidays. And she had a stepmother whom I adored. She was a very strong Catholic and taught me all the prayers. When I was in the concentration camp I was praying to the Virgin Mary. *Incroyable*, I know.

You were in the camp for how long?

Three weeks. I've got a very rare book on all the French children of the Holocaust. It has the dates of the convoys and I was saved by a day. The next day I would have been finished. So it is a bit of a miracle that we are here talking.

Did you have friends as a little girl?

They were all burnt in Auschwitz. I lost them all. [Pause, then thoughtfully] Maybe that has something to do with it. When the war started I lost all my little children friends. I hadn't thought of that.

I had two sisters but I didn't like having sisters. And my friends were gone. Dead. And once you're married, it's something else. They are the friends of your husband, they're not your friends.

What about children?

Oh, that's the most impossible love affair of all. A child is like a lover, let's face it. Like an impossible lover, whether boy or girl. And my children are not my best friends. They adore me, but they are not my best friends because I wouldn't want that, I wouldn't have it. I wouldn't want to make demands on them, or my daughters-in-law. You can't. You have no right to do that.

I do have a few girlfriends – I call them girlfriends because they're young girls. A lot of young girls want to be with me. And I'm still a born teacher, so I want to be with them to give them bad 'abits. [Chuckles] I teach them to drink and I teach them to suffer. They're usually very bright girls. We go straight away to a restaurant and drink. I listen to them and it breaks my heart, because they suffer these girls, usually about love. We did too, but not like that. And they're supposed to be more free, these girls.

Perhaps that makes it harder.

Probably, yes, because they hanker after what they discard. They have to choose.

But I don't believe in friendship, I really don't. I said that when I was twenty, thirty, forty, fifty. My friend is my work. I have my dialogue with my work. Endlessly.

I've never had a proper studio, except at 9 Collins Street, and the Rankins Lane thing, when I separated from my family. So my house has to be a studio. I can't have a dining room or whatever, everything is for the work. It's poor us if we have dinner here. [Laughs] We've got to clean and you can only have that much space because I can't move all that, you know. [Mirka indicates the table laden with great piles of books and paintings and objects. Our coffee cups and the coffee pot, from which issues superlative coffee, are perched on the very end in a tiny space specially cleared for the occasion.] I'm very sad about it because I can't entertain. I love entertaining. Because it's so important to talk, like I'm talking with you. It's such a pleasure. So you see, these are the disciplines.

And the sacrifices?

The sacrifice, yes. Call it sacrifice. Yes.

I did get quite a large amount of money at a certain time, but again I spent it all on books and perfume and paints and brushes. And when I realised what I'd done I thought, Oh, I could have built a studio on top of the house. But then it's a bit too corny. You know what I mean? It's a bit too real to have a studio. I like it difficult. It's difficult for all the so-called friends. [Laughs]

Maybe it's a way of –

Protecting myself? Yes. Probably. You're quite right. [We quietly drink the last of our coffee as the evening closes in. Mirka chuckles.] We're watching. We're waiting for the friends to come.

Are we waiting for the friends to come, or waiting for catastrophe?

Well, catastrophe, you're sure it will come. But who knows if the friends will come? You don't know. The catastrophe is that we have to die. That's a terrible catastrophe.

When you say we're waiting for the friends to come, do you really –?

I'm an optimist, you know.

But do you want the friends to come?

Oh no, because I don't know what a friend is. But I hope one extraordinary one will come. Somebody very brilliant. Yes. [Laughs] But I'm not engaged with a friend – or lover. I adore the man I love. I *adore* the man I love. That's two big words: 'adore' and 'love'. But I haven't surrendered, I'm still a free being. I don't know what it means, but I haven't surrendered to him. I'm not his slave. Surrender would be not painting. And going to live with him. Adoring him and looking after him, which is a dream. I would love to but I can't because I am a painter. I have to do my work.

Did you surrender with Georges?

No. Georges knew that I was a painter. He knew what it meant.

Were you and Georges friends?

Oh very. Oh yes.

And once you and Georges separated, did you see him?

By chance, but he never came here. I saw him before he died, I went to see him in the hospital, alternating with his new wife. But it would be too much for him to see me because it was too much to leave me. It was very hard. But it was just one part of my life. Georges was a very exceptional man, a very cultured man, very knowledgeable, but he was a French man. And I think I misled him. Every time when he started to take mistresses, I pretended I understood, but I was very sad. I wanted to be too clever. Now I would demand fidelity.

What about people who say they are married to their best friends?

I couldn't stand that. You've got to have a battle going on. That's what keeps it alive. You don't just surrender. A friend you would have to surrender to, I think.

If Joy were still alive, and Sunday, do you think you'd still be friends, or whatever you want to call that relationship?

Oh yes. For sure. I miss them. I need them. I need to talk to them. Sunday would look at the painting and she'd know. She wouldn't say a word, it would be on her face. She knew when I was on the right track. You need that in your work.

Have you had any friends since who are like Joy, or Sunday?

No, they were extraordinary. That was once in a lifetime. You don't meet people like that so often. They were outstanding people. Mind you, there are still great people now, but I can't see anybody quite like . . .

It strikes me that perhaps the things that other people ask from friendship are not actually what you want from it.

No, I want everything from friendship.

Yes, but don't you want that from lovers as well?

From a lover I want nothing. But from friends I want everything, that's different. *C'est la différence.* A lover is like a flying bird – in and out – but a friend is forever. So I would demand the impossible from a friend, it's not possible.

So you think that the ideal friend is unattainable?

Even if it were attainable it's not fair to exploit someone else. I think there's a kind of exploitation in a friendship. I don't know if the word 'exploitation' is right. You don't use someone else for your good, you don't use another person. But I don't mind somebody using me. See, that's why I am confused. Maybe I'm a mixed up kid! [Laughs] I'd love to have a friend, I really would. It must be wonderful to have a friend from whom you would learn. I'd have to learn. They'd have to be more clever than I am, without being pretentious or stupid. Joy was extraordinary. Joy and Sunday had more experience than me, and they had great lives. So I could learn from them.

I think it's Ortega y Gasset who says you must love an interesting man if you're a woman, and vice versa. You must love somebody from whom you will learn things. That's true for friendship too.

A friendship means . . . it's one of the ships, it goes away.

The ship could be coming towards you as well.

Oh, yeah.

Or you could be in it and it's taking you somewhere very interesting.

That's more like it.

If you are in the friendship, you are in the ship.

Yes, that's right. Oh, that's lovely.

You are making the journey together.

Yes, but do I want to make the journey together?

Mirka, that's the big question: do you?

I don't, really. I want to be alone. I *am* alone in this world. The sooner you know you're alone in this universe, the better you will be, even if it's hell. I like living dangerously. By myself. And you should be solitary. Even if you have a full life with a beautiful husband and children, you must still have your own garden, your own private room, that's very important. In the end you are alone, you must know that.

NOTES

FIRST THINGS FIRST
Page
4, 7   All quotes from Ralph Waldo Emerson are from his essay 'Friendship', *Essays*, George Routledge and Sons, London, n.d.

7   'all the ladders start . . .' William Butler Yeats, 'The Circus Animals' Desertion', *Collected Poems of W.B. Yeats*, Macmillan, London, 1963.

8–9   All quotes from Dorothy Rowe are from her article 'The Formula for Happy Families', *Guardian*, London, 6 Jan 1997.

9–10   'Why, I wonder . . .' Frances Partridge, *Memories*, Phoenix, London, 1999, p. 238.

10   'one soul inhabiting two bodies', quoted in Diogenes Laertius, *Lives of Eminent Philosophers*, translated by R.D. Hicks, William Heinemann, London, 1925.

10   All quotes from Cicero are from his essay 'Laelius: On Friendship', *On the Good Life*, Penguin, London, 1971, pp.175–227.

11   All quotes from Francis Bacon are from his essay 'Of Friendship', *Essays*, Everyman edition, 1983, pp. 80–86.

12–13   All quotes from Michel de Montaigne are from his essay 'On Friendship', *The Complete Essays*, translated and edited by M.A. Screech, Penguin, London, 1991, pp. 205–219.

13–14   Emerson, op. cit.

15   Regarding the conclusion that even women who describe themselves as happily married are likely to become depressed if they are for too long without a close friend, see Stacey J. Oliker, *Best Friends and Marriage*, University of California Press, Berkeley, 1989.

15 'she knew my heart and my secrets . . .' (my translation),
Geoffrey Chaucer, *The Complete Works of Geoffrey Chaucer*, second
edition, edited by F. N. Robinson, Oxford University Press, Oxford,
1976, pp. 529–533.

15–16 'you admit no sworn confidante . . .' William Congreve, *The
Way of the World*, Edward Arnold, London, 1979, lines 212–215.

16 For Vera Brittain's version of her friendship with Winifred
Holtby, see her *Testament of Friendship*, Virago, London, 1997. For
the sexuality of the participants, see Deborah Gorham's 'The
Friendships of Women: Friendship, Feminism and Achievement in
Vera Brittain's Life and Work' in *Journal of Women's History*, Vol. 3,
No. 3, Winter 1992, pp. 45–69.

17–25 The section on Hannah Arendt and Mary McCarthy is
based on Carol Brightman's *Writing Dangerously: Mary McCarthy and
her World*, Harcourt Brace, New York, 1994, and *Between Friends:
The Correspondence of Hannah Arendt and Mary McCarthy
1949–1975*, edited by Carol Brightman, Harcourt Brace, New York,
1995, with a little additional material from David Laskin's *Partisans:
Marriage, Politics and Betrayal Among the New York Intellectuals*,
Simon & Schuster, New York, 2000. All quotes are from
Brightman's *Between Friends*, unless otherwise indicated.

18 'Mary was, quite literally, enchanted by . . .' Elizabeth Hardwick
in her foreword to Mary McCarthy's *Intellectual Memoirs: New York
1936–1938*, Harvest, New York, 1993, pp. xviii–xix.

24 'could only be called sacrificial' Hardwick, op. cit., p. xix.

26 'five-star friendship': a description given by a friend of Graham
Little's of the kind of friendship that he wished for more of, in
Graham Little, *Friendship: Being Ourselves With Others*. Text,
Melbourne, 1993, p. 254 and 266. He suggested that 'a book on a

dozen five-star friendships would tell us much'.

32 'This is how it goes . . .' Margaret Atwood, *Cat's Eye*, Bloomsbury, London, 1989, pp. 118.

32 'Think of them as constantly on LSD . . .' Mary Pipher, *Reviving Ophelia*, Doubleday, New York, 1996, pp. 57, 59.

40–41 'an extra part of the brain . . .' Rieper and Hulme, *HQ*, January/February 1995, p. 51.

44 All quotes from Frances Partridge come from *Memories*, op. cit., p. 116.

JOANNA MURRAY-SMITH
Page
45–46 All quotes from Joanna Murray-Smith are from her novel *Truce*, Penguin, Melbourne, 1994, pp. 54–55.

CHRIS MANFIELD
Page
68 All quotes from Chris Manfield are from her book *Paramount Cooking*, Viking, Melbourne 1995.

MARY VALLENTINE
Page
79 'at a famously appalling party . . .' 'A Symphony Unto Herself', Janet Hawley, *Good Weekend*, 27 July 1996, p. 26.

80 'taking an indecisive, insecure . . .' ibid.

80–81 'A short, mean Adelaide critic . . .' This quote is based on Janet Hawley's article, with additions by David Marr.

95 'Mary surrounded him . . .' Hawley, op. cit.

BARBARA BLACKMAN AND MIRKA MORA
Page
215–16   All quotes from Barbara Blackman are from her
autobiography *Glass After Glass: Autobiographical Reflections*, Viking,
Melbourne, 1997. For information on Joy Hester and Sunday Reed
in both these conversations, I have drawn on Janine Burke's
introduction to *Dear Sun: The Letters of Joy Hester and Sunday Reed*,
William Heinemann, Melbourne, 1995, as well as *Glass After Glass*,
in particular the chapter 'Portrait of a Friendship'. Material on the
good ship Mora comes from pp. 169–190. Bails Myer is quoted on
p. 173. For introductory material on Mirka I have also drawn on
Max Delaney and Murray White's *Mirka Mora: Where Angels Fear to
Tread: 50 Years of Art 1948–1998*, Museum of Modern Art at Heide,
Bulleen, 1999.

BIBLIOGRAPHY

BOOKS

ATWOOD, MARGARET, *Cat's Eye*, Bloomsbury, London, 1989.

BACON, FRANCIS, *Essays*, Everyman edition, 1983.

BEIER, ULLI, *Mirka*, Macmillan, Melbourne, 1980.

BERNIKOW, LOUISE, *Among Women*, Harper and Row, New York, 1980.

BERRY, CARMEN RENEE and TRAEDER, TAMARA, *Girlfriends: Invisible Bonds, Enduring Ties*, Wildcat Canyon Press, Berkeley, 1995.

BLACKMAN, BARBARA, *Glass After Glass: Autobiographical Reflections*, Viking, Melbourne, 1997.

BRIGHTMAN, CAROL, *Writing Dangerously: Mary McCarthy and Her World*, Harcourt Brace, New York, 1994.

—— ed., *Between Friends: The Correspondence of Hannah Arendt and Mary McCarthy 1949–1975*, Harcourt Brace, New York, 1995.

BRITTAIN, VERA, *Testament of Friendship*, Virago, London, 1997.

BURKE, JANINE, ed., *Dear Sun: The Letters of Joy Hester and Sunday Reed*, William Heinemann, Melbourne, 1995.

CALLOW, SIMON, *Love Is Where it Falls: An Account of a Passionate Friendship*, Nick Hern Books, London, 1999.

CHARTIER, ROGER, ed., *A History of Private Life, Vol III: Passions of the Renaissance*, Harvard University Press, Cambridge, 1989.

CHAUCER, GEOFFREY, *The Complete Works of Geoffrey Chaucer*, edited by F. N. Robinson, second edition, Oxford University Press, Oxford, 1976.

CHODOROW, NANCY, *The Reproduction of Mothering*, University of California Press, Berkeley, 1979.

CICERO, *On the Good Life*, Penguin, London, 1971.

CONGREVE, WILLIAM, *The Way of the World*, Edward Arnold, London, 1979.

DELANEY, MAX and WHITE, MURRAY, eds., *Mirka Mora: Where Angels*

Fear to Tread: 50 Years of Art 1948–1998, Museum of Modern Art at Heide, Bulleen, 1999.

DESSAIX, ROBERT, ed., *Speaking Their Minds: Intellectuals and the Public Culture in Australia*, ABC Books, Sydney, 1998.

DICK, KAY, *Friends and Friendship*, Sidgwick & Jackson, London, 1974.

DUCK, STEVE, *Friends for Life*, Harvester, Brighton, 1983.

EMERSON, RALPH WALDO, *Essays*, George Routledge and Sons, London, n.d.

ENRIGHT, D.J. and RAWLINSON, DAVID, eds, *The Oxford Book of Friendship*, Oxford University Press, Oxford, 1991.

FILLION, KATE, *Lip Service: The Myth of Female Virtue in Love, Sex and Friendship*, HarperCollins, Sydney, 1996.

FOSTER, PATRICIA, ed., *Sister to Sister*, Anchor, New York, 1997.

GIDDENS, ANTHONY, *The Transformation of Intimacy*, Polity, Cambridge, 1992.

GILLIGAN, CAROL, *In a Different Voice*, Harvard University Press, Cambridge, 1993.

——, and LYONS, NONA P. and HANMER, TRUDY J., eds., *Making Connections*, Harvard University Press, Cambridge, 1990.

GREER, GERMAINE, *The Female Eunuch*, MacGibbon & Kee, London, 1970.

JAMIESON, LYNN, *Intimacy*, Polity, Cambridge, 1998.

KAREN, ROBERT, *Becoming Attached: First Relationships and How They Shape Our Capacity to Love*, Oxford University Press, New York, 1998.

LASKIN, DAVID, *Partisans: Marriage, Politics and Betrayal Among the New York Intellectuals*, Simon & Schuster, New York, 2000.

LITTLE, GRAHAM, *Friendship: Being Ourselves With Others*, Text, Melbourne, 1993.

McCARTHY, MARY, *Intellectual Memoirs: New York 1936–1938*, Harvest, New York, 1993.

MANFIELD, CHRIS, *Paramount Cooking*, Viking, Melbourne, 1995.

MANTEL, HILARY, *An Experiment in Love*, Penguin, London, 1996.

MARGOLIES, EVA, *The Best of Friends, The Worst of Enemies*, Dial, New York, 1985.

MATTHEWS, SARAH H., *Friendships Through the Life Course: Oral Biographies in Old Age*, Sage Library of Social Research, California, 1986.

MILLER, ALICE, *The Drama of Being a Child*, Virago, London, 1990.

MONTAIGNE, MICHEL DE, *The Complete Essays*, translated and edited by M.A. Screech, Penguin, London, 1991.

MURRAY-SMITH, JOANNA, *Truce*, Penguin, Melbourne, 1994.

NESTOR, PAULINE, *Female Friendships and Communities*, Oxford University Press, Oxford, 1985.

O'CONNOR, PAT, *Friendships Between Women*, Harvester, Hertfordshire, 1992.

OLIKER, STACEY J., *Best Friends and Marriage: Exchange Among Women*, University of California Press, Berkeley, 1989.

ORBACH, SUSIE, *What's Really Going on Here?* Virago, London, 1994.

—— and EICHENBAUM, LOUISE, *Between Women: Love, Envy and Competition in Women's Friendships*, Arrow, London, 1994.

PARTRIDGE, FRANCES, *Memories*, Phoenix, London, 1999.

—— *A Pacifist's War: Diaries 1939–1945*, Phoenix, London, 1999.

—— *Everything to Lose: Diaries 1945–1960*, Phoenix, London, 1997.

—— *Hanging On: Diaries 1960–1963*, Phoenix, London, 1998.

—— *Other People: Diaries 1963–1966*, Phoenix, London, 1999.

—— *Good Company: Diaries 1967–1970*, Phoenix, London, 1999.

—— *Life Regained: Diaries 1970–1972*, Phoenix, London, 1999.

PIPHER, MARY, *Reviving Ophelia*, Doubleday, Sydney, 1996.

POGREBIN, LETTY COTTIN, *Among Friends*, McGraw-Hill, New York, 1987.

PORTER, ROY and TOMASELLI, SYLVANA, eds., *The Dialectics of Friendship*, Routledge, London, 1989.

ROSE, GILLIAN, *Love's Work*, Chatto & Windus, London, 1995.

ROSSI, ALICE S., 'A Feminist friendship: Elizabeth Cady Stanton (1815–1902) and Susan B. Anthony (1820–1906)', in Rossi, Alice S., ed., *The Feminist Papers*, Bantam, New York, 1974.

RUBIN, LILLIAN B., *Just Friends: The Role of Friendship in Our Lives*, Perennial Library, New York, 1990.

SHAKESPEARE, WILLIAM, *The Complete Pelican Shakespeare*, Viking, New York, 1977.

SPENDER, DALE and SPENDER, LYNNE, *Scribbling Sisters*, Camden Press, London, 1986.

SPIEGEL, DAVID, *Living Beyond Limits*, Times Books, New York, 1993.

STONE, LAWRENCE, *The Family, Sex and Marriage in England 1500–1800*, Peregrine Books, 1982.

STORR, ANTHONY, *Solitude: A Return to the Self*, Ballantine Books, New York, 1989.

—— *The Art of Psycho-Therapy*, second edition, Routledge, New York, 1990.

TANNEN, DEBORAH, *That's Not What I Meant!*, Virago, London, 1992.

—— *You Just Don't Understand: Women and Men in Conversation*, Virago, London, 1996.

WARD, JANET DOUBLER and MINK, JOANNA STEPHENS, eds., *Communication and Women's Friendships*, Bowling Green State University Press, Bowling Green, 1993.

WARNER, MARINA, *From the Beast to the Blonde*, Chatto & Windus, London, 1994.

YEATS, WILLIAM BUTLER, *Collected Poems of W.B. Yeats*, Macmillan, London, 1963.

JOURNAL, MAGAZINE AND NEWSPAPER ARTICLES

ABEL, ELIZABETH, '(E)merging Identities: The Dynamics of Female Friendship in Contemporary Fiction by Women', *Signs: Journal of Women in Culture and Society*, 1981, Vol. 6, No. 3.

APTER, TERRI, 'What Are Friends For?', *Guardian*, London, 15 November 1999.

ARIES, ELIZABETH and JOHNSON, FERN L., 'Close Friendship in Adulthood: Conversational Content Between Same-Sex Friends', *Sex Roles*, 1983, Vol. 9, No. 12, pp. 1183–1196.

BERK, LEE, 'New Discoveries in Psychoneuroimmunology', *Humor and Health Journal*, Vol. 3, No. 3, 1994, pp. 1–8.

—— 'The Laughter–Immune Connection: New Discoveries', *Humor and Health Journal*, Vol. 5, No. 5, 1996, pp. 1–5.

BROWN, RITA MAE, 'Some of My Best Friends Are . . . Men', *Ms*, September 1985, pp. 66, 115–116.

DAVIS, KEITH E., 'Near and Dear: Friendship and Love Compared', *Psychology Today*, February 1985, pp. 22–30.

DeSALVO, LOUISE, A., 'Lighting the Cave: The Relationship Between Vita Sackville-West and Virginia Woolf', *Signs: Journal of Women in Culture and Society*, 1982, Vol. 8, No. 2, pp. 195–214.

DESSAIX, ROBERT, 'Kith and Tell', *24 Hours*, March 1994, pp. 58–60.

DURRANT, SABINE, 'The Life and Extraordinary Loves of Simon Callow', *Guardian*, London, 1 March 1999.

FISCHER, CLAUDE S., 'What Do We Mean By "Friend"?', *Social Networks*, 1982, Vol. 3, pp. 287–306.

FREEMAN-GREENE, SUZY, 'The Two of Us: Mirka Mora and Tiriel Mora', *Good Weekend*, 25 April 1998.

GORHAM, DEBORAH, ' "The Friendships of Women": Friendship, Feminism and Achievement in Vera Brittain's Life and Work in the Interwar Decades', *Journal of Women's History*, Vol. 3, No. 3, Winter 1992, pp. 45–69.

HAWLEY, JANET, 'A Symphony Unto Herself', *Good Weekend*, 27 July 1996.

MINNICH, ELIZABETH KAMARCK, 'Friendship Between Women: The Act of Feminist Biography', *Feminist Studies* 11, No. 2, Summer 1985, pp. 287–305.

ROWE, DOROTHY, 'The Formula for Happy Families', *Guardian*, London, 6 January 1997.

SAFE, MIKE, 'Boys to Men', *Australian Magazine*, August 2–3, 1997.

SMITH-ROSENBERG, CARROLL, 'The Female World of Love and Ritual: Relations Between Women in Nineteenth-Century America', *Signs: Journal of Women in Culture and Society*, 1975, Vol. 1, No. 1.

SPIEGEL, DAVID, ET AL., 'Effect of Psychosocial Treatment on Survival of Patients with Metastatic Breast Cancer', *Lancet*, 14 October 1989.

WHEATLEY, JANE, 'Soul Sisters', *HQ*, January/February 1995.

ZIEGLER, JAN, 'Immune System May Benefit from the Ability to Laugh', *Journal of the National Cancer Institute*, 1995, Vol. 87, Issue 5, p. 342.

Acknowledgements ¶

The women whose stories appear in this book were extraordinarily generous with their time and their experiences. I am deeply grateful to them. Many other women also spoke to me frankly and generously about friendship. I thank them all, particularly Marion Halligan, Susan Hamilton, Saskia Havekes, Drusilla Modjeska, Joanna Nicholas, Rhoda Roberts and Rae de Teliga.

I would also like to thank the gallant David Marr, my meticulous and sympathetic editor Meredith Rose, Fiona Daniel for her early editorial advice, my research assistant Hilary Emmett, and my publisher Julie Gibbs, whose heart was in this book from the beginning and whose grace and patience never faltered, even when sorely tried.

For their encouragement, support and affection throughout the writing of this book I would like to express my profound gratitude to my friends Robert Dessaix, John Berrick and William Fraser, and to my sons, Ben and Josh Ball. Ben was also, most generously, my first reader and editor and gave me invaluable advice, and Josh's incandescent energy and faith in me never flagged, even when my own had abandoned me. Together, they sustained me.

Grateful acknowledgement is due to the following for permission to quote from their published works: on pages 8–9 from Dorothy Rowe, 'The Formula for Happy Families', *Guardian*, London, 6 January 1997; on pages 9–10, 44 from Frances Partridge, *Memories*, Phoenix, London, 1999; on page 18 from Elizabeth Hardwick, foreword to Mary McCarthy, *Intellectual Memoirs: New York 1936–1938*, Harvest, New York, 1993; on page 20 from Carol Brightman (ed.), *Between Friends: The Correspondence of Hannah Arendt and Mary McCarthy 1949–1975*, Harcourt Brace, New York, 1995; page 32 from Margaret Atwood, *Cat's Eye*, Bloomsbury, London, 1989.

Ruth Cracknell
Journey From Venice

*Baggage has been sent all the way to Venice, money has been
changed, we are sitting down, and at last we have time to look at
one another. We are smiling! We are like two conspirators!*

The Serene City beckons, promising Paradise regained for
Ruth Cracknell and her husband, Eric, as they set forth on a
carefully planned holiday.

Up and over the bridges, through the maze that is the city.
Spring rain, and water on all sides, soothing. What they are
seeking is time. Time to think, time to gaze, time for each
other. But from the moment the holiday becomes an uncharted
journey, their time is measured.

Journey From Venice is confronting yet deeply comforting –
an acknowledgement of the miracle that is unconditional love.
And this story, above all, is a love story.

'A brave and honest tribute to a successful and loving
partnership.' THE BULLETIN

'Uplifting and beautiful ... the story of a once-in-a-lifetime
love.' THE DAILY TELEGRAPH